Affect, Psychoanalysis, and American Poetry

Affect, Psychoanalysis, and American Poetry: This Feeling of Exaltation

John Steen

BLOOMSBURY ACADEMIC
LONDON • NEW YORK • OXFORD • NEW DELHI • SYDNEY

BLOOMSBURY ACADEMIC
Bloomsbury Publishing Plc
50 Bedford Square, London, WC1B 3DP, UK

BLOOMSBURY, BLOOMSBURY ACADEMIC and the Diana logo are trademarks
of Bloomsbury Publishing Plc

First published in Great Britain 2018

Cover design by Eleanor Rose
Cover image © Getty Images

A catalogue record for this book is available from the British Library.

A catalog record for this book is available from the Library of Congress.

ISBN:	HB:	978-1-3500-2154-9
	ePDF:	978-1-3500-2153-2
	eBook:	978-1-3500-2155-6

Series: Bloomsbury Studies in Critical Poetics

Typeset by Integra Software Services Pvt. Ltd.
Printed and bound in Great Britain

To find out more about our authors and books visit www.bloomsbury.com
and sign up for our newsletters.

For Stephen, in lieu of *Rock Drill*

Contents

Acknowledgments

My friends, family, and colleagues made this book possible by providing the kind of holding environment with which it is concerned. Over the course of several years, I learned as much about the affects from these people as from the texts that linked us. The project began in the Department of Comparative Literature at the Laney Graduate School of Emory University under the direction of Elissa Marder, Walter Kalaidjian, and Claire Nouvet. These advisers provided unrivalled support for my fledgling efforts at scholarship, and the shape of the book owes everything to their early guidance. Among the many faculty members at Emory whose patient mentoring made this project possible, I'm especially grateful to Deborah White, Geoffrey Bennington, Cathy Caruth, Andrew Mitchell, and Jill Robbins. Fellow graduate students at Emory introduced me to the very idea of intellectual community, and their conversations, feedback, and gentle nudging helped me over innumerable hurdles. Special thanks to Adam Rosenthal, Dave Ritchie, Aaron Goldsman, Armando Mastrogiovanni, Matt Roberts, Ronald Mendoza de Jesus, Ania Kowalik, Harold Braswell, Margaret Boyle, Mark Stoholski, Taylor Schey, Patrick Blanchfield, Christina Leon, Brent Dawson, Naomi Beeman, Andrew Ryder, John Selvidge, Maya Kesrouany, Mishka Sinha, Scott Branson, Jacob Hovind, Joshua Backer, and Verena Peter. Mentors and teachers at the Emory University Psychoanalytic Institute nurtured my interest in the field when I was a student there, and I'm especially grateful to Carol Levy, Steven Levy, Patrick Haggard, and Bobby Paul.

My colleagues at Oklahoma State University and East Carolina University supported me in precarious times. Without the encouragement of these steadfast teachers and thinkers, the project would have stalled long ago. Thank you, Elizabeth Grubgeld, Ron Brooks, Richard Frohock, Katherine Hallemeier, Seth Wood, Timothy Bradford, Amanda Klein, Margaret Bauer, Tom Douglass, Jeffrey Johnson, Alex Albright, Erin Frost, Liz Hoiem, Marianne Montgomery, and Brian Glover.

During the year I spent with Scholars for North Carolina's Future, I learned from the examples of academics who saw their labor as inseparable from political action, and I owe a debt of gratitude to Bruce Orenstein, Nancy Maclean, Lisa Levenstein, Stephen Boyd, Michael Pisapia, and many, many others for this vision of alternative academia. Sarah Glick and Sam Wohns at Faculty Forward deserve a special word of thanks for their encouragement during this time.

This book was completed during my first year of teaching at The Galloway School, and I found support and encouragement from school leadership and my colleagues at every step. I'd like to thank Suzanna Jemsby, Gareth Griffith, Roberta Osorio, Peter Emmons, Cheryl Despathy, Ann Fountain, Jeanne Martinez, Rosie Seagraves, Jesus Martinez-Saldana, Scotti Belfi, Sam Biglari, Lauren Holt, Lisa Lindgren, Robin Rakusin, Anne Broderick, and Chamara Kwakye.

The project was greatly improved thanks to those who read and commented on parts of the manuscript. In addition to Stephen Ross, Jason Maxwell, Timothy Bradford, Dave Ritchie, Adam Rosenthal, Zakir Paul, Scott Branson, Seth Wood, Lisa Knisely, Elizabeth Grubgeld, Nick Sturm, and Richard Flynn, I'm grateful to audiences at the Modernist Studies Association, MLA, American Literature Association Poetry Symposium, and Affect Theory: WTF conference for the gift of their questions and comments on the work in progress. To Daniel Katz, series editor of Bloomsbury Studies in Critical Poetics, David Avital and Clara Herberg at Bloomsbury, and the two anonymous readers of the manuscript, thank you for believing in this project and shepherding it to publication over the course of several years.

The love and support of friends made writing about negative affects more bearable. From Winston-Salem, NC, to Atlanta, GA, and everywhere in between, I have been more than fortunate to have this company alongside me: Roy Blumenfeld, Lauren Links, Adam Rosenthal, Dinah Hannaford, Stephen Ross, Jane Hudson, Lisa Knisely, Aaron Goldsman, Dean Hunt, Amanda Morelli, Maria Corrigan, Kamal Menghrajani, Liz Blackford, Rachel Greenspan, Claire Hefner, Sarah Pickle, Andres Palmiter, Erica Palmiter, Jim Vickers, Ciara Cordasco, Kellie Vinal, Phillip Meeker, Jordan Chambers, Dale Donchey, Walt Hunter, Lindsay Turner, Gregg Murray, Erin Murray, Kate Juergens, Fernando Escalona, Jimmy Lo, Marissa Grossman, Krystle Brewer, Kara Moskowitz, Sarah Huener, Jamie Martina, Lola Rodden, and Jenn Poole.

My family has watched this project and waited for its completion with a patience and kindness that surpasses understanding. My grandmothers, Dorothy and Lucy, asked about the book each time I visited; I write in memory of their husbands, my grandfathers John and Bart. Mom, Dad, Bart, Autumn, Matthew, Anna, Sarah, and Andrés, let's go to La Carreta to celebrate.

Stephen Ross trekked over miles of invisible terrain, performing, in broad daylight, operations of great delicacy in support of this work.

Kathryn reminded me, in Adrienne Rich's words, that "whatever happens, this is."

Introduction

What does a poem contain? This unanswerable question has long troubled readers of poetry, who recognize in a poem's grid of lines a proprietary claim to representing the likeness of a person, the subjective truths of memory, and the varieties of affective experience. Discussions of poetry in the last century have been dedicated, explicitly or implicitly, to thinking about poems as either closed or open, as objects whose self-referentiality accounts for their unique status, or as objects whose openness to the reader precludes any fixed account of their formal parameters. What would it mean to consider poems as objects that are, paradoxically, both closed and open and, simultaneously, neither closed nor open? A model of poetic relationality would allow readers to imagine that an individual poem's relationship to its own closure or failure to close conditions its interaction with—its failure to be either closed or fully open to—the world that lies, at least supposedly, outside. Rather than fix poems as either closed or open, this study considers how a poem relates to the problem of what it contains or fails to contain, and how this relationship brings the poem into contact with the world.

Even to ask what poems contain entails an account of some of the most fundamental questions that continue to trouble readers, writers, and theorists of poetry and poetics. Is there a content proper to poetry? Must a certain form correspond to that content, whatever it is? Do poems correspond to some outside world, however conceived? If they do, how might the boundary between such a poetic inside and a worldly outside be drawn, surveyed, and maintained? What boundaries separate the poet from her poem, the poem from its addressees and readers, and these recipients of the poem from its effects? To return to the initial question, which branches off into additional questions, what does the assumption that a poem contains anything at all fail to acknowledge?

The notion that a poem contains something otherwise uncontainable is a feature of some of the earliest accounts of the genre, which is telling, since the continuity and self-sameness of the genre has been questioned just as insistently.

But rather than track the long history of answers to the question—what do poems contain?—I look to something poems have tried repeatedly to represent, but which they continually acknowledge they have failed to contain.

This study traces the status of the difficult feelings that attend poetry in the wake of Modernism. It tells the story of poetic structures overwhelmed and undone by intensities they cannot contain, and suggests that the consequences of this undoing for reading one of the most prolific periods of US verse to date are still unfolding, and remain to be appraised. Even when its effect on the sound of the poem is to mute it, feeling resonates distinctly among the determinants of an ongoing "crisis of verse," the genre-challenging moment by which Mallarmé defined the modernity of lyric in 1897. Bound by anxiety, mourning, shame, and rage, negative affects with a particular ability to upset communication, Wallace Stevens, Randall Jarrell, Robert Creeley, Ted Berrigan, Aaron Kunin, and Claudia Rankine reassert the significance of feeling in the poems of a century whose poetic history is most often indexed by its formal and philosophical, rather than its affective, coordinates.

Affect, emotion, and feeling have long been associated with lyric poetry, but in many ways their roles have been either idealized or devalued. On the one hand, feeling has at times marked the sole evaluative criterion for the effect of the poem on the reader as well as the single metric for the speaker's achievement of success within its parameters.[1] On the other, the range of possibilities for affect to change poetry at its very core, to change it or index its changing, has been underestimated by a reluctance to regard feeling as anything more than an aftereffect of more important formal, intellectual, political, or linguistic poles.[2] In contrast to both of these extremes, this study claims that the presence of intractable feeling spurs poetic innovation in a century that redefined affect as it interacts with lyric's poles of addressor, addressee, and audience.

I suggest that these feelings upset models of reading and writing in which poets first feel, then express, and finally provoke feelings in their readers. I argue instead that, in their very confrontation of the difficulties associated with handling feeling poetically in the wake of Modernism's challenges to lyric form, feeling rises to the level of a crisis for these poets and their readers. Caught between demands of Modernist form that changed the potential for poems to contain and process feelings and the continuing desire for poems to bear a relationship to this aspect of experience, feeling seems never to be "caught" or captured in these works, but rather to persist in uncomfortable proximity to them. In addition to claiming that poems no longer achieve a purgative processing or releasing of emotion for their speakers, but reflect it back as anxiety, grief, shame, and rage, I will argue that negative affects point toward the new shape of the poem and the changed parameters of its intimacy with feeling. I suggest that an atypical grouping of US poets spanning the twentieth and early twenty-first centuries integrate cacophonous sound, contemporary technology, mathematical constraint, and new media into the lyric in order to ensure the survival of the genre's affective resonance alongside its radically changing forms. Discovering the obstacles that changing aesthetic paradigms make for articulating feeling, these poems mark what is unbearable about affect as well as what structures of feeling US verse may yet be able to bear.

This book considers three major discourses known as much for their separateness from each other as for their invaluable contributions to twentieth-century intellectual, artistic, and social life: affect theory, object relations psychoanalysis, and modern American poetry. I argue, by contrast, that interweaving their contributions enables a deeper understanding not only of the logics by which each is constituted, but also of the potential clarity each brings to pressing contemporary questions. It is relevant to note that, while affect theory has enjoyed a surge of critical interest (and scorn) in the last two decades, both psychoanalysis and poetry figure as untimely interlocutors within academic discourse. With the arrival of psychoanalysis to American shores already over a century old and with the heyday of university poet-critics associated with the New Criticism well behind us, what insights remain for such critical and artistic dinosaurs to uncover? In an era that faces the onset of climate change and the fragility of democratic norms, how can the pre-Oedipal preoccupations of object relations psychoanalysts and the condensed displacements of contemporary poets sound a necessary note? Read alongside the last century's theorists of affect, poets from Wallace Stevens to Claudia Rankine turn to poems not to contain, but to reckon with the uncontainable. Their explorations of the affects point to the possibilities for representation and witness of inchoate experience, and as such provide models for engaging that which invites no understanding.

***

The term affect is as controversial as it is unavoidable for recent literary criticism and theory. It must first be distinguished from or defined with reference to emotion and feeling.[3] In this study, I use the term in two distinct ways. First, I follow theorists (Lyotard, in particular) for whom affect, as against emotion, describes the situations of feeling in which a failure to experience that feeling is most salient. That is, if "experience" demands a subject able to reflect consciously on the nature of his or her bodily and mental existence, affects, which consistently overwhelm the structures of perception and expression, cannot properly be said to be experienced by anyone. They exist, but cannot, in the "now" of their emergence, be named.[4] In this sense, affect refers to a sort of "felt unknown." In this vein, I use the term "feeling" to refer to the conceptual and experiential space that felt and consciously accountable emotions share with the felt unnamed and unknown affects. As its use in my title indicates, I take feeling as a fertile ground for exploring the constitutive and formative tensions of US poetry. I use it as an umbrella term for which affect and emotion mark subtler distinctions.[5] One of the chief arguments that link my chapters is that poets respond to the role feelings play and begin to turn explicitly toward them during the course of the twentieth and early twenty-first centuries. Thus, while I tend mostly to the unacknowledged anxiety of Wallace Stevens's poems, Aaron Kunin and Claudia Rankine engage directly with theorists of shame and rage, contesting the static objecthood of lyric production by incorporating intertextual interlocutors.

***

Given a discussion of affect that invokes such a transnational array of thinkers, the choice of US poetry deserves some explanation. First, US poetry in the last century has constantly turned to the concept of personality. Modernist poets, especially T.S. Eliot, explicitly opposed the value; confessional poets aimed to recover individuality in an expressive poetics of personal and interpersonal disclosure; contemporary poetic projects such as Lyn Hejinian's *My Life* find ways to use the pronoun "I" without asserting that poems serve to represent psychological selves. As a category, affect is capacious enough to treat each of these modes of grappling with personality. It may be singularly appropriate because, while affect shapes personality, the two remain distinct. For a body of poems that continually questions the ways aesthetic objects do or do not manifest the individuality of their makers, a concept like affect, which maintains a middle ground between unconscious and conscious life, remains a powerful analytic tool.

Second, I hope that my psychoanalytically informed readings of poems by US poets continue to show, in a tradition established by Jahan Ramazani, the many routes by which the forms of US poetry are shaped by transatlantic and global currents.[6] Several of the poets represented in this study have already been the focus of work showing their transnational influences and intertexts, while the contemporary poets represented here bear witness to the impossibility of isolating an "American" poetics from other national traditions at a moment when poetry is nearly as globalized as commerce. The fact that the term "American" represents an impossible container for the varieties of recent verse speaks, on an even larger scale, to the failures of containing with which I am concerned. Thus, while there is, on the one hand, no reason to separate American poetry from global poetry with respect to its reliance on and relationship to affects—certainly a similar study could be made of national and transnational bodies of work in different periods—I wish to use the national parameters of this work to claim that something peculiar about twentieth-century US poetry's relationship to affect deserves attention.

***

Why the focus on negative affects? Indeed, pleasurable affects play a substantial role in this era's poetry. Another study might have structured its argument about significant formal and theoretical innovations in poetics with reference to William Carlos Williams' startled surprise in poems like "Arrival" and Frank O'Hara's spontaneous exuberance in poems like "The Mike Goldberg Variations." Focusing instead on affects of unpleasure, however—those constituted, in the Freudian account, by a rising of tension rather than its lessening or discharge[7]—attends both to the analogous sense of crisis that accompanies the last century's struggle with affect as an increasingly urgent problem for poetics and to the controversial flowering of affective approaches to literature in our contemporary moment.[8]

My approach to affect, as indeed to US poetry, draws upon a deliberately eclectic roster of theorists and critics. My key interlocutors on the subject of affect span the century of poetry alongside which they are read, and demonstrate stylistic concerns that track those of their poetic counterparts. Sigmund Freud, D.W. Winnicott, Roland Barthes, Silvan Tomkins, Eve Sedgwick, and Lauren Berlant are all poetic thinkers in the sense that they push the boundaries of the forms they inherit and to which, in their own ways, they manage to remain faithful. One thinker in particular, D.W. Winnicott, provides a sly justification for this eclectic approach. Winnicott's "String: A Technique of Communication" presents the case study of a young boy whose mother was prone to depression and whose symptomatic preoccupation with string, with which he decorated his surroundings, indicated a "denial of separation" from an object to whom no other means of linkage was possible.[9] Despite the significant differences between the accounts of affect offered by the theorists represented here, this book represents a similarly symptomatic string by which any complete separation of their work from each other can be productively disavowed.

This study begins with Sigmund Freud, whose Copernican revolution began with the recognition of a profound link between language and affect. In *Studies in Hysteria*, Freud and Breuer argued that hysteric symptoms were the result of affects that were provoked by traumatic experience but then "strangulated." When, through the talking cure, memory returns to the traumatic experience and describes it, the affect can be "abreacted" and symptoms relieved. In Andre Green's phrase, Freud discovered a means by which affects could be "poured out verbally."[10]

In Freud's genetic account, the conscious experience of affect can be traced back to "very early, perhaps pre-individual experiences of vital importance."[11] As a tool for reading poetry, what's most remarkable about this observation is just how far affects can come. That is, a study of the appearance of affect in poems permits not so much a return to their genetic beginning but a glimpse of the diversity of forms they take as a result of stylistic and formal practices. The most notable aspect of Freud's account of affect is that, to use Wallace Stevens's phrase, "it must change." Affect is frighteningly dynamic, and as such can be transformed, displaced, or exchanged in the course of mental life with a variety of results. The appearance of an affect always opens a story about the ideas to which the affect has been linked and, crucially, to which it may become attached in the future. Although I will also draw upon Freud's work on mourning, I focus particularly on Freud's account of anxiety, an affect that troubled him for much of his career, and around which he developed some of the most consequential descriptions of the conscious mind.

D.W. Winnicott remains particularly relevant to twenty-first-century readers, as recent writers have acknowledged, because he offers a theory of the transitional site of aesthetic experience that recognizes the distinction between art and world without neglecting the ways in which they are inextricably bound.[12] Winnicott's theory of the holding environment, a simultaneously physical and psychical interaction that briefly makes infant and caretaker indistinguishable,[13] provides a powerful articulation of the ways that affects are uncontainable or, stated positively, relational. Discussions of affects consistently invoke figures of leakiness, of transmission and interaction, and of the powerful and often painful interactions of variously figured "insides" and "outsides."[14] Winnicott's theory, crucially, addresses not only holding, but the failures of the holding environment that produce the earliest affects, those that mark the emerging and persistent space that separates individuals. In adapting Winnicott's theory of the holding environment to discuss the work of affects in poetry, I aim to make a case for reading poems as dyads that consistently emerge in order to acknowledge and experience—or suffer—a gap that separates, though never absolutely, the poem and the poet, reader and poem, work of art and world.

Jean-Francois Lyotard's work has not often been a source for work associated with the "affective turn," and he will not appear prominently in any individual chapter of this study; nevertheless, Lyotard's explorations of affect ground my use of the term. Stemming from his 1983 volume, *The Differend*, which articulated a philosophy centered on the "universe" established by the unit of language he called "the phrase," Lyotard came to identify affect, too, as a phrase, but one deserving of special attention because it cannot be subsumed into any articulated phrase regime. I turn to Lyotard's account of the "affect-phrase" as a way of speaking about the peculiar status of negative affects in relation to the twentieth-century poems in which their prominence is often indicated precisely by their muteness. As Claire Nouvet writes, "To testify to the muteness of the affect, claims Lyotard, is the task of literature, which labors to say a 'secret affection' that a writer worthy of the name knows to be unsayable, irreducible to articulation."[15] Because Lyotard also identifies this phrase's address as a process into which psychoanalysis provides special insight, my reading of Lyotard's concept of affect, and its relationship to the speechlessness of infancy, calls on D.W. Winnicott's presentation of the early infantile holding environment as a model for understanding the significant role of the negative affects in the development of poetic modernity.

D.W. Winnicott's "psycho-analytic explorations" move more easily into the realm of cultural analysis than many other post-Freudian psychoanalytic approaches, and it is important to note that Winnicott found in poetry a prime extension of his core concepts. "Transitional space" or "intermediate experience," in which neither subjective nor objective phenomena dominate, becomes a characteristic of adult creativity after having played a chief role in the development of the child's capacity to distinguish self from other, to manage separation, and to relate to his or her own body.[16] Instead of calling on poetic examples merely to provide evidence for a preestablished conceptual framework, Winnicott, like Freud, seeks to account for creative activity as an outgrowth of psychic development. For Winnicott, not every person becomes a poet, but poetry is a model of "creative living," a result of healthy development and the consistent maternal holding environment that psychoanalytic treatment aims, when it has not been experienced, to restore.[17]

In prescient fashion that calls to mind Lyotard's mention of the affect-phrase's appearing alongside articulated phrases, Winnicott recognized that words in the analytic situation do not stand alone but are accompanied by effects that can only be called poetic:

> Although psychoanalysis of suitable subjects is based on verbalization, nevertheless every analyst knows that along with the content of interpretations the attitude behind the verbalization has its own importance, and that this attitude is reflected in the nuances and in the timing and in a thousand ways that compare with the infinite variety of poetry.[18]

The significance of the writing of D.W. Winnicott to this study, then, is threefold. First, I take Winnicott's engagement with Freud, which was sometimes oblique but always an implicit motivator of his original thought, as a model for this project's relationship to psychoanalytic literary criticism. While the excesses and reductive schemas of that tradition have been sufficiently criticized, psychoanalytically oriented readers have not yet responded with clear methodological aims that would differentiate a new project from the blind spots and symptomatic readings of the old. Because Winnicott identified himself as a Freudian, even though he also noted that reading Freud could hamper his individuality,[19] I suggest that Winnicott's modifications of Freudian theory, which were often not stated as such, provide a helpful way of continuing to read psychoanalytically without becoming suckled in a creed outworn. One of Winnicott's contemporary commentators, Adam Phillips, writes that "now more than ever before, psychoanalysis has also become something, in William James' words, 'to be going on from.'"[20] Nevertheless, it may remain, rather than something "right," a "good way of speaking about certain things like love and loss and memory."[21] Winnicott's conviction that his own observation of infants and the material his patients "taught" him in the course of their analytic work would be the inviolable source of his knowledge,[22] while his reading of the psychoanalytic tradition would remain in the background, suggests one pathway by which Philips's modest version of psychoanalysis could comment on the affective environments of literary texts.

Second, I employ Winnicottian concepts to interrogate and animate twentieth- and twenty-first-century American poems. The maternal holding environment that precedes speech and is fundamental for later development helps us to account for Stevens's conceptions of poetic space and of the poem as a container of uncontainable feelings. Within this environment, and following from its effects, the role of communication as an act just as often directed to the self as to others—and justifiable in this regard despite its unintelligibility to others—suggests a renewal of the terms by which Stevens's poetic "solipsism" has been evaluated. Perhaps it allows us to speak of the "good enough" poem, just as Winnicott emphasized the importance of a mother whose ability to fail her infant, and to avoid both depriving it and spoiling it, gave her a sufficiency more vital than perfection. Notably, Winnicott's version of psychoanalysis depends on an attention to and a validation of the patient that de-emphasizes one of Freud's cornerstone concepts, resistance.[23] As a result, Winnicott's analytic technique speaks to what is useful and unique about the peculiarities of Stevens's oeuvre, rather than, as some critics have emphasized, its deficits.[24]

Finally, aspects of Winnicottian style recommend a posture toward texts that is attentive to the "transitional space" that the poetic instantiates and is.[25] While the concept has been noted by numerous critics, to some extent its most radical gestures have been overlooked. Every act of reading enters a space in which the subjective and the objective are productively—if not without risk—blurred, and in which a certain play between dependence and independence that involves all actors on the psychic stage allows for movement and insight at a pace that is as dynamic as the interaction. It is precisely this "space between" that Winnicott's psychoanalytic writing on the development of the child allows us to posit for the adult (if sometimes childlike) reader and writer of poems; this study teases out the implications of a kind of reading that takes place in this liminal zone— implications for reading and writing, for texts and their readers that are borne out in the difficult language that aims to account for affective experience.

An image of this sort of reading appears in Wallace Stevens's "The House Was Quiet and the World Was Calm," a poem that seems at first to sponsor a merger between book and reader before showing that their difference is constitutive of a space that includes the action of reading as well as the environment in which it takes place:

The house was quiet and the world was calm.
The reader became the book; and summer night
Was like the conscious being of the book.[26]

The use of the word "like," as well as the fact that the poem reasserts the material existence of "the book" in its antepenultimate stanza, reminds us that the act of reading must be mediated—that it must cross a distance and take place in a space. The poem's last line, which compares the night to thinking itself, gives us the corollary: the world can be read like a book, and summer night can be like a book in being an organized "perfection of thought," but the reader cannot, even in fantasy, "become" the book. Even in the beginning of the poem, "summer night" is only "like" it. This resemblance, while it lessens the distance between subject and object in the same way that a Winnicottian potential space does, nevertheless, and as a matter of necessity, preserves a minimal distance that we may speak of as the poem's environment.

I first engage affect theory in chapters on Randall Jarrell and Aaron Kunin, to which the work of Silvan Tomkins, Eve Sedgwick, and Lauren Berlant is central. Writing on the "bodily knowledges" that affects produce, Sedgwick and Tomkins speak to the ways negative affects in particular turn the individual's attention to the relationship between inside and outside. Shame, for instance, "as precarious hyper-reflexivity of the surface of the body, can turn one inside out—or outside in."[27] Poems that punctuate themselves—mark themselves as distinct—with reference to shame are poems whose distinction from their environments is, like desire itself in this situation, incompletely reduced. It is, then, in the ongoing relation between two objects (since "shame is characterized by its failure ever to renounce its object cathexis")[28], rather than in the absorption of one object in itself, that an analysis of affects in poems would illuminate.

Lauren Berlant argues that some cultural logics reveal themselves affectively before they become legible in any other way.[29] Are poems one of the first, perhaps semi-legible, next stops? Might poems represent one of the first ways by which, after a defining cultural logic, can be felt, it may come to be articulated? If poets can still be said to be, as Pound wrote, the antennae of the race, attuned to the workings of the present in ways that other parts of the cultural body are not, and if something of what poems reveal when they present the findings of their groping is feeling—as it has often been assumed—then such a privileged place seems possible.

Of course, there is some reason to doubt that poets deserve, or can legitimately lay claim to, this privileged title. In fact, one of the key statements about poetry's relationship to feeling—that a poem represents emotion recollected in tranquility—suggests, even as it lays claim to poetry as a privileged site for the containing of feeling, that affect must recede into the past in order to be articulated poetically. While the complexity of the present seems to inhibit poets and poems just as readily as it inhibits the rest of us, the poems I consider are strikingly attuned to affects that emerge even in the course of the poem, interrupting its otherwise calm surface with an inarticulate pulsion. In this way, poetry asserts its persistence as a genre at a moment when the cruel optimism of our moment can be witnessed by what Berlant calls "the waning of genre."[30]

Affect theory provides a means for reading the ways in which poems outline their attachments, and it offers an important rearticulation of poetry's relationality. In some sense, all poetry and writing about it is writing about attachment and its optimism inasmuch as it involves "the force that moves you out of yourself and into the world in order to bring closer the satisfying *something* that you cannot generate on your own."[31] Berlant's description of optimism resembles Allen Grossman's claim that poetry is, by definition, an interpersonal practice: "Poetry is the least solitary of enterprises. It pitches persons toward one another full of news. Its purpose is to realize the self; and its law is that this can only be done by bringing the other to light."[32] Although poems in the grip of extreme affects turn more obviously to the project of "realizing the self" than to one of "bringing the other to light," I hope to show that the work of the former sustains the possibility of the latter, such that even those affects that inhibit sociality earn their status as relational.

***

Anxiety, grief, shame, and rage seem to give names to feelings that we can recognize. In trembling, tears, and blushing, the body shows the mind's cards and reveals what, at times, the sufferer would rather hide. But what does the interruption or intervention of writing do to these affects? Is there, for example, an anxiety proper to writing that differs from the anxiety that is written on the body? Might this anxiety be the same as what Blanchot identifies as an effect essential to all reading, an "anguish" that follows from the fact that "any text, however important, amusing, or interesting it may be … is empty—at bottom it doesn't exist"?[33] This study begins with anxiety because Freud notes that it is a common denominator of the affects, inasmuch as "all 'repressed' affects are exchanged" for it.[34] Anxiety is a particularly significant affect for this period's poetry because it reveals a reversal from what Oren Izenberg calls, quoting Valéry, poets' "confiance au monde" to a troubled mode more appropriate for what Auden christened "The Age of Anxiety."[35]

I proceed to mourning, perhaps the affect most commonly associated with—and controversial for—the history of recent poetry and poetics. The elegiac potential of poems has been almost as securely identified with lyric as its erotic goals, but the poetry of mourning after Modernism takes aim at the possibility of elegiac consolation, as Jahan Ramazani has argued.[36] Even more significantly for my argument, elegiac writing struggles with a problem of containment that cuts deeper into the promise of elegy than even that of consolation. For if the poem cannot contain or express the intensity of its grief, how can it sustain the illusion that this grief played any role in sponsoring the fantasied resurrection of what Ezra Pound calls its "lost dead"?[37] Channeling Emerson, such a poem "grieve[s] that grief can teach [it] nothing."[38] It finds itself, instead, among unwanted revenants, having become, in Wallace Stevens's apt phrase, "the haunt of unimportant ghosts."[39]

Next, I take up the affect of shame more directly. Shame has played a significant role in recent discussions of the ongoing intervention of queer theory into contemporary intellectual discourse.[40] It is nearly as difficult to define as anxiety, as significant differences among theorists concerning its relationship to guilt, to subjective experience, and to personal history place its role in obstructing communication in different registers. Shame also bears a close relationship to poetry because it makes salient the very questions about subjects relating to objects to which poems, and particularly those upset by intense affects, demand new answers.

Finally, I look to rage, perhaps the affect that most explicitly announces itself as uncontainable—related to and in conflict with the world outside its unmoored subject. The prose poems and scripts for video in Claudia Rankine's *Citizen: An American Lyric* invite readers to feel the rage of various individuals grouped, in the book, under the single pronoun "you." The condensation of so many disparate experiences of racially motivated aggression betrays an explosive affect that progressively opens Rankine's poems to non-poetic interventions, as if to show (on a glossy white page), that poetic affects interpellate the world they cannot—and should not be expected to—contain.

***

Chapter 1 proceeds from the observation that the philosophical and rhetorical bravado of Wallace Stevens's poems seems to be at odds with the disruptive contagion of their anxiety. That is, the "fluent mundo" Stevens idealizes does not always align with the "chaos in motion" that upsets so many of his poems. My first chapter extends Winnicott's concept of a "holding environment" to the space of the poem tasked with safely containing the emotions of a speaker. In Winnicott's explanation, the failure of the holding environment, often due to anxiety itself, gives rise to early childhood experiences of anxiety. I demonstrate that Stevens's poems betray just such an ongoing anxiety about the emotions poems can contain that belies his reputation as a confident and calmly masterful poet. Reading Stevens "with one's nerves" brings to light poems that contain nothing, or only anxiety, rather than the wisdom or "supreme fictions" which even his prose statements and more ebullient poems lead us to expect. Rather than staging this failure as an implicit critique of Stevens's poetry, I suggest that this anxiety imagines a new kind of poetic holding inseparable from its failure. In this light, Stevens's poems create and maintain a space where anxiety that arises from being insecurely held can itself be held, held onto, tolerated, and revisited.

The intense, subject-centered focus of Wallace Stevens's poems has often split commentators into those who deride Stevens's solipsism as self-indulgent and those who glorify his singular focus on the self. In my second chapter, I open more nuanced routes for reconsidering insight, interiority, and self-knowledge in Stevens's meditative poetics by drawing upon D.W. Winnicott's concept of "not-communicating," which recognizes a purposive interaction with "subjective phenomena" within nonsense communiqués. By focusing on ambient sound, birdsong, and nonsense in readings of four poems, I establish Stevens's reliance on "not-communicating" for negotiating the fraught boundary between self and other, thus resituating his poems at the unstable threshold between internal and external engagements.

Moving toward the midcentury, I turn from Wallace Stevens's anxiety and its associated interiority to middle-range affects of hesitation and ambivalence. Randall Jarrell's poems have attracted critical interest in recent years for the variety of voices their speakers appropriate in order to articulate novel approaches to gender, but I consider Jarrell's animation of statues and his appropriation of female voices as tentative attempts to give an account of emerging queer sexuality. The poems' voices index feelings simultaneously revealed and occluded, but their engagement of an ethically questionable interpersonal sphere situates poetic feeling a short step beyond Wallace Stevens's non-communicating interiority.

My fourth chapter refigures the time of mourning in the elegies Robert Creeley wrote for his mother. Maternal mourning returns Creeley to the site of the seemingly unrelated emotional crises that drove his early poems of erotic ambivalence and aggression. Poems in the elegiac tradition have long depended on manipulations of time to address the dead as though they were living; I suggest that midcentury technologies of mourning, including a particular reliance on photography, may also return poets to periods in their work that still need to be, in Freud's phrase, "worked through." Roland Barthes discovers an absolute and unmovable past in maternal photography that refuses to transform grief into a non-melancholic mourning. Creeley's vexed attempts to reanimate himself through the reading and handling of his mother's image suggest that recent poetry mourns the loss of elegiac consolation even as it claims more recent modes of technological intervention as building blocks in a proprioceptive poetics.

In contrast to Jarrell's reticent desire and Creeley's compounded griefs, Ted Berrigan's brash coterie poetics confronts its others directly, even violently. Pioneering a lyric mode at odds with the subjectively focused meditative poetics identified with Stevens and Jarrell, Berrigan's signature collage method, by which he created poems from lines written by his predecessors and his friends, demonstrates the forcefulness by which he hoped to attain a place in the pantheon. Brutal symbolic attacks on friends and enemies characterize a poetry bent on making poetry interpersonal by any means necessary. As his career progressed, however, Berrigan also found in collage method a way of making what Melanie Klein calls a reparative gesture. Although he mocked his poetic rivals, such as James Dickey, he also identified with their love of the art and used collage forms to pay them homage. In elegies for Frank O'Hara, Berrigan, like Creeley, struggled to find a form adequate to the ambivalence constitutive of mourning a rival without whom one's own life and career could be called into question.

Extending my concern with experimental forms of the lyric, I turn to a constraint-based poetics that has its origins in the French Oulipo and the conceptual procedures of Sol Lewitt. For Aaron Kunin, constraint becomes a means for showing the potential of shame to produce new means of poetic communication, and his 2005 volume *Folding Ruler Star* brings an argument about affect's importance to twentieth-century verse into the contemporary moment. Kunin's governing constraint, the five-syllable line, manipulates iambic pentameter and represents the obstacles to communication imposed by shame. Because Kunin draws explicitly on affect theorist Silvan Tomkins and engages with the history of poetry within his poems, I argue that contemporary poetry concerns itself with affect directly, in some contrast to the anxiety that overcomes Stevens's poems and the way that mourning inhabits Creeley's elegiac writing. Although Kunin takes up problems of shame in *Folding Ruler Star*, he does so fully aware that shame overtakes the space of even his tightly controlled pieces. A certain timelessness of affect manifests itself in the poets whose work I take up here, so that despite any historical argument, affects remain a challenge to the fallacy of progress or development in aesthetic production, even in a period of change as dramatic as the last century.

My final chapter takes up Claudia Rankine's *Citizen: An American Lyric*, which represents a landmark achievement for the lyric because it coheres around a set of feelings rather than around any single individual who feels them. As such, *Citizen* redefines its genre not only by replacing an individual speaker with a singular affect, but also by orienting this innovation toward minoritarian feelings and their presence—through sport, popular culture, law, and commerce—in the fabric of social life. *Citizen* explores feelings that are uncontainable because they result from an accumulation of everyday traumas, rather than from a single, catastrophic event. It demonstrates that exposure to racism produces not only "loneliness" and "disappointment" but a "real rage" that far outstrips "commodified anger"; perhaps more dangerously, it recognizes that a "lack of feeling" and feelings that can't even be known account for the dubious singularity of contemporary Black affective citizenship. As such, Rankine shows that certain traumatic feelings may bear witness to the violence of institutionalized racism precisely by constituting its most lethal and inarticulable effects. By depicting the affective body as one that both "absorb[s] the world" and fails to "hold/the content it is living," *Citizen* represents violent feeling as *in* conflict and an agent of conflict.[41] In keeping with such a recognition, the last chapter focuses not only on the injuries to which affects bear witness, but on the more insidious ones for which they are responsible.

***

While I have chosen to speak of anxiety, mourning, shame, and rage in these texts and the specific determinants of each in psychic life are distinct, they are all characterized by calling to what poems carry along in their margins or in their wakes. It is as though Stevens, Jarrell, Creeley, Berrigan, Kunin, and Rankine, writing in and responding to a century whose violence manifested itself in exiles, forced migrations, and unrecoverable losses, were all concerned with the *baggage* of poetry, both with what it can and cannot carry and with the penumbral impressions these extra-poetic aspects seek to project, develop, and program in the space of their reception. In some cases, these rhythms are tolerable to readers only because they cannot bring along the legacies or violences that brought them into being. In others, the absences themselves make the poems nearly illegible and burdensome in their affective resonance. Rhyme is not masculine or feminine here, not a technique these poets can be said to master, but rather the insistent troping of what is, in barely registered echoes, unbearable.

If poetic feelings and poetic desires remain significant to the contemporary project of formulating what Lyotard called "a literature, an ethics, a politics— perhaps,"[42] they do so both by being out of time, caught between past and future, and by being, or running, out of space. As befits aesthetic objects constructed out of *stanzas*, or rooms, poets have associated their work with small containers.[43] And yet the very use of these figures acknowledges what critics, enamored of "well-wrought urns," fail to see: poems fail to make their affective contents fit. They repeatedly fail to contain themselves. And the various ways in which poems transgress their borders may redefine poetry's relationship to those other supposedly self-contained or quarantined spheres of social and political life from which poems have often been excluded. Because feeling and desire cast determinative shadows upon literary form, because they show how prominently episodes of failed containing figure in formal innovation, and because they model aesthetic responses to seemingly closed or foreclosed topics, poetic feelings address themselves to futurity, and to its associated risks and potentials, even when they cannot imagine it. That is, if poems orient themselves temporally by means of spatial transgression, their time is always both now and to come.

Although this study is based almost entirely on negative affects, Berlant speaks to one way that it may be appropriate to refer to these affects as potential feelings of exaltation. Poetic optimism doesn't always look optimistic; for Berlant, "optimism might not [even] *feel* optimistic."[44] As a result, forgetting the optimism at the heart or in the residue of its negative affects fails to account for what productivity or fantasmatic generativity there is in these experiences and the forms they take or give. My title quotes the last four words of John Ashbery's decidedly optimistic 1963 poem, "A Blessing in Disguise." The poem's closing stanza speaks to the dynamic by which articulating an unfulfilled desire can give way, unexpectedly, to joy:

> I prefer "you" in the plural, I want "you,"
> You must come to me, all golden and pale
> Like the dew and the air.
> And then I start getting this feeling of exaltation.[45]

Rather than demonstrate closure with respect to the plural addressee of the poem, "A Blessing in Disguise" looks back upon the effect that the poem's own address has made on its speaker. Already, the poem's optimism is of a reflexive variety, manifesting inwardly as an effect, rather than a cause, of stepping outside oneself. The fact that the poem records this feeling as a beginning, the "start" of a feeling one acquires in stages, reveals an investment in representing feeling as uncontainable, unbounded by the lines of the poem. I take the poem's closing on a note of positive affect as a fitting close to a study that makes resolutely positive claims for the presence of negative affects in US poetry. Perhaps, at the end of anxiety, melancholy, shame, and rage, one sometimes recovers, if not "a place for the genuine," then a renewed access to the first signs of such a feeling.

1

Anxiety's Holding: Wallace Stevens's Poetry of the Nerves

"One reads poetry with one's nerves."[1] Wallace Stevens's aphorism not only hints at the poet's reading habits, but suggests how contemporary readers might proceed in glossing the texts of a poet whose reputed difficulty and diverse critical legacies prompt, already, a nervous response. The phrase relocates poetic legibility to a zone between mind and body, for reading "with one's nerves" would aim to sidestep both the anemic misreading characteristic of an overly cerebral analysis of Stevens's poetry and the overwrought sentimentality Stevens's verse itself continually disparages. After all, for Stevens, "It is not the reason that makes us happy or unhappy"[2]; for him, the poetic mind "destroys/Romantic tenements of rose and ice."[3] Beyond reading with nerves, certain of Stevens's poems call for a reading of the work of nerves, that unhappy by-product, anxiety.

On the one hand, Stevens's appeal to nerves calls on incontrovertible physical and biological proof, a certainty so profoundly embedded in the individual, as if in his or her blood and bones, that it trumps both casuistry and predilection. On the other, however, nerves are the seat of uncertainty, ambivalence, and untraceable impulses; as the pathways of the tensions that may not be containable by the mind *or* the body, nerves transmit the threat of the approach of what overwhelms the structures of experience. By recommending them as agents or catalysts of reading, Stevens indicates that it is, paradoxically, in the realm of the indirect, the subtle, and the risk-prone that his poetry sounds its longest-lasting chord. Or, beyond this, that poetry is not always the stable, legible, and intelligible expression of "emotions recollected in tranquility," but that it occurs also when nerves cannot collect or contain their stimuli, and when nervousness, anxiety, and panic disrupt the poem's progress and its style. To read with one's nerves, then, would mean to be attuned to what "Credences of Summer" calls "the secondary senses of the ear" and the "pure rhetoric of a language without words," that is, to what cannot simply be spoken in Stevens's verse and to what has not yet been heard there.[4] A significant aspect of Stevens's oeuvre, I suggest, concerns what cannot be parsed with one's mind, cannot be heard with one's ears, but only, instead, read with one's nerves. Long revered or criticized as the most calm, confident, and invulnerable of poets,[5] what has not often been heard or read in the poetry, and what can only be parsed with the aid of "one's nerves," I maintain, is precisely the presence of nerves, of nervousness, and of anxiety.

D.W. Winnicott opens pathways not only to read Stevens with the nerves, but to read the role of nerves in his poetry. Winnicott's writings on anxiety—which argue that the experience of being insecurely held fosters a contagious experience of anxiety related to holding and containing—help to gloss the affective material to which Stevens's anxious poems signal. His development of the concept of holding to describe the earliest, most intimate interactions between an infant and its mother also models, as I will show, the onset of the affect of anxiety in poetic technique.

Poetic holding is one locus of Stevens's anxiety. I derive the concept from D.W. Winnicott as a way to refer both to the explicit concern with containment, management, or treatment of affective content in poems and to the poetic strategies that Stevens uses to try hold or contain what often resists it.[6] Poetic holding, then, constellates a series of questions about the relationship between what Stevens called "materia poetica" and the poems made out of it, between poems and an oeuvre, and between the oeuvre and poetry more broadly and abstractly conceived.[7] How does a poem adapt to and manage, or find itself disrupted and upset by, its contents as a result of the affective intensities that threaten to destroy it? What can the space of a poem successfully contain, and how? What is the result for a poetics of the anxiety-producing discovery that poems cannot contain everything or that they cannot contain everything without registering, perhaps on the reader's nerves, the strain to which they have been subjected?

Fredric Jameson's negative account of the implications of Stevens's style is useful, if symptomatic of a certain distrust of the poet's innovative approach to poetic containing. Jameson writes of the tension between "an astonishing linguistic richness on the one hand and an impoverishment or hollowness of content on the other."[8] The description Jameson provides is precise, but, caught up in its negative evaluation ("impoverishment"), he overlooks what I take to be the notable significance of "hollowness" in its own right. I take "hollowness" not as an indication of emptiness or deception, but as an index of Stevens's anxiety about what poems can hold. That is, anxiety hollows his poetry of content so that questions of poetics—addressed to what and how poems hold—can take center stage. The supposed lack of content of Stevens's verse is actually content motivated by anxiety to question poetic content itself, what it means that poems contain or that they should. One of Stevens's major, explicit concerns in poetics— the role or capacity of poetry to hold—betrays one of the major, implicit ways in which his poems work. That is, so often concerned with matters of holding, Stevens's anxiety poems are aware that they demonstrate and articulate failures of holding.

The orbit of the planet on the table

The late poem, "The Planet on the Table," is a significant example of a poem concerned with an anxiety about holding. Written near the end of the poet's life, "The Planet on the Table" stands, quite literally, apart from its predecessors. Its speaker stands outside the book (rendered here as a "planet") of which it is a part—Stevens's *Collected Poems*, published in 1954—in order to offer an evaluation of its contents. Because its explicit subject is a book of poems, "Planet" is one Stevensian *ars poetica* among many, but it is also, from its first line, an example of a rare species, a poem about an affective state that results from writing poetry: "Ariel was glad that he had made his poems."[9]

In this line, Shakespeare's sprite parallels the God of Genesis who, after his creation of the world, regards his works from outside and expresses approval. But Ariel stands in, too, for Wallace Stevens, who, at the end of his own life and work, thus claims to author a work that leaves nothing out. Even as a planet (and a book *on* a table) is something contained by (and defined as such in relation to) a larger organizing system, a planet is also self-contained, a container complete in itself. To speak thus of his *Collected Poems*, to claim them as a "planet," is to schematize individual poems not as parts of an infinite and accumulative series, but as singular examples of phenomena and styles (or notes, ephemera, letters, songs, postcards, invective, cadences, reveries, etc., to name a few of the putative genres or subgenres Stevens names in the titles of his poems) that serve to fill out and complete the geology and geography of the planet as a whole.

"The Planet on the Table" is Stevens's first positive evaluation of his oeuvre, but it comes only after substantial acrobatics: suggesting that there can be no such evaluation in the midst of the oeuvre, the speaker of "Planet" has to step impractically or impossibly out of the book in which he is contained in order to proclaim his gladness at its achievement. To be confident about one's writing is, in some sense, to be dislocated from it, or worse, to recognize that it has already ended. But even beyond this strange standing apart, the creator is anything but glad. The speaker's physical orientation to the planet of which he speaks deserves attention. The planet of the poem rests on the table. The maker does not hold the whole world of his poems in his hands, but instead leaves it lying apart from him. On the one hand, as we have seen, this distance is necessary for evaluation. On the other, the distance is indicative of an anxiety that parallels the anxiety D.W. Winnicott attributes to the mothers of infants. Anxious about dropping the infant, rather than holding it, such a mother "uses the cot as much as possible, or even hands the baby over to the care of a nurse."[10] The distance she puts between herself and the infant has, in this case, a reason: the mother claims that the baby will be more comfortable in the cot. Winnicott sees such an excuse as the articulation of an anxiety that derives, perhaps, from the mother's own experience of "being insecurely held."

For Stevens, the distance between his planet and himself is one, presumably, that allows him to evaluate it and proclaim his "gladness." Upon closer analysis, however, the evaluation of the planet is vague.

> It was not important that they survive.
> What mattered was that they should bear
> Some lineament or character,
> Some affluence, if only half-perceived,
> In the poverty of their words,
> Of the planet of which they were part.[11]

Rather than actually describe any characteristics of the planet, these two final stanzas emphasize the fact (or the hope) that the "planet" of the poems resembles the planet where they were written.

The name Ariel signals not only, with reference to Shakespeare, a late comedy, which "The Planet on the Table" surely is in Stevens's corpus, but also a "tempest" that this Ariel, in his gladness and from his Archimedean standpoint, seems too quick to dismiss. Thus, "The Planet on the Table" shows that Stevens's confidence is more complex and less univocal than it is sometimes portrayed. Anxiety maintains a close proximity to its confident posture, and Stevens's poetry includes more open descriptions and enactments of anxiety that, owing to a history of criticism that gloss Stevens's project otherwise, have not received much attention.

Reading Wallace Stevens is not usually an experience that brings to mind the characterization of "anxious." As the least confessional and most rhetorically ebullient of the high Modernists, anxiety would seem to have neither a reason nor a means for finding its way into Stevens's work. Much has been made of Stevens's characteristic "evasions" by means of "as if" constructions and a proliferation of possible alternatives to what would otherwise be grand assertions, but it is not anxiety about their validity but a desire to draw attention to the process of their construction that drives this tactic.[12] Uncertainty, agitation, irritation, and fear seem more appropriate terms for glossing the work of so-called confessional poets like John Berryman and Sylvia Plath, whose psychological vulnerabilities appear closer to the surface of their finished work. (For all the charges of Stevens's solipsism, which I'll deal with more directly in Chapter 2, it's surprising what little place the pronoun "I" plays in his poems, especially when compared with the aforementioned poets.) The flow of Stevens's poems, unlike that of the confessionals, covers over the distraction, disruption, and hesitation that characterize poems noticeably defined by, or upset by, anxiety.

By "flow," I mean to suggest that Stevens often couches passages that describe states of agitation, panic, and anxiety in his typically stylized and mannered language such that we infer a distance between the situations described and their articulation by an unfazed or unaffected poetic speaker. In this vein, Stevens describes the anxiety of his addressee, a young poet whom his most famous long poem, "Notes toward a Supreme Fiction," seeks to instruct in the art:

> You lie
> In silence upon your bed. You clutch the corner
> Of the pillow in your hand. You writhe and press
> A bitter utterance from your writhing, dumb,
> Yet voluble dumb violence. You look
> Across the roofs as sigil and as ward
> And in your centre mark them and are cowed ...[13]

If, in "The Planet on the Table," a manner of holding suggested anxiety, here anxiety is itself held at a distance. In the context of the poem, anxiety results from living among people who work against the poet and unnaturally try to tame the strongest natural voices—lions, elephants, and bears—whose strength dwarfs even the poet's. The anxiety is not an anxiety of influence, for it is not predecessor poets who threaten the ephebe, but philistine progeny—"heroic children time breeds/Against the first idea"—who would silence him. In this sense, it is anxiety proper, rather than fear or fright, for it, in Freud's words, "describes a particular state of expecting danger or preparing for it, even though it may be an unknown one."[14]

Nevertheless, the style of the passage betokens tranquility. Rhetorical feints—the adjectives "writhing" and "voluble," the archaic noun "sigil," and the anaphoric "you" beginning each of the three sentences in the passage—distance the speaker of the poem from the suffering the speaker describes to the sufferer. The carefully crafted, worked-over passage is evocative of, but not affected by, the mental pain it describes. In a taxonomy of the emotions present there, it could be listed, but hardly emphasized as predominant. So far, anxiety seems to be at worst absent and at best thoroughly distanced from the reader, and without looking more closely at other poems—minor poems, as we will see—this proximal or marginal engagement with anxiety as someone else's affect would be its only appearance, the only reason to suspect anxiety plays any role at all in Stevens's poetry.

The concept of poetic holding comes into play as a result of Stevens's repeated mention and evaluation of his ability to create containers for the metaphors, ideas, and (rarely) persons that he tasks his poems with developing. Given that Stevens uses poems to comment on the role of poetry, the objects of his poems often stand in as material representatives of the poem in the world, as is the case in the famous early poem, "The Anecdote of the Jar."

"Anecdote" betrays a concern with the property of holding or containing by avoiding it when we expect it to claim the spotlight, allowing its very absence to speak volumes.[15] After the narration of the peculiar main event of the anecdote, "I placed a jar in Tennessee," there is no focus on what the jar holds until the "anecdote" is nearly at an end. The final lines of the poem read, "It did not give of bird of bush,/Like nothing else in Tennessee."[16] Critics usually take these lines to emphasize the jar's artifice—it is the only nonorganic object around—and to affirm the improbable and felicitous success of its placement by emphasizing precisely what it lacks in comparison to its surroundings. But there is also an ambiguity apropos of the jar's contents. Does it, in a simple contrast, "give of" nothing or does it, in its peculiar way, "not give of bird or bush," and as such give somehow otherwise than reproductively? Instead of assuming that the jar is bereft of content or that its contents are simply unknowable, we might think of "Anecdote" as a poem that emphasizes what such uncertainty about contents entails. That is, being unaware of what exactly a jar—or a poem—can contain forces us to attend to its relationship to the environment. Because we are also unaware of how the jar "took dominion," both questions—what does it hold and how has it taken hold—remain active and unanswerable. The enigma of the jar's contents and its dominion stands to the side of the poem's narrative, as though it were only a distraction. But both the "jar" and "Tennessee," the container and the environment, are peculiar. Why does the poem specify a jar, rather than another domestic object, if not for its ability to contain? Or for its ability to hide whether or not it contains? Why place it in a named place if the particular way that environment responded to the jar were not of some importance? Might these be the questions that would help us understand how a small jar "took dominion" over an entire environment? On the other hand, might concrete answers to these questions distract us from Stevens's concern with holding and the holding environment, from a kind of "reading with one's nerves" that shows Stevens shifting back and forth between the jar and its surroundings, unable to focus on one or the other and unable or unwilling to offer a "closed" reading of what seems to be a poem left, as it were, ajar? The problems of what is inside and what outside, of what it means for the "outside environment" to be *inside* a poem, and of what basis objects have for relating to their environment make "Anecdote of the Jar" not only an exemplary poem concerned with holding but a poem that demonstrates how often failures of containing distinguish an oeuvre Stevens himself insisted was a planet unto itself.

Despite fervent claims to the contrary—"poetry is an effort of a dissatisfied man to find satisfaction"—Stevens is not always the champion of poetry as the practice that gives relief, helps people live their lives, and interrupts the monotony of reality with the infinite variations of imagination. Instead, Stevens often doubts the ability and mission of art to cover up a more brutal reality. That is, some of Stevens's poems—those that are left "ajar"—trouble the idea that a poem is a good container for a person, for a life, or for experience. "Poetry Is a Destructive Force," for example, begins familiarly.

> That's what misery is,
> Nothing to have at heart.
> It is to have or nothing.[17]

Poetry comes on the scene against misery and its living presence successfully opposes the emptiness of misery:

> It is a thing to have,
> A lion, an ox in his breast,
> To feel it breathing there.[18]

This short poem concludes quickly but with a knife-twist. The lion, symbol of poetry, reveals the destructive force foreshadowed in the title but forgotten by the poem's second stanza:

The lion sleeps in the sun.
Its nose is on its paws.
It can kill a man.[19]

The risk accompanying poetry's role as "a thing to have" and "to have at heart" in place of misery is its "destructive force," a potential power unpredictable and alien to human concerns. To forget or deny this aspect of poetry, Stevens suggests, is to be naïve about the demands placed upon it to resolve or relieve misery. "Poetry Is a Destructive Force" goes beyond the question "What can poetry hold?" by reversing it and asking whether the human can hold poetry. I've been claiming and will show that Stevens is an insecure holder—but here Stevens claims that failures of holding may be imputed to the contents they try to contain. Winnicott's theory claims the origin of insecure holding is in the past, but "Poetry Is a Destructive Force" suggests that the threat that the object (infant or poem) poses to the holder, of annihilating him or her, accounts for much of the holder's anxiety about holding.[20]

Stevens's cautious handling of poetry, which in "Poetry Is a Destructive Force" approaches a warning to steer clear of it, is also operative in "The Emperor of Ice Cream." The poem builds up an elaborate edifice for describing (and embellishing) a funeral, only to close each stanza with the pronouncement that if any portrayal can overcome the gaudiness and unsuitability of aesthetic representation, it would have to be more spare and artless than the one he has just provided: "Let the lamp affix its beam./The only emperor is the emperor of ice-cream." As such, "The Emperor of Ice-Cream," published in *Harmonium*, may be the earliest poem in the *Collected Poems* to struggle with the problem of holding, that is, with the concern that poetry may not be the proper container for any situation it attempts to put into language. It is here that Winnicott's concept of holding and the holding environment, though it derives from a particular context in clinical psychoanalysis, will be helpful for exploring the implications of Stevens's concerns.

Holding, failing, reading (Winnicott)

Unlike Freud, whose *Inhibitions, Symptoms, and Anxiety* delivered a revised and comprehensive theory of anxiety, Winnicott speaks of anxiety mostly in the context of other developmental phenomena;[21] unlike Klein, Winnicott does not posit anxiety as one of the chief forces stimulating early infantile development. In many ways, then, it would be easy to pass over anxiety's role in Winnicott's work in order to focus on the more popularly recognized "Winnicottian" concepts of transitional objects and potential space and what seems, in many brief accounts, to be their calmer and more palatable account of the psychic life of infants than the ones associated with either Freud or Klein.[22] While emphasizing and exploring the concept of holding for a study of Stevens' poetics, I maintain that the significance of anxiety in Winnicott's account of this phase of infant development has been overlooked, and that reinserting it may help us read both the holding and the turbulent anxieties about holding that punctuate Stevens's oeuvre. Because anxiety for Winnicott is not only a consequence of the worst failures in the holding environment, but also the affect that adult analysis hopes the defensively structured analysand can return to and tolerate, to recognize anxiety in Stevens's poetry is not to defame or dismiss it. Rather, it is to approach the work from an angle that allows us to see what forces threaten the poem and how those threats shape it. More "defended" poems give less evidence of these influential aspects, and so prove less helpful for articulating how anxiety, by holding poems, holds the key to understanding Modernism's relationship to poetic forms.

For D.W. Winnicott, psychoanalysis is an encounter in which the history, consequences, and experience of holding and being held come to light. Both in the literal sense of early infantile dependence on a holding mother and in the figural senses of an adult's capacity for concern and love, holding signifies the royal road to a way of living whose hallmarks are creativity, spontaneity, and authenticity.[23] The numerous resonances of the term "holding" apart from any psychoanalytic connotations suggest why Winnicott found the word amenable to his purposes of naming a naturally occurring phenomenon and the analogous psychical phenomenon that springs from it. While the *Oxford English Dictionary*'s first definition is familiar, glossing holding as "[t]he action of [the verb] hold in various senses," the second is less obvious: holding is defined as "[t]hat which holds or lays hold; an attachment; a means of laying hold or influencing."[24] This second definition mingles agent and recipient. Holding, then, might just as well describe the holder as the person who, having been held, develops an attachment for the holder; he or she can be said to "have a holding" on the holder and to "lay hold" of him or her. This transitivity of holding, the sense in which both parties are holding and being held, suggests that there is no act of holding unaffected by the experience of having been held, and no being held without the (often anxiety-provoking) possibility and responsibility of having to hold lurking on the horizon. In this respect, holding names one of the fundamental ways in which humans attach to each other, or form the bonds and binds by which families, communities, and societies form.

Significantly, Winnicott links the physical act of holding to the affective qualities that emerge from it. The concept of holding and of the holding environment merges the mother's physical holding of the infant and her creation of the psychological environment in which, through a gradual transition from complete unity to independence, the child approaches maturity. The duality of the referent is particularly appropriate because, as Winnicott states, holding takes place at a time in development when "physiology and psychology have not yet become distinct, or are only in the process of doing so."[25] Physical holding is not only like, but, owing to the early state of the child's development, actually *is* psychological holding. When, as I will discuss later, Winnicott emphasizes a mother's technique of holding—adapting to the infant's body and not holding too tightly[26]—the significance of the double resonance of the word becomes clear: the technique of physically holding an infant influences emotional development inasmuch as it gives birth to the infant's psychological apparatus, which is at this stage indistinguishable from its physical environment, and is integral for the child's transition from complete dependence to independence.

In this way, the concept of holding presents Winnicottian psychoanalysis in a nutshell: unlike Freud, Winnicott's comments on adult analysis are never far from his thoughts about children and infants; unlike Klein, Winnicott emphasizes the role of the mother as the infant's "holding environment" over the infant's inner fantasy world; and, finally, unlike the American ego psychologists with whom he found some posthumous favor late in his career (and perhaps in contrast to his earlier views as a pediatrician), Winnicott's conceptual vocabulary inhabits a realm far from technical jargon and scientific systematization.[27,28]

In his major statement on the role of holding in infantile development and in the adult analysis, "Theory of the Parent-Infant Relationship," Winnicott posits four stages of childhood development, each pegged to the infant's progress in separating from the mother. Starting at birth in a phase of "absolute dependence," the child moves through "dependence-independence," in which the first category is dominant, to "independence-dependence," before finally achieving relative independence. Winnicott's major claim is that Freud failed to account for the first stage, in which holding is most important. "The infant exists only because of maternal care" in this stage, which precedes that of "living together" with the mother and, significantly, of alerting the mother to its needs by means of the "signals" of crying and kicking.[29] During absolute dependence, however, the interaction between mother and infant is not only such that the infant cannot yet produce signals in order to indicate its needs, the good-enough mother should not need to receive such signals. A mother's ability to adapt to her infant's needs (a major part of holding) derives from her "devotion" to the child, and as such is part of what Winnicott calls her "knowledge," something she brings to the interaction with her infant that has little to do with the "learning" she must undertake to master from external sources such as doctors.[30] Feminist critics have been quick, and astute, to point out that Winnicott depicts motherhood as an easy, natural, and immutable relationship to sustain, and indeed, essays such as "Theory of the Parent-Infant Relationship" and "Transitional Objects and Transitional Phenomena" bespeak a reductive understanding of a relationship that, as Elissa Marder has explored, is too quickly regarded as natural.[31] It's only in essays such as "Hate in the Counter-Transference," which lists reasons a mother may hate her baby, that Winnicott more accurately accounts for the dangers inherent for self and other in the work of mothering.

While Winnicott emphasizes the role of the psychological environment, he also believes that the physical must not be forgotten, inasmuch as it is a means of communication: "Holding includes especially the physical holding of the infant, which is a form of loving. It is perhaps the only way in which a mother can show the infant her love."[32] Just as Freud was attuned to the minimally verbal communicative potential of the Fort/Da game, Winnicott stresses that communication during the holding stage is different from that of other stages. The child does not send signals to the mother because it does not yet need to, but the mother, in her knowledge of what the infant needs, is able to communicate via holding. Holding thus figures a different sort of relationship between language and emotion, and it is at this intersection that Stevens focuses his poetry.

Before we start to think that Winnicott's analysis of mothers and infants is too rosy, a critique that many Kleinians have leveled against him, it is important to cite the continuation of the above quotation: "There are those who can and those who cannot hold an infant."[33] While Winnicott allows for—and even seems to accept the other qualities of—such mothers, he does not omit the sometimes catastrophic circumstances that can befall an individual as a result of having had such a mother. The key to failed holding is not a lack of devotion to the infant or ambivalence about it; for Winnicott, the mother's anxiety leads to insecure holding, to an environment in which the baby's own anxieties and insecurities cannot be contained or consoled.

Most of Winnicott's theory of anxiety, and the majority of the discussions of the term in his work, come by means of, and through a link with, this concept of holding, which refers to the chief characteristic of the mother's care of the newborn infant and to the adaptive process by which the mother's care changes in order to allow the infant to achieve independence. For Stevens as well as Winnicott, then, anxiety and holding are inseparable; its grip on those it affects, and on the writing produced under its disturbing effect, is tantamount to an insecure, anxious holding of the topics or concerns it treats. Anxiety's hold makes for anxious holding.

Outside of explicit reference to holding, anxiety was of central importance to Winnicott's understanding of the aims of psychoanalytic treatment, not only (as with Freud) in the theoretical underpinnings of neurosis but as a generative factor in the workings of a psychoanalytic therapy that could provide relief from it. Without disregarding the lasting damage that anxiety could set in motion, Winnicott also saw anxiety as necessary, normal and at times productive. As such, Winnicott provides one avenue for seeing anxiety as more than a problematic concept to be theorized. Inasmuch as the affect can be located and taken note of, it can be significant, and even illuminating, as an indicator that something otherwise undetectable is happening.

Winnicott's theory of anxiety focuses on the infant's relationship with the mother and with the transitional object or objects that stand in for her. Like Freud, Winnicott claims that anxiety has its determining causes in the earliest infancy of the child. For Winnicott, the child's ability or inability to tolerate anxiety based on environmental and temperamental factors is an important gauge of his or her healthy development. What he calls "intolerable anxiety" is a sign of disintegration and nascent psychosis, whereas an ability to tolerate a high level of anxiety indicates a certain strength of personality in its progress toward independence. And finally, in some adult analyses, by means of regression, the analyst aims to help the analysand become able to experience anxiety again and to unravel the layers of defenses that mask an inability to tolerate it that had its beginnings in early childhood.

In his characteristically simple style, Winnicott announces in "Anxiety as Insecurity" that "we are near the well-known observation that the earliest anxiety is related to being insecurely held."[34] He explains that insecure holding forces the child to prematurely, and without the necessary resources, respond to the "impingements" of the external environment. Notably, Winnicott adds that this contingency, rather than the infant's "inherited potential," can structure the infant's entire personality: "if maternal care is not good enough ... the personality becomes built on the basis of reactions to impingement,"[35] by which Winnicott indicates both the ways that unmet physical needs threaten the baby from outside and the ways that a mother's own emotional deficits or demands can upset the baby's development.

Winnicott argues that "[a]nxiety in these early stages of the parent-infant relationship relates to the threat of annihilation."[36] This is because the ego goes "from an unintegrated state to a structured integration," at which point "the infant becomes able to experience anxiety associated with disintegration" where it previously had not been possible.[37] Thus, the importance of the "holding environment," which Winnicott says "has as its main function the reduction to a minimum of impingements to which the infant must react with resultant annihilation of personal being."[38] Holding is so powerful and consequential for later life that failures in this environment result in extreme anxieties. And so powerful is anxiety at this stage in an infant's life that the characteristic defenses of an entire personality structure can be traced back to this stage.

Winnicott notices something peculiar about anxiety in relation to the mother. That is, the mother's own anxiety is determinative of her child's. Anxiety might lead a mother or a sibling to hold the infant too tightly for fear of dropping it, or not to hold it at all, believing mistakenly that it is happier in the crib.[39] In this situation, anxiety interrupts knowledge and prevents one of the basic functions of childcare from taking place, often with the effect of passing on an anxiety to the infant him- or herself.

One of the most important facets of the concept of holding is Winnicott's application of it to adult psychoanalysis. Jan Abram notes that, often in his published work, the concept of holding appears as a rough synonym for "management" as it applies to the care of those who are so severely mentally ill as to be unable to function.[40] So important is holding in these situations, Winnicott insists, that instead of "interpretations that might be made on the material presented" in a schizophrenic's analysis, the focus should be on the patient's "main need," which is "for an unclever ego-support, or a holding. This 'holding,' like the task of the mother in infant-care, acknowledges tacitly the tendency of the patient to disintegrate, to cease to exist, to fall forever."[41] In the analysis of a more neurotically organized patient, holding allows for the creation of a potential space through the transference that would otherwise have been impossible: instead of interpretations, which would be received as impingements, this analytic holding environment often functions in silence as the analyst conveys a sense of empathic understanding. As with infantile development, the very notion of health and psychological growth in the analytic setting depends on the successful creation of a holding environment against impingement, even when the most likely culprits are words themselves.

Winnicott draws a number of parallels from his psychology of infants to the technique of adult analysis and it is, in part, this work of relating holding in one case to holding in another that allows us to use the concept in reading Stevens. When Winnicott discusses the role of holding in adult psychoanalysis, he will speak often of the technique of regression. The analyst offers a holding environment not in order for the patient to progress, at least not immediately. Instead, the analyst hopes to allow for regression back to the time of insecure holding, where the defenses were organized and the neurotic or psychotic personality determined. Winnicott claims that feeling anxiety might even be a part of recovery or progress in the analysis:

> [D]efences are formed in relation to anxiety ... the infant experiences intolerable anxiety with recovery through the organization of defences. From this it follow that the successful outcome of an analysis depends, not on the patient's understanding of the meaning of the defences, but on the patient's ability, through the analysis, and in the transference, *to re-experience this intolerable anxiety* on account of which defences were organized.[42]

Stevens's poems demonstrate an exemplary ability to display intolerable anxiety at the moment that defenses against it—almost always those of his rhetorical evasion—are being formed but have not yet obscured their inciting causes.

Winnicott's most clear statement of the relationship of holding to the adult analysis comes from a later paper, the 1963, "Psychiatric Disorder in Terms of Infant Maturational Processes":

> You will see that the analyst is *holding* the patient, and this often takes the form of conveying in words at the appropriate moment something that shows that the analyst knows and understands the deepest anxiety that is being experienced, or that is waiting to be experienced.[43]

If Winnicott previously defined anxiety in terms of holding ("being insecurely held"), we can now do the converse. Holding happens when the analyst's words make clear that he or she grasps the threat—"the deepest anxiety"—facing the patient. If infantile holding happens just on the threshold of the use of signals and is itself the indicator and determiner of future anxiety, so it is that holding and failures of holding take place in analysis at the zero degree of language, where words become intelligible out of silence. This is the constraint of poetry and our reading and analysis of it. Reading Stevens with one's nerves will be a kind of holding of the poetry in which Stevens's own concern with holding can be viewed, and along with it perhaps the deepest anxiety that his body of work confronts.

Winnicott's theory of holding, and of the anxiety that often accompanies it, does not simply map onto the reading and writing of poems. That is, rather than suggest that Stevens is the anxious, motherly holder of the poem-infant that reflects and in turn transmits the same anxieties to which it has been exposed, I take Winnicott's theory as a sign of the ways that holding and anxiety are inseparable, of the ways that anxiety escapes containment and betrays a certain contagion through everything it touches, of the ways that the words in poems bear witness to both a concern for holding and an exposure to anxiety, and of the possibilities for innovation that this anxiety makes available to poetry in its moments of crisis.

Stevens's "Chaos in Motion and Not in Motion"

Dating from the middle period of Stevens's career, "Chaos in Motion and Not in Motion," like "The Snow Man," sustains repeated encounters, paradoxically because it is the poetic account of an encounter that cannot be withstood. On the surface, "Chaos" is a poem with a narrative at its center. The story is that of Ludwig Richter, a nineteenth-century German illustrator who appears in the poem as a "spirit" and, to use the title of another Stevens poem, as a "connoisseur of chaos." The poem's account of Richter, the purported subject of its chaos, is interesting because it is rare for Stevens's poems to feature characters, much less historical figures. I suggest, however, that Richter's story is not the only event of the poem. In fact, "Chaos in Motion and Not in Motion," a poem full of the language of the stage, performs a catastrophic drama in its own speech behind the masque of its master narrative. The chaos of the poem exceeds the character for whom the leading part was written and reveals the problem of anxiety in the oeuvre as a problem of holding.

Several problems beset "Chaos" as a poem tasked with containing or holding emotions, especially those of a man who has "lost the whole in which he was contained." The poem, which speaks to the problem of movement in its reference to "motion and not in motion," moves from its beginning to its end in view of an insolvable problem it nevertheless continues to confront. Furthermore, the poem's ellipses and unquestionably short stanzas of two lines leave the poem more open than most of Stevens's poems, as though the poem itself were at the same time ephemeral and physically insistent.

> Oh, that this lashing wind was something more
> Than the spirit of Ludwig Richter ...
> The rain is pouring down. It is July.
> There is lightning and the thickest thunder.

It is a spectacle. Scene 10 becomes 11,
In Series X, Act IV, et cetera.
People fall out of windows, trees tumble down,
Summer is changed to winter, the young grow old,
The air is full of children, statues, roofs
And snow. The theatre is spinning round,
Colliding with deaf-mute churches and optical trains.
The most massive sopranos are singing songs of scales.
And Ludwig Richter, turbulent Schlemihl,
Has lost the whole in which he was contained,
Knows desire without an object of desire,
All mind and violence and nothing felt.
He knows he has nothing more to think about,
Like the wind that lashes everything at once.[44]

Read from start to finish, "Chaos in Motion and Not in Motion" introduces a character (lines 1, 2), describes a tumultuous environment as a projection or dramatization of his turmoil (3–12), and returns to a more direct explanation of the character's chaos (13–18). But how much does "Chaos" lend itself to such an ordered reading?

Although the poem opens in the voice of a speaker bemoaning Richter's presence on the wind and wishing for "something more," it never again addresses the problems of its speaker. The poem will never be more concerned with the subjectivity of its speech and the possibility for the speaker's relating to Richter than in the nonfluent sigh of its first word. From here, the poem slips into the third person and never returns to the speaker's situation. On the one hand, Richter's drama overwhelms the speaker's desires for "something more," an excess or supplement he never receives or has time to describe. Perhaps the reason he bemoans Richter's appearing is nothing more than this: the speaker will never return to himself because he is, against his will, caught up in Richter's chaos. The character impinges on the environment of holding and containing, and all the subject can do is comply. (As we shall see in Chapter 2, Stevens does not like anything to keep him from interiority.) On the other, however, the poem's shift from first-person wish to third-person narration after its first stanza suggests something less readily apparent. If the speaker wants "something more," how does something so insubstantial manage to pull him under? How might the appeal to Richter's drama, which takes the form of the speaker's wish to be rid of Richter, be an excuse to avoid its own utterances and to stifle any explanation for its opening "oh"?

Roman Jakobson's discussion of the "emotive function" of language permits a gloss of the first word of "Chaos," which may contain its most dramatic index of anxiety. He writes that the "emotive function" is "focused on the addresser [and] aims a direct expression of the speaker's attitude toward what he is speaking about … [t]he purely emotive stratum in language is presented by the interjections."[45] According to Barbara Johnson, who calls on Jakobson to make the argument, the word "oh" has a special role when it appears in poems. As a signifier of pure subjectivity, it opposes the "O" of apostrophe, which is perhaps the fundamental trope of the lyric and the sign of the pure conative function in its trajectory toward an addressee.[46] In "Chaos," Stevens's speaker's "oh" places the poem under the sign of a plaintive subjectivity before it turns aside, focusing most of the poem's energies on a middle ground between "oh" and "O" that is the narrative of Ludwig Richter's theatrical turbulence. That is, what is odd about this poem is how completely subjectivity is erased following the strength of its presence in the first two lines and how no other apostrophe ever takes its place. Although the first stanza ends in ellipses, it closes off the speaker's explicit involvement in the drama of the poem. In an attempt to contain "Chaos," I argue, the speaker quarantines himself from the storm and spectacle in a strategy that seems destined to fail.

Chaos not only is the subject of the poem, then, but is at work in it. In the figure of Ludwig Richter, whose own chaos is the putative subject of the poem, chaos becomes an anxiety that runs against the poem's story. That is, instead of either a narrative about the speaker's resolution of the Ludwig Richter problem or a narrative of that problem alone, "Chaos in Motion and Not in Motion" displays the particularly lyric anxiety that besets a poem that cannot articulate what it so urgently needs to signal.

The poem's context in history and Stevens's career offers one explanation for the anxious tone and content of "Chaos in Motion and Not in Motion." Stevens's letters suggest July of 1945—weeks before the United States would drop the atomic bomb on Hiroshima—as the most probable date of composition for the poem.[47] Stevens was attuned to the situation and described the summer in a letter as "most defective" because "the benumbing effect of the war seems to grow constantly worse."[48] We get a sense of the workings of Stevens's imagination in his disjunctive equation of thunderstorms and atomic bombs, as his letter to Henry Church continues, "And if the war doesn't quite put an end to us, the weather will, if it stays as is."[49] In the summer of 1945, annihilation could come from any direction, even, it seems in the poem, from a long-dead German illustrator named Ludwig Richter. Even the letter's mention of a desire for a small road trip to Pennsylvania finds him dwelling strangely on confused tongues, dead ends, and spectres. Deciding against the trip, Stevens wrote, "It doesn't sound worth while merely to see … the haunts of unimportant ghosts whom I could not understand, since they would be certain to talk to us in Pennsylvania Dutch."[50]

I take the locus of anxiety in "Chaos" to be beyond history, and even beyond Richter's anxiety, his "desire without an object of desire." We have to account for the anxiety of the speaker, the voice that tries and fails to contain Richter within the whole of the poem. This leads us to see the poem as an interpersonal drama, something rare enough in Stevens, though the affect attached to it here makes the poem representative and illuminating of a dynamic that runs through the oeuvre. Is Richter's anxiety, the anxiety the speaker attributes to him, separate from his own?

Why does Richter come forward in a "lashing wind"? Before the catalog of its destruction (stanzas 4 and 5), we perceive the "lashing wind" as a threat. And, in fact, "wind" is a term Stevens often uses to depict crisis, confusion, and uncertainty.[51] The speaker's tone in "Chaos" hardly befits a "lashing" wind, however, and it is the discrepancy between the adjective "lashing" and the style of these sentences that is our clue that something is awry. The speaker's opening apostrophe sounds like weariness with a tired subject: "something more" would be something more interesting or more contemporary than a "turbulent Schlemihl." As the poem continues and the lashing wind gives way to a destructive storm, Stevens's unaffected tone is even more at odds with the content to which it, like Odysseus to the mast, is lashed: the short sentences (each with its "to be" verb) and concrete words (modified by adjectives speaking only to the physical characteristics of the storm) suggest a continuation of the speaker's opening attitude of weariness and boredom. The only thing missing is the speaker himself, who remains, during the storm he describes, closed off within himself. Another Stevens speaker had claimed, in "The Man Whose Pharynx Was Bad," "I am too dumbly in my being pent,"[52] but the voice who speaks "Chaos" is so imprisoned that he is unable to give words to his condition.

The third stanza offers one solution to this problem, introducing a theatrical metaphor. Perhaps this is no strong storm at all, and only "a spectacle" where "Scene 10 becomes 11,/In Series X, Act IV, et cetera." This storm would warrant the speaker's detached style because it is staged, and the turbulence of the poem, if it is contained in the disaffected tone of the poem, is resolved thereby. But, as it turns out, this is a false calm, only the eye of the hurricane: the storm grows stronger in the following stanzas, and reading the weary "et cetera" of line 6 more closely leaves us no doubt. While we could assume that the throwaway

Latin phrase indicates the speaker's alliance with a reader who would no doubt also be bored to be further oriented in this drama, the speaker of "Chaos" only hopes we will be content with such an inference. Instead, this "et cetera" masks the speaker's unwillingness to orient himself in a "spectacle" that is much more threatening than he is ready to admit.[53]

On the one hand, this seems to be an apocalyptic poem, with the "massive sopranos" and the drama progressed to the late and perhaps final "Series X." But both of these references indicate, not weariness at a *long* play but an anxiety about infinitude, about something that doesn't end, or whose ending cannot be certain. In the idiomatic expression, "it's not over till the fat lady sings," but here multiple sopranos do their worst in a present continuing sense—they "are singing," and their "songs of scales" warm up to some final song of whose beginning (not to mention an ending) we are uncertain. If this is "Series X," when does it all end? And the disorientation that accompanies it? If this is a spectacle, it makes the speaker more, rather than less, anxious. Perhaps less able to keep his distance than ever before, this speaker's defense crumbles alongside the world he describes. The theatrical metaphor and the spectacle it introduces does not solve the tonal problem, but rather brings it into full view.

Despite the chaotic movement caused by the storm as described in the fourth and fifth stanzas ("People fall out of windows, trees tumble down … "), the first half of the poem describes chaos as unmoving. That is, the disorder does not, in these stanzas, move the speaker, who resists its disorganizing effects by treating even the most threatening movement—even the theater from which he watches this "spectacle" is "spinning round"—as a matter not worthy of additional explanation or concern. But, revealingly, neither does the unmoving chaos of these lines move or progress the poem, which stays with a single, descriptive tone for its single matter of concern and cannot reach any conclusion except "et cetera." It is only the speaker's return from the remove of the atmospheric disturbance to the individual who seems to have conjured it that sets the threat of chaos in motion. The speaker's anxiety comes full circle even though the narrative of their relationship never receives explicit attention.

But haven't we seen the change coming? Helen Vendler calls line 13 the "human beginning"[54] of the poem (she explains that it is often the case that Stevens delays the personal and emotional until late in his poems), but the shift has already taken place when we learn that "The theatre is spinning round." The drama Stevens's speaker narrates is not the only spectacle about to give way. The one he performs and participates also draws to its climax. The crisis is not only Ludwig Richter's, but also that of the poem.

The poem does change stylistically, but not in the way as we might expect. "Has lost" is the first verb of "Chaos" not to be in the present tense, and this longest sentence of the poem is also the first one not to contain a "to be" verb, signaling that the poem's heightened language tries to meet the heightened threat level, since the threat that the speaker will lose his way asserts itself here with the most disorienting force. Abstract nouns replace concrete, and the polysyndeton of "mind and violence and nothing felt" replaces the asyndeton of stanzas four and five in a first indication that chaos is now in motion, not only for Richter but for the speaker who must account for his state of mind. The poem reaches its stylistic as well as thematic climax in a missed encounter, a confrontation between the speaker and the irritating figure of the lashing wind he has bemoaned, avoided, and finally pronounced "lost." The nonconfrontation seems motivated just as much by the speaker, who runs away from it. Despite a sustained interest in Richter—he devotes three stanzas to him—the pace becomes faster as the poem draws to a close. The "motion" of "Chaos in Motion" is that of the speaker's attempt to escape from a danger he has avoided admitting by any means possible. What is the nature of this threat, however?

The speaker's opening claim is that he wants "something more" than Richter's spirit. It is because such a spirit is not substantial enough for the speaker that he continually slips through his fingers upon any attempt to grasp him, that the threat he represents to the speaker is that he cannot be held within the bounds of the poem. On the one hand, this is an anxiety about writing poetry: the speaker of this poem identifies a subject who must be given proper lyric treatment but whose insubstantiality and turbulence resists this, whether this is, as Vendler suggests, because of the speaker's similarity to Richter or precisely because of a difference that nevertheless cannot prevent the anxiety from being held in common. If Richter eludes the poem, anxiety scripts Richter's absence precisely because his affective turbulence risks becoming the speaker's, too. The threat that Richter is or could become the speaker of, or the voice intoning, "Chaos" is what explains the distance this speaker tries to keep from him. Richter's anxiety is contagious, and it is the speaker's unspoken understanding of this, rather than any identification between poet and character, that leaves Ricther lost in a wind and still lashing as the poem ends.

It is the contagion of anxiety that Winnicott describes as one particularly debilitating consequence to being insecurely held: one risks becoming an insecure holder. In a lecture to mothers called "Knowing and Learning," he writes that having "a mother who was not very good" at holding makes the anxious mother "afraid of passing on to her own baby some uncertainty belonging to the past,"[55] and that this fear causes her to hold the baby either too tightly or not at all. These remarks on infant care concern the mature Stevens poem, one that Vendler claims identifies "one of the fundamental miseries of the old,"[56] because the speaker relinquishes control of Ludwig Richter, just as the anxious mother seems to be controlled by her child even as she holds it. While he attempts a defense against Richter's lashing wind, his indifference and compliance cannot withstand it. Instead, Richter, turbulent and anxious about the absence of his own "object of desire," retroactively creates or instantiates the speaker of "Chaos in Motion and Not in Motion" as a speaker anxious about what he cannot securely hold. The speaker's fear that his voice is not his own, and further that his fate is determined by that of his historical subject, long dead but somehow unvanquished, produces a poem that brings Richter into view only to obscure and eventually escape him. The time of the poem is the brief window of time in which the speaker can tolerate or endure what Winnicott names as the job of the analyst—"being used." Like an anxiety attack itself, the poem is a spilling over of what can no longer be contained by one person, but whose duration is also almost unendurable.

The anxious have no worse anxiety, and no worse experience, perhaps, than watching anxiously as their anxiety repeats itself. In this sense, the opening "oh" of the poem reads as weariness at the inevitable return to the beginning of a poem that never, like the play it describes, seems entirely finished. For Stevens, the anxiety that cannot be held or contained within "Chaos in Motion and Not in Motion" spreads to his other poems, permeating—and uniquely motivating—an oeuvre that seeks "intenser calm" in the midst of an affect that, by returning again and again, "lashes everything at once."

I have suggested that Stevens's poems are concerned with holding and that they demonstrate the consequences of insecure holding. Winnicott's holding environment concerns not only infant development but the surround of poems threatened by characters, topics, and affects that are uncontainable, and in so doing suggests a vocabulary for reading some of Stevens's least read and most powerful documentations of affective experience as it is simultaneously registered and escaped. In the next chapter, I speak to another aspect of Winnicott's work that helps us to read Wallace Stevens's poems, namely a "non-communicating" interiority that is inseparable from the problematic experience that, for both Winnicott and Stevens, grounds the possibility of aesthetic experience, that of holding and being held.

Threshold Poetics: Wallace Stevens and D.W. Winnicott's "Not-Communicating"

By turns hidebound and exuberant, recondite and sententious, Wallace Stevens's poems task their readers with tracking the orientation of an ever-changing self. "What counted was mythology of self," he writes in "The Comedian as the Letter C," but especially in that poem, whose main character stands apart from and then, suddenly, among human and inhuman others, the self is rarely still enough to locate, much less to lend a mythos.[1] Two epigrams in the posthumously published collection of Stevens's aphorisms, *Adagia*, suggest the tension at work in constituting the poetics of the self in transition. The first urges the poet to advance from the individual imagination to a fictive poetics that would address a community outside the poet: "The transition from make believe for one's self to make believe for others is the beginning, or the end, of poetry in the individual."[2] Such a mandate is consistent with Stevens's bold, if critically contested, claims about the ends of poetry in society, that it may "help people live their lives."[3] But Stevens checks his own boldness in a second adage, one that suggests that the difficult labor of poetry consists of making the opposite movement, from external concerns to a resolutely inward site: "We have to step boldly into man's interior world or not at all."[4] Noticeably, however, neither adage speaks to the fixity of an external or internal location. Rather, both speak from the threshold of "man's interior" and exterior worlds of a necessary "transition" or "step" toward the proper, if recently unsettled, location of poetic experience. These prose fragments suggest that the self imaged and articulated in Wallace Stevens's poems dwells fitfully between solitude and society. In the analysis that follows, I suggest that the poetic strategies of this space, which marshal sounds and speech at the limits of audibility and intelligibility, are consonant with this poetic self's transient and transitional temperament.

Wallace Stevens has only recently been regarded as a poet whose investments in the exterior world—history, politics, and news—deserve an important place in his poetic reputation; since the 1950s, most assessments of Stevens have granted pride of place to a world-avoiding interiority that some critics have scorned as solipsism and others have praised, hyperbolically, as American poetry's closest approximation to the quintessence of lyric. Only in the last two decades, led by Alan Filreis, James Longenbach, and Jacqueline Vaught Brogan, has a new perspective, one that recognizes Stevens's engagement in the events of his day, emerged as a corrective.[5] Of course, none of these scholars claim that contemporary history was, to use a phrase from the late "Of Local Objects," the "absolute foyer" of Stevens's work, but they furnish the necessary reminder that his poetry privileges change, variation, and modulation—the desire for a foyer than the sense of already inhabiting it.[6] While critics have argued that Stevens's poems demonstrate movements in accordance with natural cycles (Lensing), the mercurial variations of mood and emotion (Vendler), and the instability of language (Miller), I would add that a dual obligation to the challenges of self-knowledge and the conflicts of ethics drives Stevens's poems. The endless, restless movement that his poems observe and demand describes, too, the lability characteristic of this writing's oscillation between internal and external sites of concern.

Writing roughly contemporaneously with the earliest poems of *Harmonium*, Freud claims in his *Introductory Lectures to Psychoanalysis* of 1915–1916 that psychic defenses play a role analogous to flight in the "fight or flight" response.[7] Rather than provide a physical escape from danger, however, defenses permit the conscious ego a mental escape from threats by means of denial, splitting, reaction formation, and other unconscious processes of reality distortion. Rather than rush to psychologize the author of such motion-centered poems as neurotic, or even to apply the analogy, however, I propose a psychoanalytically inflected reading of Stevens's poems because Freud's discourse—especially as it is adapted by its heirs in the British Independent school of psychoanalysis—develops a vocabulary for discussing the constant transitions of psychic economy and thus aids the reader in limning the characteristic hoverings, approaches, and withdrawals from the threats of the interpersonal world and the comforts of the mind—or the promises of contact and the threats of self-knowledge—that mark the language of Stevens's poems from beginning to end. While I turn away momentarily from a Freudian perspective for discussing Stevens's poetic selves,[8] Winnicott's conceptual vocabulary offers an alternate, but resolutely psychoanalytic approach to the language of the moving self.

By focusing on what is gradual, precarious, and transitional, Winnicott's account of the self offers a rich conceptual vocabulary for describing the changes—rather than the fixity—of Stevens's psychic negotiations of the real world. Adhering neither to Freud's developmental stages nor to Klein's more suggestive "positions," Winnicott "tends ... to write of capacities"[9] and to interpret otherwise pathological phenomena in light of their function for the individual's continual striving toward health. Trained as a pediatrician, Winnicott emphasized the intimate link between the capacities acquired during childhood and the quality of adult mental health; instead of the product of overpowering instincts for sexuality and aggression, Winnicott argued that the child's movement toward independence—a state characterized by the capacity for creative and spontaneous living—necessarily takes place in relation to other people and things. Such "objects" constitute an environment that, owing to the child's nascent ability to perceive differences between self and other, exists neither completely inside nor outside her mind. In order to develop this capacity to distinguish between fantasy and reality, the child alternately relies upon and tests her environment. Shuttling back and forth in this way now only allows the child to differentiate between inner and outer reality but also to negotiate the demands of his or her needs with respect to both. This demand, of course, is never completely resolved, and as such characterizes the struggles of adults, too: "It is assumed that the task of reality acceptance is never completed, that no human being is ever free from the strain of relating inner and outer reality."[10] Unlike Freud, who saw the persistence of the tasks of childhood development into adulthood as an indicator of neurosis,[11] Winnicott recognized that certain conflicts first encountered in childhood would require outlays of energy throughout life. Given the constant pressure to foreclose one or the other arena of experience, the task of bringing inner and outer reality into relation was ongoing. Wallace Stevens's poems enmesh themselves in the intricate labors of such a task.

By a foray into Winnicott, readers of Stevens can better track multiple motive forces that shape a poetic language made to grapple with the movements of a self torn by allegiances to itself and its others, or "inner" and "outer reality." In the adages above, Stevens speaks from what D.W. Winnicott calls a "transitional space" between self and others, or on the way from self to others or the converse, such that the desire to be in the world or in one's mind is always mediated by the change it would take to arrive there. In several recent readings to introduce a Winnicottian perspective to Stevens's poems, Gina Masucci and Daniel T. O'Hara helpfully suggest that the "absolute foyer beyond romance," which seems to mark the highest desire of the restless poetic mind, bears a resemblance to Winnicott's "space" because it, too, serves mainly as an anteroom for other, more fulfilling encounters. Instead of "a space with its own function, or definitive identity, [the foyer is] a liminal gate-keeping space, a place to pass through to other, large, more important and definite places or actions."[12] Their analysis, by suggesting that Stevens's poems occupy their hard-won foyers provisionally, calls upon another Winnicottian concept's explanatory power. "Not-communicating," a concept Winnicott developed late in his life, suggests a paradoxical variation of positive, normative communication that helps to account for the poetic strategies by which movements between the self and its others, or from foyer into other, occupied rooms, are represented.

Winnicott's "Communicating and Not Communicating Leading to a Study of Certain Opposites," published in 1963, promotes the significant developmental work performed by silence and by self-directed or self-interpreted practices of speech; all of these means may, Winnicott asserts, nourish an internal world that must reach a threshold of safety and communicative confidence in order to engage with the social aspects of the external world. Analogously, Stevens's singularly difficult strategies for setting "materia poetica"[13] adrift between what Winnicott called "subjective and objective phenomena"[14] substantiate a poetic outlook preoccupied with structures of feeling and experience peculiar to the self at the threshold of internal and external worlds. Against critics who accuse Stevens of a pervasive solipsism or global disengagement, the concept of "not-communicating" identifies an inward turn not identifiable with any simple withdrawal from common concerns. Inasmuch as Winnicott's term claims a general validity for the psychological phenomenon and Stevens's creative application of the strategy speaks not only to his own interiority but also to the contours of inner space as such, "not-communicating" reveals private, "cul-de-sac" communication itself as a common concern.[15] In Stevens's poems, "not-communicating" is a necessary precondition of any incursion into the social world. In the poems I take up later, such strategies depict unknown, internal space as a necessary site of poetic attention; mirror and amplify the frustrations of communication; access otherwise hidden sources of knowledge or memory; and establish necessary preconditions for crossing the threshold from privacy into social engagement.

The oddly hyphenated phrase "not-communicating" exemplifies the vocabulary Winnicott derived from clinical experience and the vernacular.[16] The phrase refers not only to an individual's communication with "subjective phenomena" instead of with persons or objects perceived of outside the self, but to the fact that this form of communication must be seen in its relationship to "communicating." In fact, Winnicott writes, "not-communicating" often takes the place of logical communication, and as such can still be characterized as a form of interaction between two persons. This interaction, crucially, retains an interpersonal index because potential interlocutors not only perceive the dynamic but perceive it as directed or addressed toward them. Winnicott's contribution consists in his recognition that this "active or reactive" relationship to typical communication has its role to play in the development of the healthy subject: only by having access to the refuge or consolation of "not-communicating" can the developing subject regard the alternative, a less private form of communication, as something more than an exacting or impinging demand on the resources of the self.[17]

For Winnicott, the term "self" does not describe a subject's full and conscious presence to herself. In fact, as Winnicott describes in his foundational article, "Ego Distortion in Terms of True and False Self," the individual is split from the start between a set of capacities and feelings that are authentic and proceed from within, and a set of defensive reactions to the external world that can, in certain cases, dominate psychological functioning. Despite its aim of protecting the True Self from damage, reliance on the False Self's knowledge of rules for interacting with others and its complicity with demands can stifle the individual's sense of authenticity. "Whereas a True Self feels real, the existence of a False Self results in a feeling unreal or a sense of futility."[18] Notably, Winnicott derives the concept of "not-communicating" from this split and regards the inward turn of communicating with subjective objects that it accomplishes as an attempt to make contact with a True Self that has been threatened by "the fact that communication so easily becomes linked with false or compliant object-relating."[19] "Not-communicating" makes reparations for the damages of the external world on the development of the self and simultaneously signals the extent of those damages.

Thus, despite the negative phrasing, "not-communicating" is Winnicott's term for a phenomenon of health; it describes the way that individuals actively engage with "subjective phenomena" and ignore or disengage from objective events and others. The term is valuable for allowing us a more complex view of such disengagement as not simply withdrawal, but as a shift of focus highly motivated by the ongoing process of development. "Although healthy persons communicate and enjoy communicating, the other fact is equally true, that *each individual is an isolate, permanently non-communicating, permanently unknown, in fact unfound.*"[20]

Instead of needing to see Wallace Stevens as the epitome of health or illness, a confidently self-aware or withdrawn, antisocial character, "not communicating" allows us to situate Stevens in a middle ground. To critics who understand Stevens's social disengagements as evidence of a disturbed vision of reality, the phenomenon of "not communicating" counters that what appears to be pathological may actually serve the healthy person's desire to protect a center.

Underlining the developmental necessity of participation with "subjective phenomena" at the expense of the objective phenomena which communication is expected to engage, Winnicott reveals that what appears to be withdrawal is actually active and even outwardly engaged, a communication both to the self and to others, albeit by other means. Stevens's inclusion of echoing, nonfluent sounds and ambient noise constructs a repertoire of noncommunicative strategies integral to an apology for meditative interiority haunted by, responsive to, and engaged with its others, and it is in both the hard-won stability and the precise—more true and more strange—representations of linguistic isolation that this conflicted and transitional poetics affords Stevens that the originality of his poetics' stance toward private and public worlds consists.

Although it would be reductive to claim that critics fall into only two camps—one of praise and one of blame—critical appraisals follow a few predictable paths in dealing with Stevens's interiority. Mark Halliday faults Stevens's "omissions and distortions" of social practices and devotes his book, *Stevens and the Interpersonal*, to a critique (and eventual qualified defense) of Stevens's social disengagement.[21] Gerald Bruns claims that we can locate a disruption of Stevens's poetry in what it knows it neglects: "[Stevens] is a poet troubled by the sort of poetry he is not writing and perhaps can't bring himself to think of as poetic … the poetry of the other."[22] He goes on more forcefully: "It is not, as Hugh Kenner once put it, that there are no people in Stevens's poetry … it is that people in Stevens's poetry never answer back."[23] Coming to Stevens's defense, Harold Bloom praises the "selfhood-communings" that set him apart as "the twentieth century poet of that solitary and inward glory we can none of us share with others."[24] Helen Vendler claims that it is in Stevens's difficult, self-reflexive poetic process that we discover their originality. Although "baffling to the ordinary reader when they enact the thinking of thoughts, or the sensing of sensations, or the supposing of suppositions," these techniques comprise the "second-order" processes for which Stevens is renowned.[25]

Set against this handling of interiority, a trend in the recent criticism positions Stevens's poetry in relationship to the historical and political issues of his day. Examining his Second World War-era output, Jacqueline Vaught Brogan situates her claim that Stevens matured to become "one of the most compelling and ethical poets" within an argument about the progress of his poetics throughout his career.[26] She also notes that a critical predisposition for seeing Stevens "as an aesthete, removed either by inclination or economic position from any involvement with the political realities of his time," led to the dismissal of earlier critical appraisals of Stevens's political involvement, such as Joseph Riddel's 1958 article, "Poet's Politics."[27] The work that has come out of this recent trend is not always in conflict with an understanding of Stevens as a poet of inner issues in relation to outside ones. At times, even scholars most invested in the project of exposing Stevens to the light of historical and social issues admit that he was insular. Alan Filreis's archival research in *Wallace Stevens and the Actual World* shows that Stevens does approach and engage with what the poet termed "the actual world," but Filreis concedes that the phrase "actual world" is not always an indicator of devoted involvement. Stevens used it "at times to denigrate his interest in such externalities as the last resort of a man whose already famous interiority made him feel desperately irrelevant."[28] As Winnicott's theory of development has prepared us to accept, the world of actual objects is often the horizon of multiple approaches and retreats in a transitional space characteristic of subjective and objective phenomena intermingling. Stevens could, out of a (subjective) feeling of desperate irrelevance, malign the same (objective) world he would approach later as the locus of pleasure and affiliation. (In a poem like "No Possum, No Sop, No Taters," the maligning has to precede the affirmation: "It is here, in this bad, that we reach/The last purity of the knowledge of good.")[29]

That is, if the "actual world" came to mean both a repudiated or repudiating place and a site of subtle investigation in the poems, it is time to investigate anew how interiority is at work in a poet whose relationship to the external world has been shown to be continuous and complex. Interiority would not be the simple opposite of an "actual world" in Stevens. Rather, it would be an aspect of the "actual world," a response to it, and a buffer between it and the self never completely free from its predicates. I read Stevens's interiority differently from both Halliday and Bloom by demonstrating that the poetry's resistance to social convention is a more complex phenomenon, neither an oversight nor the overarching thematic keystone. Rather than simply rejecting or accepting society, Stevens directs our attention to the process of an individual self's becoming separate as a response to, and in some way a prelude to engagement with external pressures. As such, the poems constitute an anatomy of the struggle to achieve solitude as well as an apology for its eventual, always deferred achievement. In my readings of four poems, I show that the individual relates to the outside world and to the self simultaneously, and does this by means of a modification of positive communication that Winnicott calls "not-communicating."

I begin with "The Comedian as the Letter C" because "Comedian" radically upsets any notion of interiority in Stevens as a space of indulgent withdrawal from ethics, and it is thus useful to begin an analysis of Stevens's relationship to private communication with this early poem's recalibration of privacy itself. The early long poem's deliberation—over dozens of lines in its first canto—of how its main character becomes "an introspective voyager" is the first and fullest poetic treatment of what is, after all, a deliberate turn inward, rather than an already-established interiority.[30] By tracking the progress of this turn, I show that shifts of tone and ambient sounds in the poem threaten the main character's introspection. A seminal moment of self-regard parallels the purpose Winnicott announces for "not-communicating": to create "something that corresponds to the state of the split person," something that "communicates silently with subjective objects."[31] This "something" would attempt to make contact with a self that remains "an isolate ... permanently unknown, in fact unfound."[32] In the same way that, for Stevens, sensory perception mediates and even creates the outside world, in which "things seen are things as seen,"[33] only establishing contact with the self by communicative means can provide evidence of its existence. The self-beholding of "Comedian," in its search for self, grounds the poem's defense of interiority as the unreachable destination of a perilous voyage, rather than an indulgent escape from reality and the obligations of social presence. I turn to readings of "Autumn Refrain," "Depression Before Spring," and "Waving Adieu, Adieu, Adieu," in order to trace Stevens's tentative engagements with (and disengagements from) the self and the external world, emphasizing a dislocation from both outside and inside that remains on the threshold—consistently provisional, hesitant, and incomplete. In all of these poems, nonfluent, inhuman sounds are the media of noncommunication; these departures propel the inward turn and its movement away from a social other who is always nearby. Crucially, however, by terming these movements "divagations," Stevens belies their finality. It may be in his response to the other as a threat and an *eventual* ally that readers best account for Stevens's relationship to the social world; strategies of not-communicating, which defer such relationships and strategize as to their possibility in the future, present the strongest evidence that critics like Bruns who argue that society is wholly absent from the oeuvre are mistaken.

Crispin's loss of a "mythology of self" and his becoming "an introspective voyager" happen amid peculiar tonal variations and a menagerie of unarticulated sounds that complicate our sense of interiority in the poem. Always conflicted, and most often parallel to or intercalated with an external world, inwardness is never simply inwardness in Stevens. The problem of self-knowledge, or more basically, of obtaining a space in which such knowledge could be gained, serves to complicate what is already an involved drama of the individual's location in the world. "Comedian" suggests that, for Crispin, unable yet to contact interiority, the sounds addressed to and received from the external world are even less intelligible than those of "not-communicating."

Within *Harmonium*, a volume of poems that advertises its many genres or subgenres in its title—invective, explanation, anecdote, theory, hymn, sonatina—"The Comedian as the Letter C" delivers its comedy as part treatise and part travelogue. The relationship between these genres is that of commentary to original text, in the sense that the poem turns to the exegetical and synthetic mode precisely when its narrative needs, as Helen Vendler puts it, "punctuation."[34]

The scholarly treatise of "Comedian" follows the humbling of its protagonist. The story of his own transition from complete control of his surroundings to the recognition that his surroundings control him does not so much conclude as find itself "benignly ... clipped" in its own final lines so the story of the world around him can continue.[35] The poem's movement progressively strips Crispin of his sovereignty, his aspirations, and his role in the poem whose title bears only a truncated version of his name, "the Letter C." To read this progressive stripping or, as the poem has it, "dissolv[ing]," is to recognize the travails—rather than the indulgent triumphs—that follow from a decisive "introspective" turn in its first canto.[36] Instead of "inward glory," as Bloom has it, Crispin's reflections first increase his "apprehensions" and then are powerless to stop his disappointment and eventual demise.

As for the other genre of "Comedian," the poem's travelogue is only briefly that of a geographical voyage. Although the opening contrasts the sovereignty of humans on the earth with their alienation at sea, the speaker narrates the way that mental travel turns up on the itinerary. Mary Watson, who also suggests a Winnicottian intertext for this early poem, suggests the two journeys happen simultaneously: "the outward quest *is also* directed inward."[37] "Bordeaux to Yucatan, Havana next,/And then to Carolina" is the geographical trip, but along the way, rather than after it or during a hiatus, "Crispin/Became an introspective voyager."[38] By what poetic strategies does "Comedian" manage to travel in both directions at once?[39]

In the poem's opening lines, Crispin adds "a touch of doubt" to the claim that man's status as "the intelligence of his soil ....principium/And lex" is applicable once he is at sea, surrounded by "porpoises, instead of apricots."[40] Crispin's "verboseness," a habit, when on land, of acting as "general lexicographer of mute/And maidenly greenhorns,"[41] is the first casualty. The speaker, verbose in his own right, distinguishes between his own voluble tongue and Crispin's by claiming that the latter errs by giving language, or worse, a nonfluent "haw of hum"[42] to things that do not need it. Crispin oversteps his bounds, becoming not just the "intelligence" of his soil, but also its spokesman.[43] The only sounds of "Comedian" at this point are those made by Crispin, but if the environment has already struck back in muting him, it will soon do so by its own deafening sound.

The poem's move to countermand a certain kind of address to nature has a companion in Stevens's poem "Nuances on a Theme by Williams," which dates from the same time period as "Comedian." There, Stevens uses an indictment of false relationships between humans and objects to distinguish his poetry from Williams's. "Nuances" reiterates an injunction against prosopopeia even as it personifies and addresses the "ancient star" Williams had commanded to "Shine alone in the sunrise/Toward which you lend no part."[44] Stevens's speaker, in ironic contrast, demands that the star not recognize any gesture that grants it such power: "Lend no part to any humanity that suffuses you in its own light."[45] One of the emerging tropes of *Harmonium* is a call for attention to be placed where it is due, at the moment when objects from the outer world and the inner world come into contact.[46] Williams, and Crispin at this point in his voyage, takes too much for granted about possible relationships to the inhuman external world. Stevens makes the case for a different kind of communication, one that would aim to exhaust communication with the local (though not always more knowable) inside before it addresses the outside and thus risks devaluing it with its own suffusing light.

Indeed, Crispin's environment defines him in the next part of canto I. Once the voyage begins, it is not the unfamiliarity of "porpoises" or even their "inscrutable hair in an inscrutable world"[47] that bothers him: "the lost terrestrial" upsets his sovereignty, but his concomitant, and now inaccessible "mythology of self,/Blotched out beyond unblotching"[48] motivates a terrifying new vision.

> Crispin ....now beheld himself,
> A skinny sailor peering in the sea-glass.
> What word split up in clickering syllables
> And storming under multitudinous tones
> Was name for this short-shanks in all that brunt?
> Crispin was washed away by magnitude.[49]

The poem first indicates that Crispin's voyage will turn him into an "introspective voyager" when (after many lines in this poem, and at the end of a long sentence) a sea-glass grants Crispin his first sight of himself. Certainly, such a re-vision of sight comes at the cost of viewing the external world with any real accuracy: in order to use the "sea-glass" to see himself, Crispin must invert it and use it as an ersatz mirror. The telescoping effect allows Crispin to watch himself watching himself as from a distance, though the word "beheld" indicates a more reverent encounter for a man who nevertheless lacks a mythology. Alienated by the environment, which has demanded everything he owns and stripped him of it, Crispin manages to hold on to only one thing, an image of himself constructed out of equipment intended to permit a vision of the distant ocean. With this reversal, the poem's figure matches Winnicott's concept: at the moment an impinging environment threatens the integrity of a developing self, "not-communicating" grants inward vision out of tools forged for social and public use. As "Comedian" continues, setting a precedent for Stevens's oeuvre, it also turns to language turned inward:

> The whole of life that still remained in him
> Dwindled to one sound strumming in his ear,
> Ubiquitous concussion, slap and sigh,
> Polyphony beyond his baton's thrust.[50]

How to even isolate a singular self for observation if, as Stevens states in "Theory," another *Harmonium* poem evokes the relationship between self and environment, "I am what surrounds me"?[51] How indeed, if what surrounds "me" is a polyphony? Crispin's self-beholding comes at the expense of seeing the external world, but is also the result of significant labor, artifice, and, given his inverted telescope, even innovation. If the failure of sounds to ever "dwindle to one" indicates the failure of Cripsin's introspective voyage, it does so in order to remark that the difficulty of inward turning inheres not only in what it turns away from, but in what it turns toward.

The critical commonplace on the poem's sonic register, which notes only that many of its sounds relate to the letter C, might be updated to note that even this one sound creates a polyphony, that this polyphony remains external to the poem's Comedian, and that it manages to draw out—like an emetic—all "the life that still remained in him." The vampiric sound represents what Stevens would later call "the violence without," the threat of an outside world's chaotic intrusion into inner life. Such a violence can only be countered by the agonistic struggle of the imagination, a "violence within," and it is to such an internal conflict that Cripsin turns next.

> Against his pipping sounds a trumpet cried
> Celestial sneering boisterously. Crispin
> Became an introspective voyager.[52]

"Comedian" represents audibly that the vertiginous visibility of self-seeing can hardly be spoken. The external environment's "sneering boisterously" cannot be met by speech of the kind that Crispin, formerly a "general lexicographer," has been accustomed to utter. Instead, the noise from outside turns Crispin inward, and to a kind of speech appropriate in this realm. The archaic adjective "pipping" describes, according to the *Oxford English Dictionary*, "the action of a chick in cracking or puncturing its shell prior to hatching." Instead of hatching, however, or heading into the external world, Crispin, in the tradition of Ben Johnson's "brave infant of Saguntum," returns to the womb. Winnicott writes of this motivated return to inner speech: "because of the fact that communication so easily becomes linked with some degree of false or compliant object-relating[,] silent or secret communication with subjective objects, carrying a sense of real, must periodically take over to restore balance."[53] Stevens's poem goes one step further, though. Not only does Crispin's turn aim to restore balance: it is actually an act of courage because it confronts even stranger phenomena introspectively than it had in the "starker, barer world":

> Here was the veritable ding an sich, at last,
> Crispin confronting it, a vocable thing,
> But with a speech belched out of hoary darks
> Noway resembling his, a visible thing ....[54]

The speech inside, hardly spoken by Crispin but confronted there in all its unfamiliarity, suggests two significant theses. First, rather than choose or fall back upon such strategies as a crutch, Stevens's writing stumbles upon or discovers forms of communication alien to externally directed speech in response to the environment. And second, the mantle it takes on by addressing the interior world is not easy. Stevens will spend a career seeking an "interior paramour," but Crispin's inner world opens to him as a space of "hoary darks"; it is a realm just as unintelligible as the outside, with the only advantage of being the "thing in itself" instead of a draining polyphony. It is in this sense that Winnicott claims such speech "carr[ies] a sense of real" and recalls Stevens's lifelong claim that the only authentic grasp of reality would necessarily be obtained by means of the imagination. And it is in this approach to inner reality as a horizon sought for both refuge and exploration that Stevens's poems suggest a solution to the pressing ethical question they raise. Because "not-communicating" both protects and discovers, finds solace for itself and charts the inherent dangers of interiority for all, poems that partake of its pipping sounds simultaneously "step boldly" into the reality of "man's interior world" and substantiate an imaginative voyage with an ethical vector, a "make-believe for others."

In the aftermath of skepticism about psychoanalytic concepts in both literary criticism and the broader culture, readers of canonical Romantic and Modernist poetry have turned to Winnicottian concepts to renew a dialogue about such fundamental concepts to the study of lyric as address and mourning.[55] As of yet, however, no study has attended specifically to Winnicott's writing on language or, as he more often calls it, communication. Where to date Lacan has provided the account of language in psychoanalysis most provocative for literary studies, I suggest that Winnicott provides a compelling alternate route. Like language for Lacan, communication for Winnicott is a key element of the subject's development, but in Winnicott's theory the process carries a much less violent and negative valence. For Lacan, the linguistic signifier violently interrupts a dyadic relationship between mother and infant in the form of the *nom du père*"; this linguistic introduction to triangular relationships presages, for the child, the confusion, displeasure, and growth constitutive of the Oedipal-phase sexual dynamics. In contrast, Winnicott relates significant aspects of the acquisition of verbal language to the pre-Oedipal phase of development. The beginning of communication between mother and child marks a less violent transition from a preexisting silent rapport to spoken words; achieving linguistic competency does not foreclose, but instead marks a continuation of, the child's capacity for nonverbal communication with the mother.[56] As a result of this continuity of communicative capacity, the child may use communication, in the service of development. The nonsensical, unaddressed self-communication Winnicott calls "not-communicating" does not so much contrast or negate communication at this stage as form a vital part of its integration into the developing individual's repertoire of relational techniques. By "not-communicating," the infant invests in a practice of selfhood not overly compliant to the environment's demands, which at times include the demand for intelligible, signifying communication at the expense of growth. As we have already seen, the toggle between investing in the reality of the self and the reality of the external world continues throughout adulthood in behavioral and linguistic arenas. Rather than a rejection of either social obligations or poetry and poetics in general, what I call the "not-communicating" of Stevens's poetry also demonstrates, on the level of content, a negotiation between self and environment. At the level of language itself, such a poetics resists the demands of a poetic tradition that would reject the potential of nonsense, nonhuman sounds, and labyrinthine syntax structures in order to reenvision the poetic signification of selfhood.

In my use of Winnicott's term to highlight aspects of literary language, "not-communicating" bears some resemblance to Roman Jakobson's identification of a poetic function whose orientation "toward ... the message for its own sake" distinguishes it from both the "referential" or "cognitive" function that focuses on the context of a message and the "emotive" or "expressive function" directed toward its addressor.[57] I insist on speaking of "not-communicating," however, for several reasons. First, "not-communicating" cannot be defined by any fixed combination of Jakobson's linguistic functions: speech that addresses the self in the presence of an other, and does so as part of a movement between these two poles can only be said to be transitional. Second, as a part of Winnicott's theory of development, the concept's ability to go beyond the description of linguistic function in order to identify possible precursors and effects of the stylized and less readily intelligible language of poetry proposes a psychological index of poetic language that does not depend on psychologizing the poet for its conclusions. The apparent retreat into a private language of such "cul-de-sac" communication demarcates a space in which poetic speech can explore and assert the authenticity of the nascent self, temporarily resist demands of the environment, and shore up resources for an eventual return to referential speech. As such, poetic "not-communicating" actually communicates significant data, for it is at these sites that poetic speakers report their perception of heightened external threats and their intentions to develop resources to meet them by poetic means.

After the conceptual introduction of noncommunicating as an inward turn in "The Comedian as the Letter C," Stevens frustrates communication and engages in "not communicating" in the poems by including sounds at the expense of intelligible speech. At times, these noises resemble human speech enough to mimic its failures but depart from it enough to sound alien; as such, they "signify on" such speech and remain communicative in their not-communicating. In a reading that, like Winnicott's own theory, takes issue with Freud's failure to theorize the process of language acquisition, Mutlu Konuk Blasing claims that Stevens's sounds signal—though they cannot by their very nature as nonfluencies narrate—a history of the developmental process of language acquisition. I differ from Blasing's approach by situating the nonfluent sounds in Stevens's poems apart from indicators of any personal or individual history; instead, I take them as placeholders for a poetic strategy that sustains and investigates the ongoing development of the self as a general concept, finding in this generality the very generativity of the technique for a consideration of Stevens's ethics. As Rachel Cole suggests, referring to "Of Modern Poetry," Stevens's style of writing often chooses aural abstraction over verifiable meaning: "instead of truth, he communicates aural arousal, sonic intensity, an asemantic condition of emphasis, of heightened degree."[58] Moreover, Cole claims, by means of this form of communicating, the poems refuse to presume knowledge about the desires of their addressees. As such, what seems at first like deliberate withdrawal from the milieu of others may in fact indicate the groundwork for an even more radical commitment to ethical engagement, a reverence for the ineffable otherness of others.

A large portion of the ambient noise of the oeuvre consists of birdsong. In "Depression Before Spring," Stevens turns away from lexical speech and to translations of birdsong when the subject at hand (and the cause of the speaker's "depression") is a failed address.

> The cock crows
> But no queen rises.
> The hair of my blonde
> Is dazzling,
> As the spittle of cows
> Threading the wind.
> Ho! Ho!
> But ki-ki-ri-ki
> Brings no rou-cou,
> No rou-cou-cou.
> But no queen comes
> In slipper green.[59]

The short poem contains repeated attempts at describing a call that brings no response, with birdsong emerging as one strategy for uttering the narrative otherwise. The first stanza contains the only narrative the poem advances, and the final stanza repeats it. But between these utterances, the speaker lapses into nonsignifying sounds, reenacting the call first with an expression whose sound contains the quintessential "O" of apostrophe (cf. Johnson). This unanswered cry of "Ho! Ho!" contains, at the lowest limit of signifying speech, the same lament as the relatively protracted version of the first and last stanzas. But the speaker pushes past this limit and in the next stanza turns to the more evocative (because even less linguistic) "ki-ki-ri-ki" and "rou-cou-cou," using these sounds to counter human speech at the moment such speech as used in the first stanza fails to signify the absence that unexpectedly and melancholically attends it.[60] If positive speech expects a response, expects the queen to come "in slipper green," noncommunicating sound comes between call and failed response to reveal what is unbearable and other to speech, namely its own failure. At the same time, and unlike the descriptions that bookend it, this nonhuman, noncommunicating speech accomplishes what human speech cannot, bringing the sound "rou-cou-cou" to the surface of the poem, allowing the speaker to "hear" the sound whose presence and absence he had thus far failed to evoke.

In "Depression Before Spring," Stevens communicates first with positive speech and then turns to "not communicating" before a closing reappearance of positive speech. The modified speech parallels its positive, unmodified counterpart even at the syntactic level. The conjunction that begins the line, "But no queen comes," does not contest the previous stanza's assertion; instead, by reaffirming it, "but" emphasizes a repeated protest. "Not-communicating" picks up in the poem where human speech leaves off in order to reiterate its particular failure; when the poem returns to human speech in the closing stanza, the work of not-communicating reveals a transformation of the poem's linguistic register. Rather than a narrative recounting and resolving a scene of failed seduction, the poem performs a failed mourning of that failed seduction. As with the polyphonic "C" of "Comedian," the plaintive note of poetic not-communicating—here a shrill keen of "ki-ki-ri-ki" and its long "e"—not only does not provoke response: it fails to even end. The call echoes back not once but twice in the "queen" and "green" of the poem's last line, signaling that, beyond failure, the poem's "sonic intensity" consists in returning one's own call to its speaker as if begging for response.[61] Once again, interior speech, instead of repose, poses a threat to the self more grave even than its external counterpart. Like the persistent and cloistering melancholy of depression itself, the foreclosed closing of "Depression Before Spring" calls attention to the punitive recriminations that attend the self newly burdened by its incorporation of a lost object.

A haunting repetition and return of sound also imbues the mournful register of "not-communicating" in "Autumn Refrain." The poem, a modified sonnet, begins with a movement of stripping away characteristic of "The Snow Man," "The Comedian as the Letter C," and so many of Stevens's late poems. However, instead of the personality, it is the layers of the environment's sights and sounds that "Autumn Refrain" strips away to allow an encounter with the interior world. The speaker of "Autumn Refrain" recounts the sounds that are "gone" once night has fallen: "The skreak and skritter of evening gone/And grackles gone and sorrows of the sun."[62] After he narrates the silencing of these sounds, however, he speaks of an absence of a different quality. Also gone is

> ... the moon and moon,
> The yellow moon of words about the nightingale
> In measureless measures, not a bird for me
> But the name of a bird and the name of a nameless air
> I have never—shall never hear.[63]

The poem evokes the nightingale by means of its current absence as well as its future inaccessibility. Yet again mimicking the structure of elegy, this speaker conjures up sounds and sorrows both to say they are gone and to prove that in some other sense they survive.[64] Hardly any word or sound occurs in this passage without being immediately repeated, and at a rate that far surpasses the returns of "Depression Before Spring." Like that poem, sounds and sound-makers of twilight are both gone in the refrain and, by means of this repeated evocation of absence, diegetically present, produced by the poetic process itself. Unlike an elegy that conjures up the dead in order to dismiss them finally, the "skreaking and skrittering" of "Autumn Refrain" reasserts itself as the speaker reveals that what had seemed "gone" is, in fact, recoverable. It remains to be rediscovered "beneath/The stillness of everything gone." This line marks the "turn" of the sonnet in at least two senses. What has been stripped away can now be claimed as something that "resides" as a "residuum," but it also proves, as such a residuum, to be an ambivalent resurrection.

> And yet beneath
> The stillness of everything gone, and being still,
> Being and sitting still, something resides,
> Some skreaking and skrittering residuum,
> And grates these evasions of the nightingale ....[65]

The residual "skreaking and skrittering," by its grating or shredding, overcomes the nightingale's evasions and brings it—and its song—near. This is an important moment, because it shows that an inarticulate and partial sound, here contrasted even to the fullness of the inhuman sounds of birdsong, has a power to evoke what only a moment ago the speaker had asserted he would "never hear." In doing so, the poem accomplishes the reverse of Keats's "Ode," which begins in the presence of a nightingale's song and ends by exclaiming, "fled is that music." But why try to recapture the Keatsian nightingale, and how could "skreaking and skrittering" play any part in such an aim?

"Skreaking and skrittering" constitute, at the beginning of "Autumn Refrain," ambient noises that, having no definable origin or addressor, disappear quickly. Their "residuum," however, is quite different. Once all of the ambient sounds have been removed, internal sounds remain, making this new "skreaking and skrittering" a no more peaceful, but nevertheless different phenomenon because it is personal and internal. These screeching or scattering sounds can only be heard when one is "Being and sitting still." The song of the nightingale approaches by the speaker's communication with subjective objects, that is, by listening to what remains "beneath/The stillness." In the absence of external noises, it must be internal sounds, like those from the "hoary darks," that the listener perceives.[66] When stillness sings in the same key as a nightingale's, subjective communication becomes the "key" to productive solitude.

"Autumn Refrain" comments on the access that "not communicating" provides to what would otherwise be inaccessible sources of knowledge and memory. Traditionally, the nightingale sings to palliate the pain of its own memory of violence.[67] By means of sounds that have both their origin and their destination in the self, the speaker can gain some access to the nightingale and, perhaps, to that same relief. If Keats's nightingale was the symbol of poetic imagination—or the flights of fancy too dangerous for everyday soaring—Stevens cozens no illusions about the availability of such transport for his own era's poetics. On the other hand, if the private and not-communicating song finds the same key, the poem's discovery compensates for any mournful loss of Romantic imagination by resituating its site in a mind of autumn. Recalling once again the lesson of "Comedian," such an internal sound is no sure cause for rejoicing. The nightingale's is "a desolate" sound, and whether or not its transformation into a voice heard internally preserves its desolation, its stillness betrays any hope of its capacity for flight.

Although nothing recovers the exact song, at the very least the speaker can experience "stillness … in the key of that desolate sound." Stevens need not engage the social order because he can access the "hungry generations" of the outside world by means of subjective communication. If "Depression Before Spring" laments the inaccessibility of the social, "Autumn Refrain" mediates access to social advantages while deftly avoiding its dangers.

In contrast to the confident speech of "The Idea of Order at Key West," the poem that follows it in *Ideas of Order*, "Waving Adieu, Adieu, Adieu," tests the limits of "not communicating" as a means to its end. The poem's preoccupation with death stands in stark contrast to the youth and liveliness of the singing girl of "Key West" and foregrounds saying goodbye to the material world that the second poem "rages" to classify and understand. Like "Autumn Refrain," the poem has Keats's "Ode to a Nightingale" as its chief precursor. An echo of that poem's famous closing stanza, which also repeats "adieu" three times, introduces the concern of "Waving Adieu, Adieu, Adieu" as a return to the reality of the self from the illusions that threaten its integrity. In Keats's ode, "adieu" serves both as a command for the nightingale to leave and as a benediction after it has gone. Stevens's poem, too, must first push the old regime away before it can come to a place from which to look back on it with new eyes.

"Waving Adieu, Adieu, Adieu" takes departure, rather than encounter, as its point of departure, though it will lead up to an encounter in its closing lines. It, too, dramatizes a "toll[ing] back" to the "sole self," taking Keats's ending (and the theme of ending in general) as its beginning so as to showcase the poet's need to disengage from what would otherwise be a smothering, ever-present contact with a world of which he disapproves. Stevens's attention to the act of separating, to that which allows a personal world to develop, makes possible a reading of the poem's "not communicating," which takes place through difficult syntactical maneuvers, delays, and repetitions or echoes. The poem works through the possibilities for a zero degree of communication, trying to understand how, without "crying and shouting," or even moving, the speaker could still communicate a "farewell" to life and to the old order of religious understanding.

The first noncommunicative strategy, which appears in the poem's first stanza, is grammatical. Hyperbaton, a radical disjunction of syntactical elements from their expected order, leaves the grammar of each stanza-length sentence unclear until the final line.

> That would be waving and that would be crying,
> Crying and shouting and meaning farewell,
> Farewell in the eyes and farewell at the centre,
> Just to stand still without moving a hand.[68]

The poem begins unconventionally, as many of Stevens's poems do, embedding their hermeneutic-disclosing roots late in the poem. Such a strategy suggests the priority of self-communication in Stevens: the opening lines' inward turn figures, metonymically, the process writ large in poems like this one, which use not-communicating in order to approach communicating at a later, more appropriate time. Here, a demonstrative pronoun without an antecedent leaves the grammar in question almost before the poem begins. If the rhythmic cadence of the lines, the polysyndeton, and the repetition of "that," "crying," and "farewell" seemed to cushion the opening's difficulty, the eventual predication of the sentence in the last line of the stanza interrupts the reader's ease by reversing the understood meaning of the opening lines. "[T]o stand still without moving a hand" must be parsed as the suppressed antecedent of the opening stanza's "that," indicating that the static tableau on which the stanza ends, its standing still, is somehow equivalent to "waving" and "crying" and "shouting and meaning farewell." The last line stills the dramatic movement of farewells as we have seen them, subsuming them under an odd, motionless, and speechless kind of "bidding farewell" that it will take the rest of the poem to explain. In what world could such inaction constitute the communication of farewell?

It is not until the third stanza of "Waving," that the speaker turns away from the performative gesture of arresting dramatic farewells by grammatical means to a more direct statement of the reason that such stillness is desirable. The delay in itself is an additional obstruction to the communicative potential of the poem, although not an unfamiliar one in Stevens's poems. One often gets the sense that the beginnings of Stevens's poems are tangential to their eventual poetic concerns. This tangential quality derives sometimes, as here, from grammatical obstructions and sometimes from a calculated triviality that gives way to the poem's strongest lines. Helen Vendler points out a similar phenomenon and makes it an axiom for reading Stevens that one should look not at the beginning of the poem but toward its end for the "human narrative."[69] She also suggests that such a strategy is characteristic of Keats's odes, where discovering a "secret beginning" of the poem allows us to return to the actual beginning with a better understanding of the poem's chief concerns.[70] Instead of focusing on a "secret" place in the text, as in Keats, or in the hidden "human narrative" in a Stevens poem, the motivation to obscure and secret away clear narratives is itself a matter of great importance. While Winnicott makes an explicit reference to artists in "Communicating and Not-Communicating," suggesting that it use derives from an "urgent need" in "the artist of all kinds,"[71] it may be better to suggest that Stevens's writing performs the oscillation between both types of communication as a demonstration of poetry's contested relationship with the psychological self as an entity that desires attachments in the world and finds itself threatened by a world that can subsume these desires with its own demands for compliance.

Such a dilemma manifests itself in "Waving Adieu, Adieu, Adieu," by a certain kind of endlessness—signaled by means of repetition—that appears at the very moment that individuality becomes an important term. Oscillating between the need to be found and the need to "not be found,"[72] the speaker "not communicates" and communicates at once, winding his long sentence through clauses that repeat not only the "to" that precedes the infinitive form of verbs, but also the words "little," "be," and "just." In the repetition of these words a diminutive, barely visible subject, existent, or "being" emerges against the language that obscures it:

> To be one's singular self, to despise
> The being that yielded so little, acquired
> So little, too little to care, to turn
> To the ever-jubilant weather, to sip
> One's cup and never to say a word,
> Or to sleep or just to lie there still,
> Just to be there, just to be beheld,
> That would be bidding farewell, be bidding farewell.[73]

These stanzas do, of course, communicate. For the third time in this short poem, the poem makes a claim about "bidding farewell." Such a conditional adieu would involve not just being still, not participating in the overdramatic performances of farewell undertaken by those who expect "heaven to follow"; rather, or more succinctly, it would be "to be one's singular self," which, unlike the kind of living that "yielded so little," would entail a whole series of actions that, for the first time, could give a coherent identity to the individual who bids farewell. These two stanzas, too, consist of a long periodic sentence, the same grammatical structure of the first two. By now, however, we recognize the pattern, and the accord between the opening dependent clauses and the predication that will follow them. Furthermore, the infinitive constructions are less jarring than the pronominal constructions of the first stanzas. And while the periodic sentence requires a grammar driven by its final clause, its opening phrase is the point around which the poem turns. "[T]o be one's singular self" drives the meaning of the sentence by grouping the actions that follow it under its name. Despising, turning, sipping, and saying all fall into the category of actions necessary for constructing a "singular self" in the midst of a world where "bidding farewell" has been radically redefined. These actions oppose the deliberate farewells of the first two stanzas.

To be one's singular self, though, comes at a certain cost—not just of the way of "being that yielded so little," but also of the trappings of a language that communicates to an external world by means of words, gestures, and even tears. Only not communicating promises the speaker a way of accommodating himself to death—and, as it turns out, to life—in a postreligious world. The movement of the poem has been a familiar stripping of the unnecessary qualities of communication (compare the stripping of the self in "The Snow Man" and of Crispin's sovereignty in "The Comedian as the Letter C"), but in the final lines the speaker regains some of his lost "spirit," notably from a different source than those who believe in heaven. The kind of life that not communicating allows begins when, in a provocative enjambment, he notes that "to be one's singular self" requires a "turn/To the ever-jubliant weather." The enjambment on the key word "turn" puns on the poem's own decisive shift. In the final stanza, the adjectival phrase "ever-jubilant" becomes a vocative, and "ever-jubilant" sounds the poem's first apostrophic address: "Ever-jubilant,/What is there here but weather, what spirit/Have I except it comes from the sun?"[74]

Instead of a God, the speaker's question posits (as only Stevens's questions can do) the invisible force and will of weather. Mimicking the grammatical conceit of the entire poem, the last line reverses a general pattern of movement. Most of the poem had obeyed a movement outward from the speaker, in a concern about how to communicate differently. Once he has learned to do so, he can communicate, even if a personifying apostrophe to the weather is an odd form of communication. More importantly, perhaps, the speaker can also begin to receive communication in the form of a sun-borne "spirit." "Not-communicating" clears a path for the reception of communication from others. "Waving Adieu, Adieu, Adieu," a poem that never specifies the addressee of its farewells, only issues a specific address once it has justified not addressing, having "never to say a word." The assertion of a "right not to communicate," and the elaboration of how not communicating might be achieved, alone makes positive communication possible in Stevens.[75] That it does make this possible reveals how often Stevens's poems end at the moment of such contact between inner and outer worlds, as though the work of the poem itself were in arriving at this point, where a social self no longer mediated by poetry could begin to interact.

The ever-changing self to which Stevens's poems give voice, in an array of tones beset or harmonized by alien sounds, measures its progress by means of creative modifications, transformations, and deferrals of modes of communication that serve to address others. In this way, Stevens's poems turn aside from accepted and expected registers of poetic involvement in the social sphere, and do so to the extent that some critics find distressing for an oeuvre that spans two world wars, a domestic economic Depression, and rising awareness of American influence on international affairs. Nevertheless, this experimental retooling of poetics represents a poetic attempt to respond to that world's "chaos in motion and not in motion" by other means. The poetic space cleared by temporarily separating an inward self from the external world points not only to the extremity of external crisis, but also to the hope that hard-won internal resources could better engage with that world once they have been heard, understood, and used as a catalyst for growth. The fact that this attempt to engage always remains in the realm of the possible, and thus holds Stevens's poetry at the threshold of self and other, inner and outer phenomena, the "interior world" and the "actual world," represents no failure. It may present, instead, an opportunity to read the Stevensian corpus as a repertoire of tactics for a genre—one recognized for its violent seductions and premature definitions of its addressees—to inch more humbly toward newly ethical encounters. The Winnicottian conceptual universe, with its defense of "the right to not communicate," suggests that it is at a continual threshold that Stevens's poems take their boldest step.

Randall Jarrell's Beards

Like Wallace Stevens, the affects proper to interiority lie at the heart of Randall Jarrell's poetry. In his review of Stevens's *Collected Poems*, Jarrell recognized and celebrated a strange joy at the heart of Stevens's world of the mind. In "these poems from the other side of existence,"[1] he wrote, "the realm of the dramatic monologue ... is over, and the motion of someone else's speech has been replaced by 'the motion of thought' of the poet himself."[2] At the same time, "at the bottom of Stevens's poetry there is wonder and delight, the child's or animal's or savage's—man's—joy in his own existence, and thankfulness for it."[3] Jarrell's poetry, which is similarly interested in figures of children and animals, by contrast to Stevens, aims to sustain the "wonder and delight" of existence while remaining firmly within the "realm of the dramatic monologue." If Stevens's poetry poses the question of the extent to which interiority can be an engagement with the social world, the counterpart in Jarrell's work may be the extent to which the engagements and relationships of dramatic personae may reflect the interior world of a single speaker's feelings and desires. In Jarrell's case, identifications with others, especially women, serve to articulate a form of anxiety, and a kind of shame, proper to midcentury masculine sexuality.

Jarrell's is a poetics at odds with many of the currents of midcentury poetry in both its confessional and experimental modes.[4] Jarrell's poems represent the voices and experiences of a constellation of figures—children, women, and soldiers among them—and turn, if more rarely, to his own past for explorations of childhood, art, loss, and death. If a constant of Jarrell criticism has been a preference for the poet's reviews and lectures to his poetry, more recent work has found in Jarrell's poems a vital resource for reevaluating sex, gender, and desire in the American midcentury. At a moment in American literary history when a clear boundary distinguished poetries sympathetic to non-normative sexuality from the mainstream, Jarrell's work provides no such clarity. Eve Sedgwick has drawn attention to a line Jarrell wrote to describe his mother's fainting spells: "that it was queer, it is certain."[5] To a certain extent, and as a result of its failure to contain its desires in any normative way, Jarrell's work as a whole merits this descriptor.

For most of his recent commentators, to read Randall Jarrell's poems is to reconsider the relationship between midcentury poetry and sexuality. It suffices to compare the sexual dynamics at work in Jarrell's poems—always subtle, metaphorical, and often strange—with those at work in the poems of the contemporaries to whom he is most often compared. The explicit and at times predatory sexuality of poems like John Berryman's "Dream Song 4" and Robert Lowell's "The Dolphin" pairs strangely with the innocence of Jarrell's "A Girl in a Library" and the sexual disappointment of "Next Day." While a new frankness about sexuality emerged around him, Jarrell's poems, like his person, remained reticent, even childlike. Nevertheless, or perhaps for this very reason, various aspects of Jarrell's work encourage critical interventions into his poetics of desire, and recent attention to the sexual dynamics of Jarrell's poetic families, the gender politics of his critiques of mass culture, and the tension at work in his relationships with Elizabeth Bishop, Adrienne Rich, and Hannah Arendt has proved fruitful for reviving interest in a poet and critic whose renown dropped off in the decades after his early death in 1965.

The single, peculiar figure and feature of the beard lies at the heart of many of Jarrell's explorations of sexual desire. Beards appear consistently in Jarrell's life and his work: he was famous for wearing a long beard and shaving it dramatically near the end of his life; he idealized and wrote about bearded men; and crucially, as I wish to explore, women in Jarrell's poems serve as beards for the homosexual desires of male speakers. To read many Jarrell poems is to find oneself reading through a beard. The extent of Jarrell's investment is such that his poetic logic draws its metaphorical tenor from the subjective, interpersonal, and aesthetic functions performed by bearded figures, female beards, and acts of bearding or shaving. Inasmuch as these beards are poetically legible—and the signification of a beard is notoriously ambiguous—a poem becomes, for Jarrell, a way of bearding oneself, of entering an arena of potential identifications and using this arena to articulate a desire that would otherwise be entirely inarticulable. Although Jarrell's poems have become an object of critical interest for their unique depictions of women, they have rarely been viewed with an eye toward their articulations of queer desire. The beards in two of Jarrell's best-known poems, "The Bronze David of Donatello" and "The Woman at the Washington Zoo," as well as the act of shaving that takes place in one of Jarrell's final poems, sanction such an approach. And although I want to push back against readings that regard Jarrell's identification with women as primarily feminist,

Jarrell's voicing of queer desire adds to his poetry's explorations of some of the vulnerabilities to which women in particular are exposed.

The face of the poet

Jarrell's beards were biographical as well as literary, and, in his life as in his art, they served several purposes. The stages of his physical beard represent distinct epochs of his life and serve as augurs of his death; a beard is the common feature shared by the eclectic group of male poets and artists Jarrell idealized; a beard served him as a sufficiently personal and impersonal topic of pedagogical conversation and neighborhood intrigue; it permitted him a certain number of disguises, as well as the ability to remove the mask at will and change himself instantly.

According to his wife, Mary, Jarrell began growing a beard because he wanted to resemble Chekhov. Or, rather, because, to a guest in his home who mistook a portrait of the Russian writer for Jarrell's father, Jarrell already resembled him.[6] In response, Jarrell reportedly said, "Is there no limit to what people don't know?" Nevertheless, "the next day he stopped shaving."[7] Modeling himself off of his idols may have led Jarrell to grow a beard; having a beard led him to more bearded idols:

> Years after, when people said he looked like Renoir's gentleman with the opera glasses in *La Loge* or like Donatello's head of Goliath, he'd ask with innocent joy, "I declare. Do you really think so?" Gradually, with no overt plan, bearded pictures outnumbered the others in every room. Solomon, Odysseus, Constantine, John the Baptist, and *der heilige Hieronymous* became household favorites.[8]

Jarrell was careful to protect his beard from wayward significations, and the possibility that it revealed his Beat or even his communist sympathies occasionally surfaced. Just before his appointment as Poetry Consultant at the Library of Congress, when he was accused by a detractor of a communist past, he received postcards "rebuking him for his 'Castro-beard.'"[9] The distinction between Jarrell's beard and those worn by Beat poets was the point of departure for a 1961 local newspaper profile titled, "No Sign of Beatnik behind Poet's Beard."[10] Jarrell openly decried the Beats's aesthetic spontaneity; he had witnessed it firsthand when Gregory Corso stayed with him in Washington, DC.[11] Less openly, however, Jarrell may have been concerned that an affiliation with Beat work was tantamount to an acceptance of homosexuality. His teacher,

John Crowe Ransom, became embroiled in a debate with Robert Duncan after the publication of the latter's "The Homosexual in Society," and the association of Beat poetry with queerness was widely known by the early 1960s.[12] It's easy to understand, then, the article's urgency to distinguish between the unkempt and untraditional facial hair Jarrell sported and any nontraditional poetics or sexuality it might have led readers to attribute to him. In the same article, however, Jarrell spoke adamantly about the strangeness of artistic works, and his anxiety lest they be regarded as the products of any single or dominant current. As in the lines from "Hope" to which Sedgwick would call attention, Jarrell admitted, "Works of art are queer things."[13], [14] A beard may have been Jarrell's easiest way to access, rather than avoid association with, queerness.

Jarrell's beard, and the fact that he shaved it in the last year of his life, appears repeatedly in the memorial tributes made by his friends. There, it served as a convenient site for metaphorical constructions of psychological and poetic value as well as a tidy marker of early, middle, and late Jarrell. Robert Lowell uses Jarrell's beard to mark him as anachronistic and labile. No static feature, the beard seemed just as significant in its removal as in its cultivation:

> Poor modern-minded exile from the forests of Grimm, I see him unbearded, slightly South American-looking, then later bearded, with a beard we at first wished to reach out our hands to and pluck off, but which later became him, like Walter Bagehot's, or some Symbolist's in France's *fin-de-siécle* Third Republic. Then unbearded again.[15]

Unbearded, Jarrell is anonymous, deracinated, "South American-looking." His beard gives him, in Lowell's tribute, roots in particular historical, literary, and psychological contexts. Stanley Kunitz's comments on the same occasion follow a similar course, identifying Jarrell's beard with culture and artifice, and his shaved face with a startling essence. When Kunitz and Jarrell first met, "He was bearded, formidable, bristling, with a high-pitched nervous voice and the wariness of a porcupine." Even Kunitz's description—"bristling" and "porcupine"—derives its qualities from the beard. Kunitz continues:

> That was my dominant image of him for a decade, until the turn of '65 when he came north for a visit from Greensboro, with his beard deleted, and I saw at dinner for the first and last time the naked vulnerability of his countenance. A few months later he was dead.[16]

From this description, Kunitz transitions directly into a reading of "The Woman at the Washington Zoo," whose emphasis on self-transformation Kunitz reads as symptomatic of Jarrell's work as a whole: "All the voices in all of Jarrell's poems are crying, 'Change me'. The young yearn to be old in order to escape from their nocturnal fears; the old long for the time of their youth ....'[17] Kunitz's description has analogues in several more recent critical perspectives, which remark at length on "change" as the central plank in Jarrell's aesthetic platform.[18] I consider the poem's relationship to the beard, and to the questions of vulnerable countenances, as an even more direct one than Kunitz suspects.

Walter Benjamin claims that for Baudelaire the experience of the crowd, although rarely mentioned, imbued all aspects of poetic experience: "it is imprinted on his creativity like a hidden figure".[19] Even the lines of his poems represent what Benjamin calls "a phantom crowd: the words, the fragments, the beginnings of lines, from which the poet, in the deserted streets, wrests poetic booty".[20] A beard was, for Randall Jarrell, an analogously ubiquitous marker of poetic experience. Jarrell mentions beards frequently in the poems, but his beard surrounds and crowds in upon the poem as it is spoken, as it emerges from the bearded face. Drawings of bearded faces in the drafts of Jarrell's poems attest to this awareness of the poem's source in the mouth. For Jarrell, the process of troping the speech of his chosen speakers—soldiers, children, and women, among others—involves a reference to the physical and biological determinants of vocalization and to the face that the reader would have seen were she present at its first utterance. To some extent, the poems' affected speech patterns serve Jarrell's aim of reconstituting the uniqueness of faces by poetic means.

Jarrell's poetry has an inscrutable but undeniable relationship to the face, and specifically to the mouth, and further the facial hair that by circumscribing, embellishing, and obscuring the mouth visually tropes that organ. As hirsute signals of the singularity of midcentury poetics, beards, in the very variety of their shadings, surroundings, and encroachings upon the privileged site of orality, metaphorize the demands that poets, so insistent that we give speech to others in our own voices, make on the mouth.

Jarrell's women

Jarrell's poetics of desire is characterized by a slippage between this facial feature of the beard and the relational figure of a beard, a woman whose accompaniment of a homosexual man disguises the non-normativity of his desire. Jarrell's women have not yet been regarded in this light and have instead been regarded as sufficient evidence of Jarrell's nascent feminism. While Jarrell's reputation during his life rested on his review essays and public lectures, on his frequently anthologized war poem, "The Death of the Ball Turret Gunner," and, later, on his children's books, in the years since his death critics have invested more attention in Jarrell's poetry, and specifically in those poems' fascinating constellating of women and children. Notable essays by Langdon Hammer, James Longenbach, Stephen Burt, Suzanne Ferguson, Alan Williamson, and Richard Flynn all speak to his peculiar and peculiarly nonconformist approach to gender, most notably the fact that, for a series of poems that read like dramatic monologues, Jarrell adopts a woman's voice.[21] "Next Day," for example, imagines the substitutive satisfaction an older woman hopes to find in the male gaze after relinquishing her desire for love to coincide with marriage and a family:

> When I was young and miserable and pretty
> And poor, I'd wish
> What all girls wish: to have a husband,
> A house and children. Now that I'm old, my wish
> Is womanish:
> That the boy putting groceries in my car
> See me. It bewilders me he doesn't see me.[22]

As these lines make clear, if Jarrell is a protofeminist, as some critics would have him, his feminism is problematic. Even if Jarrell does more in these lines than appropriate the female voice, and instead manages to challenge a traditional masculine norm by ventriloquizing masculinity through women, his achievement may hardly be praiseworthy. As Judith Butler argues, not every challenge to gender binaries challenges gender norms or the "sexual regulations" to which they are often linked. A strange zone of gender ambiguity is notable precisely for its failure to challenge sexual norms, and some gender performance affects normative sexuality precisely in exerting a force to maintain it.[23] In its portrayal of a vulnerable woman inviting the gaze of a male stranger, "Next Day" aligns masculine sexuality not only with invulnerability, but with the power and purpose of rescue.

At the same time, the gender ambiguity operative in Jarrell's poems of female impersonation has yet to be read with an eye toward its determination of sexuality. If Jarrell's poems' explicit aim is to render visible the tropes by which individual subjects articulate their desires, to what extent do these desires, which are so often coded as gendered in Jarrell's poems, include alternatives to sexual norms? To what extent, on the other hand, is the scope of these desires, their claims to universality or representativeness notwithstanding, artificially limited to a sexual norm that the (shock of the) gender ambiguity of their speakers serves to conceal? Lastly, to what extent is that supposed concealment a question deserving further attention?

Critics have upheld a version of Jarrell as if not a feminist like his friend Adrienne Rich, then at least an opponent of traditional masculinity. James Longenbach suggests that Jarrell was content to reject, in his poems as in his life, a masculine style, and was instead actively concerned with "developing a socially respectable way of dramatizing his own divided sensibility." To this end, he nurtured a "semifeminine" style that valued "the process of thinking, rather than the completed thought," in sympathy with Elizabeth Bishop. Nevertheless, Bishop, for her part, was the first to recognize the peculiarity, within this project, of Jarrell's female voices. They "'seem to be like none I–or you—know,'" she wrote to Robert Lowell.[24] Even Longenbach agrees that "the female speakers of Jarrell's poems are closer to a man who doesn't drink or participate in locker-room banter but who likes to read fairy tales and shout 'Baby doll!'" Stephen Burt, in a similar vein, observes that "Some of Jarrell's best poems in the voices of women could almost have been spoken by men" (183). It's certainly possible to read these markers of masculinity as a sign of a failed or at least imperfect representation of women on Jarrell's part. And there is certainly evidence, namely in Jarrell's poem "Woman," that Jarrell at times believed in and wished to list a finite set of defining characteristics of woman. To claim that his experiments in doing so from a female perspective fall short of the mark, and for the obvious reasons that such projected embodiments always suffer from the distortions of the fantasies that motivate them, may effectively head off any valorization of Jarrell's empathetic midcentury masculinity, but it fails to account for another possible reading. What if this body of poems represents precisely what readers recognize there, namely the voices of men speaking as women? That is, what if, rather than making women speak, Jarrell's poetic women speak on behalf of men? Can a queer reading of Randall Jarrell perform a reparative function by suggesting that his women act on behalf of an emergent queer sexuality?

Queer Jarrell

Randall Jarrell makes brief but meaningful appearances in Eve Kosofsky Sedgwick's writing that generate a vocabulary and an impetus for exploring a Jarrell committed, despite his admittedly weak attempts at feminism, to a form of queerness. Jarrell is, for reasons already outlined, an unlikely figure for this form of attention; at the same time, the progression of desire in his poems—especially the poems he wrote in the last weeks of his life—is often capable of a surprising and disarming openness to parts of the self whose emergence is incomplete. Sedgwick's attention to Jarrell hinges, at times, on his simply being in the room. In *A Dialogue on Love*, Jarrell plays a role in helping Sedgwick believe that her difference from her therapist need not be an insurmountable obstacle to their work together. Although he is "not even Jewish" and she "had to conclude … wasn't gay," Shannon's proximity to Jarrell proves that he can meet some of her needs. The poem titled "Sh" consists of a gentle list of the therapist's shortcomings; the last lines, as a reparative gesture, offset the complaint: "But say it's Jarrell I need./He reaches to the bookcase,/ he has it, *The Lost World*."[25] As a poet whose work is based almost entirely on surprising identifications with and desires for others, Jarrell needs to be in the room for this queerly therapeutic interaction to take place.

Sedgwick's selection of Jarrell's poem "Hope" as an epigraph to an essay on the queer "displacements of meaning" that link public demonstrations and pedagogy points to the constitutive displacements in Jarrell's own poetry.[26] The poem's speaker recalls his mother's fainting spells, but he does so while watching his wife sleep:

> She resembled a recurrent
> Scene from my childhood.
> A scene called Mother Has Fainted.
> Mother's body
> Was larger, now it no longer moved;
> Breathed, somehow, as if it no longer breathed.
> Her face no longer smiled at us
> Or frowned at us. Did anything to us.
> Her face was queerly flushed
> Or else queerly pale; I am no longer certain.
> That it was queer I am certain.[27]

While the poem explicitly claims that queerness inheres in the ambiguity of the mother's inactive actions or active (and troubling) inaction, its last line suggests the dawning recognition that the speaker's present situation, the fugue-like state in which a sleeping wife in the present has been displaced by a fainting mother in the past, has its queerness, too. A preliminary description of Jarrell's queer poetics would call attention to the workings of poems in which a strange displacement in the poem's content saturates and determines the situation of its speaking. And this is the case especially in poems that seem to conceal by the peculiarities of their displacements and the desires that motivate them by means of a beard. It's because these poems present, in Eve Sedgwick's phrase, "strange and recalcitrant" problems of interpretation that I turn to Jarrell's beard for help in elucidating a means by which his poems take on meaning in relation to the speech and desires of others, as well as the artifice, the displacements by which that desiring speech is articulated.

The desire of Goliath: "The Bronze David of Donatello"

Jarrell wrote both "The Woman at the Washington Zoo" and "The Bronze David of Donatello" during what he regarded as a relatively dry spell for his poetry. Living in Washington, DC, and working as the Poetry Consultant to the Library of Congress, he was also working on a psychoanalytic approach to T.S. Eliot's poetry, a project he never completed. About the poem, he reported in a letter to Elizabeth Bishop in September 1956,

> I haven't written too many poems lately—I wrote a long one about Donatello's David, the bronze one, I just wrote a poem about "The Woman at the Washington Zoo," and I've done eleven or twelve Rilke translations.[28]

While the published version of *The Woman at the Washington Zoo* reverses the poems' order, placing the title poem first and "The Bronze David of Donatello" last, the first poem's treatment of issues of male desire undergoes a transformation in "The Woman at the Washington Zoo," which can be read as its counterpart. While "The Woman at the Washington Zoo" will find and attach to a complicated object of desire, "The Bronze David of Donatello" narrates an attempted rejection of desire that it deems misplaced. Most notably, the ekphrastic poem redirects the viewer's attention away from an unbearded, naked, and triumphant young David and toward the severed, bearded head of the defeated Goliath. Jarrell not only took Donatello's cultivation of David as a "shameless" and "self-mirroring" figure as, in Stephen Burt's formulation, a "bad model for art," but regarded him, as I will argue, as a bad, or threatening, model for desire in contrast to the strangely magnetic Goliath.[29]

Randall Jarrell's aesthetic life was sustained by periodic all-consuming "Enthusiasms" for a surprisingly diverse range of authors, composers, and artists.[30] His letters recount both newfound and lifelong fascinations with figures outside his expertise in American poetry including Freud, Russian novels, and opera. Extensive reading and excited recommendations to friends followed.

The sculpture of Donatello was an abiding interest for Jarrell, and, in addition to visiting his works at museums throughout Europe, he nurtured his interest through art books. Like Tatyana Larina in his poem, "A Girl in a Library," the statue of David and Goliath and its story of desire emerge, long before they enter his poems, from the pages of a book.[31] More specifically, Jarrell's interest in Goliath may have taken shape from the fact that Robert Lowell sent him a copy of Ludwig Goldscheider's *Donatello*, to which Jarrell replied in thanks that Donatello is "all in all my favorite sculptor."[32] Jarrell may even have reproduced images from the book to post on his wall next to photographs of his soon-to-be wife. Teaching at Princeton in 1951, he reported in a letter to Mary (Von Schrader) that "I've put up photographs of Donatello sculpture [and] photographs of Mary Von Schrader."[33] Sustaining an aesthetic attachment to bearded men simultaneously with, and on the same level as, his romantic relationships with women suggests that Jarrell recognized Sedgwick's queer space in which the "slippage" between identification and desire is particularly close.[34]

Jarrell's preference for Goliath and rejection of David follows Goldscheider's lead. Remarkably, the head of Goliath appears in close detail a page before an image of the full statue. Goldscheider's remarks earlier in the book suggest that he considered the Bronze David overrated, as it is "entirely lacking in the pathos and terror-inspiring qualities of his riper works."[35] Presenting the Goliath head as the statue's only redeeming quality, Goldscheider may have convinced Jarrell that something had gone awry in the statue's representation of David. The back view of the David, which appears next in Goldscheider's volume, may have highlighted this fault. As Raymond-Jean Frontain notes, a rear view of the bronze David affords a view of one of the sculpture's most explicitly homosexual aspects. It "makes all the more noticeable the snake-like movement of Goliath's helmet's plume towards the ephebe's buttocks. Rarely had homosexual desire been put so publicly on display."[36] Jarrell, for his part, recognizes this part of the sculpture, noting that Goliath's "wing reaches, almost, to the rounded/ Small childish buttocks."[37] Alan Williamson reads these lines as a further way of vilifying David by means of a "passive sexual implication." "If David, the 'swan-maiden,' has taken on his victim's strength at all, it is by being anally penetrated. No wonder Jarrell goes on to imagine that Goliath is still the real presence, even in death, and David is reduced to Goliath's dream."[38] In the 1950s, the figure of David had to come to stand in for homosexuality, as Michael Bronski observes.[39] Strangely, Jarrell draws attention to David only in order to turn the gaze away from him, tacitly rejecting David's signification in favor of a more disguised, if still non-normative, sexual desire. If David represents and rejects the "shamelessness" of a passive homosexual position, what alternative does he find in the severed, bearded head of Goliath?

While the entirety of "The Bronze David of Donatello" can be classified as ekphrasis, the poem reserves its imaginative reverie for Goliath. It keeps the tempting body of David, "a labyrinth the gaze retraces," at a distance with exacting, if ornate, description.[40] While David holds his stone and "a sword alien, somehow, to the hand," Goliath's head "dreams what has destroyed it/ And is untouched by its destruction." If David had been penetrated, Goliath is impenetrable. Unlike in the scriptures, "there is no stone in the forehead."[41] But if David is passive, Goliath is hardly an exemplar of active masculinity. He is represented as sleeping and "snor[ing] in satisfaction."[42] As the poem continues, Goliath almost completely disappears under the weight of the now-reviled David, who "is like a bird/Standing on something it has pecked to death."[43] David's passivity, his need to receive the gaze of the other, shuts him off from the world with a "line of delimitation, demarcation" that even the dead Goliath manages to avoid. For Jarrell, desire can only be sanctioned if it is concealed, and, even then, it often comes at the price of death. "The Bronze David of Donatello" intervenes in the dynamic of the sculpture, challenging its demand for the viewer to gaze upon David, precisely in order to defend a closeted sexual politics, one in which sex acts must occurs secretly, almost unconsciously, and in a state that culminates in "blessed death." The bearded figure of Goliath and his inactive activity represent a fraught, if non-normative, sexuality, but one that Jarrell could sanction. As "The Woman at the Washington Zoo" will suggest however, the sleeping figure could not put the desire at work in Jarrell's poems to rest.

The man at the Washington Zoo

Like "Next Day," "The Woman at the Washington Zoo" takes on the voice of an older woman who has been left behind by love. In an essay about the poem written for a new edition of Robert Penn Warren's *Understanding Poetry*, Jarrell claimed that he "wrote, as they say in suits, 'acting as next friend'; I had for her the sympathy of an aging machine part."[44] Reading against Jarrell's claim, it seems more likely that the reverse is true, that the woman speaks "as next friend" for a man who has carefully arranged to not show his cards. I want to explore the consequences for Jarrell's poetics of reading the poem's speaker as a "beard," a woman tasked with participating in and disguising the same-sex desire of a man.

What orbit of sexual politics and social life would Jarrell's bearded poems then occupy? Perhaps it's in Jarrell's "on behalf of" that we might be able to negotiate among claims that these poems register projections of Jarrell's feminine affects, that the women in the poems speak "like" men, and that their constant concerns are those of visibility, recognition, identification, and desire.

Unlike "The Bronze David of Donatello" and Jarrell's late, unpublished poems, "The Woman at the Washington Zoo" features no facial hair. Instead, the woman in the poem goes along as a beard to the extent that she contributes to an appearance of heterosexuality in a place and at a time when the visibility of currents of same-sex desire is undesirable. In such moments, those currents need to be, like the mouth accessorized by a beard, veiled but not masked, covered but not hidden.

The poem opens with its female speaker watching foreign women, the wives of Washington diplomats, dressed in saris, walking through the zoo where she, too, is walking:

> The saris go by me from the embassies.
> Cloth from the moon. Cloth from another planet.
> They look back at the leopard like the leopard.[45]

As opposed to these vibrant garments, the uniform the speaker wears to her government job is the outward manifestation of a lonely, ignored body, one more comparable to zoo animals than to other women:

> Only I complain ....this serviceable
> Body that no sunlight dyes, no hand suffuses
> But, dome-shadowed, withering among columns,
> Wavy beneath fountains—small, far-off, shining
> In the eyes of animals, these beings trapped
> As I am trapped but not, themselves, the trap,
> Aging, but without knowledge of their age,
> Kept safe here, knowing not of death, for death—
> Oh, bars of my body, open, open!
> The world goes by my cage and never sees me.[46]

In the poem's closing lines, the speaker addresses a vulture, asking it to turn into a man who could make her an object of desire:

> Vulture,
> When you come for the white rat that the foxes left,

Take off the red helmet of your head, the black
Wings that have shadowed me, and step to me as man:
The wild brother at whose feet the white wolves fawn,
To whose hand of power the great lioness
Stalks, purring ....
You know what I was,
You see what I am: change me, change me.[47]

The poem is full of—or progressively emptied by means of—its displacements. The opening line's metonymy, in which "saris" stands for the women who wear them, registers the logic by which the poem names objects at the moment it renders them invisible. The speaker walks out of the government buildings where she has gone unseen—"dome-shadowed" and "withering among columns"— and enters the zoo. There, however, the zoo animals immediately give way to the noncaptive birds, insects, and vultures that feed there. Finally, one of these vultures is addressed not as a bird but as a man who may be able to "change" the speaker, to "open the bars of [her] body" and return her to "what I was." These displacements retroactively comment upon the displacement that allows the speaker to begin speaking as a woman. That is, the first question the poem calls us to answer is, "Who is speaking thus?"

This is, of course, Roland Barthes's question in the opening lines of "The Death of the Author." The essay begins with a quotation from Balzac's *Sarrasine* in which the narrator describes "a castrato disguised as a woman."[48] Curiously, however, the narrator begins, "This was woman herself, with her sudden fears, her irrational whims, her instinctive worries, her impetuous boldness, her fussings, and her delicious sensibility." Barthes goes on:

> Who is speaking thus? Is it the hero of the story bent on remaining ignorant of the castrato hidden beneath the woman? Is it Balzac the individual, furnished by his personal experience with a philosophy of Woman? Is it Balzac the author professing "literary" ideas on femininity? Is it universal wisdom? Romantic psychology?[49]

It is significant that Barthes turns to a literary performance of gender impersonation in order to demonstrate the difficulty or impossibility of determining who is speaking in writing. In doing so, he makes Balzac's lines the epitome of writing after the "diminishing" of the author, "that neutral, composite, oblique space where our subject slips away, the negative where all identity is lost."[50] As such, implicitly, Barthes demonstrates the interpretative uncertainty, even the panic, to which such a strategy may give rise.

Layers of possible identities and desires underwritten by a fundamental uncertainty about just who is speaking and to what end—this is characteristic, too, of the poems Randall Jarrell wrote "as a woman." The poems' speakers, by their distance from (or suggestive nearness to) the biographical facts of their author, seem to ask with heightened intensity, "Who is speaking thus?" Is it, following Alan Williamson, Jarrell the individual who, by appropriating a woman's voice, projects his own feminine characteristics that had no other home in poems of his time? Or Jarrell the satirist of midcentury popular culture, dismissive of the "feminization" of culture through mass advertising and consumerism, as in poems like "A Sad Heart at the Supermarket"? Or, as Randall Jarrell himself claimed, the poet speaking "as next friend," the poet of dramatic monologues that seek to understand the languages by which their diverse personalities speak? Or finally, a speaker in need of disguise? As Jarrell went on to say in his *Understanding Poetry* essay, "If I was also something else, that was just personal; and she also was something else."[51]

The speaker refers to her life as a cage: "The world goes by my cage and never sees me." At this point in the poem, readers have just been privy to a description of the woman's dress; the poem itself grants visibility to the speaker, making her complaint, "The world ... never sees me" untimely. Unless, that is, the fact of the female speaker's becoming visible is a further reminder that the obscurity of the man for whom she speaks is at that moment additionally magnified. Or, to rephrase, that the crisis of occluded or obstructed visibility does not only concern a state that precedes the poem, but one that is coterminous with it. On the one hand, the poem addresses a problem that is extrapoetic, a condition of the speaker's age and her state of dress, but on the other it aims to resolve, as it proceeds, a problem for which the poem must bear some responsibility. Inasmuch as the speaker's speaking as a woman accounts for the crisis of visibility, for the concealing of the male desiring subject, the poem both makes the speech of desire possible and obscures the gender of the one who desires to speak it. If this conceit of speaking and desiring as a woman satisfies one need, it reveals that the cost of this artifice is twofold. Neither the man nor the woman are fully constituted subjects of the speech they either desire to speak or for which they serve as mouthpiece.

The desire to speak and to desire as a woman, to access the somewhat limited, always vulnerable but nevertheless socially permissible and recognizable space in which a woman can desire a man represents the motivation for the governing conceit of the poem. What's more, if the speaker desires a man, and the trope that allows that desire to take on a public face, to become something other than unspeakable, is a woman's voice,[52] "The Woman at the Washington Zoo" does not merely grant the woman's voice, but encodes the process by which the voice can be, if only partially, accessed. Several, sometimes conflicting, desires circulate within the economy of the poem: the desire to be loved by a man, the desire to obtain a voice by which to make this desire known, and, finally, the strange, erupting force of a desire to be changed in the course of this speaking into an object worthy of unconcealed address.

Stephen Burt suggests that Jarrell's poems in a woman's voice are most interesting because they "show what male ideas of Woman are, and (at their best) how those ideas come to be."[53] It's possible to go one step further, however, and to suggest the speech of the poems leaves women's desires behind, concealed even more than those of the males for whom they speak. The poems don't speak to male "ideas" of woman, and certainly not of "woman herself," or even of male desires for women; which isn't to say that these constellations don't concern women at all—a point at which it's worth pausing. In effect, this restates the thesis of Sedgwick's *Between Men*, in which the distinction between male identification as men and male desire *for* men cannot be so rigidly maintained, even or especially when it routs that desire through women. By presenting male desires for men as routed through women, the poems register one way that heteronormative culture, and poetic culture in such an age—one in which such circuitous speech acts are necessary, or at least comprehensible—subordinates women's interests, their desires, to the speech of men. In this light, it can only seem ironic to consider Jarrell's ventriloquism of women sympathetic or feminist; it seems poetically just that Elizabeth Bishop wrote to Robert Lowell of Jarrell's women, that they "'seem to be like none I—or you—know.'"[54] And what better name than beard for a woman who is neither like Bishop's women, a woman who desires women, nor like Lowell's women, a woman who desires a man, but a woman whose words speak desire on behalf of someone else who cannot?

To read "The Woman at the Washington Zoo" as a register of the opportunities and the costs of the logic of poetic beards, and thus to push back against readings of the poems that account for Jarrell's female speakers by referencing the concepts of empathy and projection, may not be tantamount to claiming that any interpretative claim for a queer Jarrell comes at the expense of his protofeminist poetics. To give Jarrell the benefit of the doubt, perhaps the poem's logic is less a way of manipulating a female voice than of demonstrating how vulnerable to manipulation such voices are. By wearing its beard on the sleeve of its displacements, "The Woman at the Washington Zoo" maps out the subtle violence carried out by even the most vulnerable lyric voices. When this "woman" cries, "You know what I was," she not only points to the other speaker of her desire, but also seems to register her resistance to the bearding logic that made her speak in this way.

In this formulation, Jarrell's is a poetics that announces the precarity of the vicarious. A passage from the opening pages of *Between Men* illustrates this problematic and suggests one avenue by which "The Woman at the Washington Zoo," alongside Jarrell's other poems in female voices, may contribute to an understanding of midcentury sexuality, even though its handling of sex is routed through a beard and, even then, muted.

> To draw the "homosocial" back into the orbit of "desire," of the potentially erotic, then is to hypothesize the potential unbrokenness of a continuum between homosocial and homosexual—a continuum whose visibility, for men, in our society, is radically disrupted. It will become clear, in the course of my argument, that the hypothesis of the unbrokenness of this continuum is not a *genetic* one—I do not mean to discuss genital homosexual desire as "at the root of" other forms of male homosociality—but rather a strategy for making generalizations about, and marking historical differences in, the *structure* of men's relations with other men.[55]

While Jarrell's poems seem, at times, so starkly different from the poems of his contemporaries for taking on women's voices, it may be that, as a variant of poems written between men, they present an especially useful perspective into dynamics that the poems of other (physically) bearded midcentury poets— Ginsberg, Berryman, as well as Robert Lowell—demonstrate less visibly. Because Jarrell's poems wear their constitutive and determining displacements on their sleeves, they serve as a prompt reminder that "the *structure* of men's relations with other men" and that structure's reliance on women achieve a new singularity in its midcentury iteration.

In a formulation appropriate to much of Jarrell's work, a poem is a way of bearding oneself, of entering, if only partially and by means of others, an arena of potential identifications that remains unavailable in the social world. A significant aspect of Jarrell's verse lies in his conscious, at time overwrought, troping of the social speech of others in order to manage his own shame and gain access by poetic means to varieties of individual experience that shame inhibits. A Jarrell poem is a place where, by means of a beard, a kind of desire that is not permissible in social life can become briefly accessible, if only through the poetic others it burdens with that task.

Jarrell at the end: "Shaving" and "Rabbit"

To return to Eve Sedgwick's interest in Randall Jarrell, Axiom 7 of "Axiomatic" suggests a possible explanation. It registers the "strange and recalcitrant" nature of allo-identification, one of the central mechanisms by which feminism, queer theory and, in some accounts, queer desire locate and attach to objects.[56] While a homophobic account of heterosexuality depends on a common-sense distinction between identification (with men) and desire (for women), contemporary understandings of same-sex desire "expose [the] factitiousness" of any such distinction in order "to show how close may be the slippage ... between identification and desire."[57] By so doing, such understandings allow "an entire social region of the vicarious [to] become peculiarly charged in association with homo/heterosexual definition."[58] Sedgwick's interest in Jarrell may derive, in part, from the cathexis of vicarity that his noncombat soldier's perspectives on combat, his adult-authored poems of childhood and his male-authored poems of female experience indulge. The aim of identifying across boundaries is problematic in that it depends on the power to speak for others, but the concept may suggest an account of the "naked vulnerability" of the clean-shaven face Jarrell wore in the last year of his life.[59]

Few images from the last year of Jarrell's life survive. As Mary Jarrell recounts, John F. Kennedy's assassination may have marked the beginning of a serious depression for Jarrell, one that combined with a new awareness of aging, which he called, in the German vocabulary he picked up from Hannah Arendt, Torschlusspanik, or door-closing panic.[60] At some point during this tumultuous last year of his life, part of which he spent in a mental hospital, Jarrell shaved off the beard he'd been cultivating for over ten years. As we've already seen, Stanley Kunitz associated Jarrell's clean-shaven face with a surprising, almost terrifying vulnerability, as if the beard had served him as a buffer, a barrier between the part of Jarrell with which many readers identify in the poems and the part exposed to public, social life.

The act of shaving and the new fact of Jarrell's clean-shaven face appear in Jarrell's final, unpublished poems and offer a new perspective on beards in the poet's work. "Shaving," which Jarrell left in manuscript form in a notebook from the last year of his life, records his attention to the natural beauty of a newly revived ritual. The short observation recognizes that, as the speaker begins shaving, he undertakes anew a task he performed yesterday:

As I lift the can
The dry fluff of yesterday's lather
Falls from it as last week's snow
Fell from the pine bough when the squirrel jumped to it.[61]

Unlike the stilled, dead, or sleeping bearded Goliath in "The Bronze David of Donatello," the man in "Shaving" is active, alive, and energetic. Unlike Stevens's "pine bough shagged with snow" in "The Snow Man," Jarrell's tree is shaken by the arrival of a squirrel, thrust into motion by the quotidian activity of natural habit. "Shaving" flags a moment in Jarrell's life when a new ritual enhances his ability to perceive the world around him. It meets the present moment, when "yesterday's fluff" falls away, in a way that "The Woman at the Washington Zoo" hardly could.

The late, unpublished poem "Rabbit" recognizes and turns against the logic of bearding by which Jarrell's work had proceeded for years. The poem is a playfully intimate extended conversation in which the speaker acknowledges that he looks like, and therefore is, a rabbit. Its closing lines shift, however, to "a little story about beards." If, as I've argued, a beard had previously provided Jarrell self-protective shielding from social interactions he regarded as threatening, immoral, or simply undesirable, now a beard is "more trouble than it's worth" because it hides an identity that the speaker is finally willing to accept. Even though he'd "look better with one," the speaker will forego a beard, he claims, not so much for what it allows him to do or be as for what it allows others to see. The poem's crushing final lines argue that a clean-shaven face will allow others to see feeling's ravages: "I don't want the erosion of habitual emotion/Of sorrow and of cruelty, not to show." As opposed to the bearded poetry he wrote during most of his life—poems about other people whose identities he could briefly adopt—Jarrell sought, in his final year, a new poetics of vulnerability.

Jarrell's last poem may be the only one in which his desire almost completely foregoes a beard. Written in all caps and dated October 13, 1965, the untitled, unpublished poem is housed in the New York Public Library Berg Collection.[62] It addresses Jerry, a fellow patient at the UNC hand clinic where Jarrell was receiving treatment for wounds sustained in a suicide attempt in April of 1965. The poem mimics a vacation postcard from the hospital, informing Jerry, who has been released, of "how much we miss you." As it continues, it carries its desire more openly, if somewhat more facetiously: "Of all the Eskimos/Or Canadians or men from the pole/You're the longest-haired and nicest-looking/ come back to us and things will start cooking." In the poem's final couplet

Jarrell articulates a desire for men, and although he once again routes it through women, he manages to speak more openly on his own behalf than ever before: "The girls say nobody else will do,/and we know how they feel—we think so too." More significant even than the expression itself is Jarrell's use of the first person plural pronoun, which indicates that his position with respect to desire is not maintained or abandoned alone, but alongside a community of others. His death the following day cut short an exploration of unbearded affect that had just entered a new stage.

Mourning the Elegy: Robert Creeley's "Mother's Photograph"

Nearly a decade has passed since Robert Creeley's death and the publication of his *Collected Poems, 1976–2005*. Because many of Creeley's most frequently anthologized poems were already written by the mid-1970s, his work of the 1980s has been, with a few notable exceptions,[1] largely overlooked. The last ten years have been especially valuable, then, for the renewed attention they have brought to the notable shifts in form and content characteristic of Creeley's middle and late poetic output.[2] Among these shifts, critics note that, against what Charles Altieri has called the Spinozan "conativity" of Creeley's early work,[3] many poems published after *Life & Death* memorialize friends and acquaintances. Recognizing the prevalence of this mode adds to the poignancy of the tributes offered to Creeley, which seem to recognize that they mourn a prolific elegist. Due in part to the reputation assigned him after the success of his first collections, Creeley has not often been considered an elegiac poet.[4] Even recent critical work, which has helpfully drawn attention to the poet's handling of aging and death in his final collections, does not discuss elegy.[5] In response, this chapter considers the series of elegies Creeley wrote for his mother during the fourteen-year period following her death in 1972 and argues that their intervention into a poetics of mourning is a major, if unrecognized, achievement. After alternating between reverent tributes to the mother and restless bids for release from her haunting posthumous power, the series culminates with a poem that turns to a photograph of the mother in an attempt to conclude its prolonged work of mourning. "Mother's Photograph" ends up providing, however, an account of losses sustained during its attempt to find resolution in the extra-linguistic resources of the photograph; in so doing, it mourns the "lubricity" of the genre of elegy. One task that remains essential to the ongoing work of mourning Creeley, then, is a more nuanced account of the poetic work accomplished during the course of Creeley's mourning.

By way of introduction to the first poems of the elegiac series that culminates in "Mother's Photograph," I take as noteworthy both the serial nature of Creeley's project and the concepts of maternity to which his poems are indexed. For example, while some of Creeley's individual elegies fit Jahan Ramazani's description of the "melancholic" "anti-elegy,"[6] the subgenre characterized by its aim of exposing, rather than burying, its lost objects, others hew more closely to seemingly conventional, consolatory aims. Ramazani's model, which attends to individual lyrics, can theorize neither the plurality of Creeley's elegies nor their oscillation between elegiac and anti-elegiac modes of acknowledging the mother. As such, the roles of both the elegies' duration, the span of fourteen years over which they were composed, and their economy, that "sporadic" and "chaotic" whole containing such varying approaches, remain to be considered.[7]

Because they are discontinuous and distributed among four volumes of Creeley's verse (*Away, Echoes, Mirrors,* and *Memory Gardens*),[8] the maternal elegies do not figure among the experimental "serial" poems of the late 1960s and 1970s, which Alan Golding regards as among Creeley's most inventive work. Nevertheless, I identify an implicit series formed by the thematic coherence of the elegies that resembles such book-length poems as *Hello* and *Pieces*. These poems, too, aim to be, in Rachel Blau DuPlessis's words, "accretive *pensees.*"[9] In practical fact, they differ by their failure to accrete; each elegy responds to an identical, continual (rather than continuous) call to elegiac writing that issues forth from grief that remains as inconsolable after each poem as before. Such a repetition also aligns with one aspect of the Freudian account of mourning, in that the reality of loss must be accepted over and over again because its "existence … is psychically prolonged" by a libido that is "reluctant to abandon" it.[10] Unlike the Freudian model of healthy mourning, in which such a loss is eventually accepted, the successive poems both repeat the trauma of the mother's death indefinitely and change only in their need to address new crises raised by the situation's growing urgency. In the tradition of Mallarmé's *Un Tombeau Pour Anatole,* of Roland Barthes's *Camera Lucida* and *Mourning Diary,* and, more recently, of Anne Carson's *Nox,* Peter Gizzi's *Threshold Songs,* and Susan Howe's *The Midnight,*[11] Creeley undertakes a nontraditional *work* of mourning that serves less as a single tribute to a lost loved one than as a testament to grief's problematic ongoing.

In *The Mother in the Age of Mechanical Reproduction,* Elissa Marder emphasizes that alienation, separation, and mediation are just as constitutive of motherhood as of fatherhood. By unraveling and specifying the artifice of the "quintessentially 'natural'" mother, and the "meanings attached to the maternal body,"[12] Marder displaces the mother's association with the beginning of life in favor of the nonlife intimated by the technological prostheses of the maternal: "birth and death … are brought into an intimate and disturbing proximity with one another" and the womb becomes "structurally indistinguishable from the tomb."[13] Creeley's elegies address just such a mother, one who, as "Mother's Voice" has it, "frightens me" by haunting the voice, body, and memory of her son and watching more closely over his death than his birth. Rather than an idealized mother-son relationship, Creeley's elegies point to the ghost of a "maternal function" in the machine of his mourning. Marder finds that "the photographic medium is often represented as a prosthetic maternal body";[14] in the process of reading a photograph, Creeley will discover the elegiac consequences, for the genre of elegy, of the fact that the photograph's most intimate link is not with the mother, or even with the fact of her death, but with the death that a haunting maternal function presages for the speaker.

Creeley's series begins on a different note, however, and it is by marking the dramatic change that occurs between the first poem, "For My Mother," and the last, "Mother's Photograph," that the increasingly urgent crises characterizing Creeley's work of mourning may best be recognized. By far the longest and most narrative poem of the series, "For My Mother" is also the most temporally specific, confining itself to the weeks of the mother's final illness and the hours after her death. The unprecedented decision to publish the poem as an individually bound chapbook before its appearance in *Away* suggests that Creeley regarded the poem's occasion as one tied closely to the time of the mother's death, not that of his mourning.[15] Unlike later poems in the series, its service is that of eulogy, not elegy. Even at this earliest moment, though, the poem raises questions about its ability to accomplish its aims, to make satisfactory tribute "for" the mother. The speaker twice revises his verb tense (e.g., "Is it,/was it, ever/you") and then recognizes the inadequacy of his speech to provide closure; such speech leads, in fact, in the opposite direction:

> I feel
> the mouth's sluggish-
> ness, slips on
> turns of things
> said, to you,
> too soon, too late,
> wants to
> go back to beginning.[16]

The desire to, rather than end, return "to beginning" and hear the mother's voice drives several poems in Creeley's series, including "Mother's Photograph," which records its search for the proper time in the lost object's life to begin mourning. This temporal reversal occurs even as, or perhaps because, the poem concludes with the speaker's realization, also repeated in "Mother's Photograph," that her death guarantees his own death in the future: "I am here,/and will follow."[17] The backward movement is consistent with Barbara Johnson's revised understanding of the relationship of poetic speech to the maternal voice. If she had once spoken of poetry's "endless elaborations and displacements of the single cry, 'Mama,'" mother-centered poems by Baudelaire and Plath suggest that poems often "attempt not to address the mother but to *hear her voice*."[18] While Creeley's first elegy includes "the single cry" of maternal address ("Mother, I/love you"), the mother's voice inflects later iterations. As they shift toward their less admiring register, however, Creeley's poems will add a footnote to Johnson's account: while it is sometimes the desire to *hear* the mother's painfully absent voice, it is at others an urgent need to silence its posthumous echo that motivates poetic speech. This work of silencing is the project of "Mother's Voice." As the first poem in Creeley's series to depict the fear of the dead mother and of her potentially murderous vengeance, it establishes a crucial link to "Mother's Photograph," in which the threat of violence drives the speaker to photography.

"Mother's Voice" laments the persistence with which maternal speech outlives its body. The poem goes on to suggest that even when she predeceases them, a mother always outlives her children and ensures their eventual deaths:

> I hear
> mother's voice say
> under my own, I won't
> want any more of that.
> My cheekbones resonate
> with her emphasis.[19]

Against the movement toward the mother of the previous poem, "Mother's Voice," which Creeley chose as the title poem of a mimeographed artist's book he completed with Tom Clark,[20] articulates a desire to achieve distance from the mother precisely because her own "distance ... from/common fact of others" threatens the speaker's desire to continue living:

> I look out
> at all this demanding world

and try to put it quietly back,
from me, say, thank you,
I've already had some
though I haven't
and would like to
but I've said no, she has,
it's not my own voice anymore.[21]

Despite different grounding attitudes toward the mother's death, both "For My Mother" and "Mother's Voice" pit desire against crises to which mourning itself gives rise. Both reckon with the unstable image repertoire of the object, whether lost or irritably present. Read together, they outline a genre in which the surviving speaker and the dead object vie for control, leaving the subject and object of elegy constitutively unstable in a "confusion of tongues" that attends the dissolution of the body. At this pivotal, or simply dizzying, moment in his series, Creeley, like Roland Barthes before him, turns to a photographic image. When the mother's voice becomes a threat, Creeley employs a photograph, which does not speak, to silence it; when the elegy discovers that neither poem nor photograph will be so easily manipulated, it must mourn both the resistance and the ephemerality of elegiac practice.

***

In both its history and its critical reception, no medium reprises the oscillation between certainty and instability, authenticity and artifice, so insistently as the photograph. And this oscillation helps to account for the significant role that photographs, in which the dead seem to live again, have come to play in rituals of grief and mourning. Indeed, the rapid expansion of photographic technologies in the twentieth century allowed the photograph in its many iterations (from professional portrait to personal snapshot) to challenge the nineteenth-century preeminence of the poetic elegy as a document of remembrance.[22] In recent years, elegiac writing in both the narrative and poetic vein has integrated and interrogated photographic evidence as a means for coming to terms with the role of the image in structuring contemporary lives while they are lived and as they are remembered and represented posthumously.[23] For both Barthes and Creeley, this coming to terms occurs because, while the photograph does not speak, it produces referents with a certainty that "no writing can give."[24] Recognizing that a photograph can—or that it promises to—accomplish something that memory and words cannot leads both writers to consider its potential at a moment when grief has stalled language.

Apart from the direct treatment of photographs, Creeley's poetic vision maintains a rapport with photography for reasons that appeal directly to the maternal and to the physical body. At the age of two, Creeley's left eye was injured when shards of glass from a broken car window pierced his cornea. Creeley's parents were divided on how to treat the injury, however. His father fought to preserve the eye even when an infection threatened vision in his son's healthy right eye. Shortly after Dr. Creeley's death from pneumonia, however, the poet's mother, a nurse, arranged for an operation to have it removed. She informed the young Creeley only moments before the procedure began, and Creeley later reported feeling upset at "being tricked in this curious way."[25] Parallel to the concern in "Mother's Voice" that a maternal voice had been added to the speaker's own, overpowering it, Creeley's mother's removal of the poet's eye just as his father died multiplies her impact on Creeley's sensorium. From seeing two parents in two eyes, Creeley would suddenly see only one parent with one. The figure of the mother would, by necessity, loom large for him; and due to his single eye, she would loom there in a vision that can best be described as photographic. Thus, even in poems that do not explicitly reference photography, such vision is mutely at work.

And even apart from elegiac content, Creeley's innovations in poetic form transcribe physical limitation into poetic strategy. While Creeley's inheritance and adaptation of the short line owes much to William Carlos Williams, I want to suggest that Creeley also manipulates line-length in order to implement a photographic and maternal poetics; the truncation of each line refers to and repeats the maternally inflicted trauma of halved sight.[26] Reflecting on a photograph of Creeley and Robert Duncan (who suffered from double vision), poet Eleni Sikelianos notes that Creeley's isolation of single words as poetic lines demonstrates a "morphology of the monocular."[27] The short line becomes, in this view, not only a tribute to Williams's perceptual precision[28] but a marker of Charles Olson's "proprioception," which regards the "tissues" of "the 'body' itself" as the privileged site of poetic labor.[29] For Allen Ginsberg, even Creeley's reading voice demonstrates his poetic preference for the "mono." Creeley stuttered into the microphone "monosyllable by monosyllable," allowing Ginsberg "to hear speech so bare that the modifications of mind syllable by syllable were apparent."[30] Inasmuch as Creeley's mother was to some extent the problematic agent of his single vision and, for much of his early life, its only object, the proprioceptive axis by which Creeley developed a poetics out of his single vision bears a maternal imprint. In this light, the mother's death is a loss and a significant threat to poetic organization.

Of all of Creeley's elegies, "Mother's Photograph" presents the most dramatic demonstration of this threat to poetic orientation. In a project uncannily similar to that of Barthes's *Camera Lucida*, the poem derives the precariousness of the speaker's own life and death from the mother's mortality as figured through a photograph of the mother in her youth. Barthes locates this revelation not in interpretation, but in the photograph itself:

> By giving me the absolute past of the pose (aorist), the photographer tells me death in the future … In front of the photograph of my mother as a child, I tell myself: she is going to die.[31]

According to Barthes's well-known description, the photograph has a special relationship to the work of mourning; *Camera Lucida* laments a "rather terrible thing which there is in every photograph: the return of the dead";[32] in this way, the photograph becomes an obstacle rather than an aid to mourning. A photograph is "without culture," "undialectical," and "violent," "fill[ing] the sight by force"; its bluntness mimics nothing so much as the raw, unredeemable fact of death itself. As a result, a photograph only renews the searing pain of loss—what Barthes calls "grief"—and provides no incentive to the work of Freudian mourning, to accepting the reality of the object's loss and agreeing to find satisfactions in substitutive loved objects. That is, "[n]othing in [the photograph] can transform grief into mourning."[33]

Nevertheless, according to Elissa Marder, one redemptive possibility of the medium of photography lies in the kind of reading and writing that the photograph demands. If, for Barthes, the power of the photograph is its referential certainty, a "power of authentication [that] exceeds the power of representation,"[34] then a photograph demands that its viewer fill this gap: "The Photograph uses its power of certainty to disable the latent potentialities of language: it neither reads nor writes."[35] In response to its muteness, Barthes engages in a kind of writing that is itself photographic. He "reproduce[s] the photograph in his own psyche," which takes on the functions of a dark room—or a womb.[36] There, the pasts to which photographs refer can be developed and imagined differently. As Marder explains:

> This "photographic writing" cannot show anything directly; it animates a potential field of associations through which the time "before" is awakened otherwise and, when read, brings the "déjà vu" of a possible, impossible future to life.[37]

Most importantly, if the psyche functions like a "womb" for the reproduction of the uncanny, which Freud ties to the strange familiarity of the body of the mother, Barthes's writing uncovers a conceptual link that is otherwise hidden by the strangeness and difficulty constitutive of responding to images: "photographic reading is intimately connected with the figure of the mother."[38] In this inner, uncanny space, the possibility remains "to create new temporalities that unfold from dormant histories that are embedded in its inscriptions."[39]

Creeley, too, had grappled with the temporality of grief. While "Mother's Voice" demonstrates that the endurance of maternally inflicted psychological wounds can forestall the sought-after closure of healthy mourning, "Mother's Photograph" demands that the photograph provides access to just such a new temporality by which the mother's innocence, as well as her life, could be recovered. As Barthes and Creeley recognize separately, the paradox of such an effort is that, to absolve her of the crimes of motherhood, the son must return her to childhood, the time before she was a mother at all. By erasing the maternal relation in search of consolation, the son repeats the very violence that set him to elegize the mother in the first place. Rather than provide closure, for both writers the photograph illuminates the constitutive double binds of the work of mourning.

Lastly, both writers call on a nonwritten and nonrepresenting medium to access a period of "history," something Barthes defines as "the time my mother was alive before me," of which they have no memory and to which their mourning can provide no access. Oddly, Creeley and Barthes's texts concern not only the same figuratively "historical" time, but also the same chronologically historical time. Henriette Binger Barthes was born in 1893, and Barthes places her age in the "Winter Garden photograph" at 5. Genevieve Jules Creeley was born in 1887, and "Mother's Photograph" presents her "aged/ten." Barthes's mother died in 1977, at the age of eighty-four, while Creeley's mother died at eighty-five in 1972. The two photographs, neither of which is reproduced, may have been taken only months apart, in 1898 and 1897, respectively. Moreover, despite the fact that Creeley's poem predates Barthes's book by some seven years, the two contemplated their mothers' photographs when the images were themselves between eighty and ninety years old. For each author, the fragility of the physical image must have paralleled the mother's final fragility. Despite this, "Mother's Photograph" begins by contrasting the mother's contemporary embodiment with the youthfulness depicted in the photograph:

Could you see present
sad investment of

person, its clothes,
gloves and hat,
as against yourself
backed to huge pine tree,
lunch box in hand in
homemade dress aged
ten, to go to school
and learn to be somebody
find the way will
get you out of the
small place of home
and bring them with
you, out of it too,
sit them down in a new house.[40]

Beneath the central narrative of the poem, whose celebratory evocation of the mother's role in establishing the speaker's own life (she brought him out of a "small place" and into a "new house") would seem final, the poem's structural elements suggest an alternative. And alternating is the operative word, since, as Jonathan Culler claims, "elegy … replaces an irreversible temporal disjunction, the move from life to death, with a dialectical alternation between attitudes of mourning and consolation, evocations of absence and presence."[41] As we shall see, the syntax and prepositions of "Mother's Photograph" oscillate between two opposing parsings to dramatic effect.

More specifically, the syntax of "Mother's Photograph" presents difficulties to the reader who would parse its single sentence; the ambiguous tense of its main verb only compounds this difficulty at the level of basic legibility. The poem's first word, "could," may signal either the opening of an unpunctuated question or an unpredicated conditional statement. In either case, a grammatical deferral marks the poem; as a result of this fundamental uncertainty, the poem proceeds by multiplying its possible referents and occasions—the virtually present and actually absent mother, her photograph as it is virtually presented and represented to her, and the possibility of either an answer to the question or a predicate to the conditional statement—without verifying or concretely situating any of them. This conflict between the interrogative and conditional moods, in addition to amplifying some of the temporal confusion constitutive of the experience of maternal mourning, brings the poem's emphatic concern for futurity to the fore. By deferring the most basic aspects of the poem's legibility to a future time, the poem represents one effect of a psyche overtaxed by grieving—the inability to cathect other objects or responsibilities—and it continually asks whether the most overlooked dimension of mourning is its futurity. If "For My Mother" and "Mother's Voice" regard the future as a site of elegiac consolation for the mother's death and as the scene of intolerable maternal haunting, respectively, "Mother's Photograph" is structured by the explosive tension that results from admitting both urgent expectation and anxious deferral to the same poetic space.

Finally, the play of prepositions in a poem already primarily concerned with the virtual relationships between persons suggests that we read "Mother's Photograph" as a special kind of self-elegy, one less singular in its challenge to conventional elegy than Ramazani's "anti-elegy." Like its syntactical possibilities, the prepositions of "Mother's Photograph" alternate: the poem's concern with containing and ejecting, incorporating and expelling, and birthing and dying turns on its repeated use of the words "in" and "out." Will the speaker be held or ejected? Has death removed the mother from him or brought her even closer? How does her escape "in" to death or "out" of life prefigure his own? "Mother's Photograph" becomes, through these words and the questions they propose, an elegy for the self that takes place within—and takes the place of—the body of the mother. As such, the language play of "Mother's Photograph" asks a provocative question of poetics and the genre whose conventions it so radically upsets: is the elegy a womb—or a tomb?

This question has antecedents in twentieth-century verse that contextualize the poem's labyrinthine dynamics of maternal time. Parsing the opening words of "Mother's Photograph" as an interrogative aligns Creeley's words with those of the aging speaker of Yeats's "Among School Children." The fifth stanza of that poem also anachronistically juxtaposes a young mother with her aging son and returns to a time in the past in order to posit the present as a hypothetical possibility rather than a lived certainty:

> What youthful mother ...
> ...
> Would think her son, did she but see that shape
> With sixty or more winters on its head,
> A compensation for the pang of his birth,
> Or the uncertainty of his setting forth?[42]

Both Yeats and Creeley ask if the past contains the seed of the present by necessity, or if it is radically separated from the present by its necessary ignorance of it.[43] In both cases, the speakers grant their mothers a posthumous ability to judge their lives, invoking the threatening possibility that the speakers' respective mothers' posthumous examinations could, anachronistically, upset the actual courses of the speakers' lives: since each mother could have decided not to bear children, it is possible that neither of these speakers would have ever been born. Exploring this disconcerting possibility is nevertheless necessary, since it lengthens the history of maternal haunting. For both Yeats and Creeley, reestablishing one's birth as a contingent rather than necessary event creates a consoling parallel with the otherwise unthinkable contingency of the present. For Creeley, whose elegies recognize with increasing alarm the extent to which one's present life and potential death have been determined entirely by the mother's death, asking an unanswerable question also demonstrates, helpfully, the impotence of apostrophe. That is, the ability to mourn at all is here predicated on the assumption that elegiac temporality is defective, that his maternal apostrophe is to some extent ineffective; otherwise, the mother could respond, change her mind about giving birth, and even exercise the power to kill him that she has always retained. By granting a choice to a mother whom he knows cannot respond, the speaker takes her choice into his own hands, not merely to justify his own birth, but to give birth to himself so that he may take on the role of her mourner in the future. In full recognition that elegiac conventions fail to resurrect or to mourn the mother completely, Creeley's speaker makes the poetic case for the extension of his work of mourning into an infinite, circular futurity.

Parsing the poem's opening words, "could you see," in the conditional mood, which leaves the poem's single sentence incomplete, suggests an alternate reading of the poem's temporally oriented tensions. As a poem that sets up an expectation for and then defers its own predication, "Mother's Photograph" would defer even its precise stance on the futurity of mourning to a future in which such a statement would, perhaps, be possible. Like the famously undecidable nature of the question asked at the end of "Among School Children," the grammar of "Mother's Photograph" is undecidable. But if Yeats's question has rhetorical implications, Creeley's poem implies a revolution in poetic time. That is, because limiting himself to the present moment had always been Creeley's recourse against the violent impingements of the unintelligible world, "Mother's Photograph" explores the fact that the mother's death and the generic conventions of elegy threaten the present moment from two directions. If the process of introjection would rob the speaker of his present and situate him entirely in a past life with the mother, elegiac manipulations of time threaten the present by their promise of a consoling future. Added to this, the mother's ability to haunt the speaker and guarantee his death diminish his hope of any future at all. If "Mother's Photograph" turns to the photograph in order to resist, in addition to the past, the actual present in which the mother has died, the hypothetical present determined by a posthumously revised past, and any predetermined future, what does such resistance recognize about the genre to whose conventions it still, if only minimally, adheres? In what follows, I suggest that if the temporal confusion caused by the coincidence of the mother's death in the past and its threat to the speaker's future calls Creeley to the photograph, whose "'absolute pastness'"[44] would seem to redeem time, it also called him to relinquish any expectations that poetic photography could provide solutions to intractable elegiac problems.

The first stanza of "Mother's Photograph" presents the poem's frame as a presentation of the photograph of the mother *to* the mother herself. The poem's content thus moves from presentation to representation of the photograph. Its turn to a description of the photograph follows from the suggestion in the conditional "could" that the mother cannot actually see herself in it, and that any vision—or psychic development—of the photograph will be the speaker's own. Following the mode of Barthes's photographic reading and writing, as against the photograph's own muteness, the poem reproduces the photograph in words. Notably, and in distinction to Barthes, the poem's reliance on voice stands in even more direct opposition to the photograph's muteness, making the paradox of a "photographic poem" in the oeuvre of a poet known for incorporating silence into the spacing of the poem on the page, particularly salient.

As it does so, a portrait of the mother as a ten-year-old child emerges that contrasts the sad outfitting of her old age. She is self-sufficient with "lunch box" and "homemade dress." Nevertheless, in these stanzas the mother herself is hardly to be found. Instead of a description of her body, as even "For My Mother" had it, only the garments and accessories that surround what should be her body find a place in the "now" of the discourse. In one possible reading, these stanzas have their counterpart in Barthes's mention of "a kind of stupefaction in seeing a familiar being dressed *differently*."[45] But for Creeley, the dress precludes any description of the "familiar being," as though to bring her body into the poem were also to enter the fact of her death in the space of death's elegiac denial. The "presencing" of the mother that the poem's apostrophe enacts stands in tension with the "absencing" that is the work of its metonymic substitutions.

This maternal metonymy, while it refrains from using her parts to retrieve a composite substitute image, serves a significant purpose in "Mother's Photograph." Not even pictures of her from the past, from a time in which she was alive, can make her "present": even then, her body was missing. For Creeley, this is no "Winter Garden photograph" in which "I studied the little girl and at last rediscovered my mother."[46] So complete is the loss of the mother for Creeley that her presence in memory and as an object of poetic address is spectral, an absence outlined by the objects that typically define the limits of the body.

So far, my reading has pushed back against the poem's seeming celebration of the mother's story, which affects the speaker's own: if not for her "getting out," the speaker would not have been raised in the "new house." But the tribute of the last stanza of the elegy crosses a different threshold by means of its prepositions to the extent that even this story confronts problems of death and mourning. Against the word "in," which is repeated in the first half of the poem, the final two stanzas repeat the word "out." The word echoes a phrase in Ginsberg's "Kaddish" that Creeley quoted in "For My mother": "Death's let you out."[47] In a letter to Ginsberg dated January 28, 1973, Creeley describes how he came to include the phrase:

> I wanted to tell you ... that while my mother was dying in Marin General, just worn out at last physically, 85, I kept hearing in my head as I'd be there, watching the catch of her breathing, how the body was all going "in"—anyhow those words of yours, "Relax and die"—also "Death's let you out."[48]

Instead of a heroic escape from poverty that benefits her young family, placing Ginsberg's phrase in the background of Creeley's own use of the preposition "out" recasts the mother's journey as a successful flight from life itself. What makes the fourth stanza so haunting is the sense that this new flight into death retains its collective predicate. When the mother dies, she will "bring them with/you, out of it, too." As a commentary on the work of mourning, "Mother's Photograph" suggests a more desperate scenario. Unlike the more traditional, "healthy mourning" of "Mother's Voice," in which the speaker desires more of life than his mother's voice sanctions, the mourning speaker of "Mother's Photograph," lacking what Freud calls "the narcissistic satisfaction ... derive[d] from being alive," indexes the deaths of his entire family to the mother's demise.[49] In the context of the poem, the verb "bring" is spoken, like those that immediately precede it, in the infinitive, as among the actions that the mother's pose in the photograph suggest she intends. She is dressed this way in order "to go to school" and to "learn to be somebody." By the poem's last stanza, however, with three lines intervening between the last verbs in the series, "bring" reads like a command. As such, the mother's capacity for causing death encompasses both readings, albeit for different reasons. On the one hand, to read "bring" as a verb in a series linked directly to the young, photographed mother's intended actions is to use her pose to establish the link between her death and her family's.

In this reading, the photograph of the mother is, far from a means of recovering life, the very instrument by which death tightens its hold. No longer the giver of life, here the function of the maternal is to kill. Reading "bring them out of it" as a command suggests, similarly, that holding the photograph of the mother, far from offering consolation, only deepens his grief. By bringing him to a place in which he can only desire his own death (and that of the other survivors), "Mother's Photograph" demonstrates one route by which the aims of elegy give way to those of self-elegy.

Reconceiving the elegy from this perspective—in which self-elegy is so often its immediate derivative—refigures the role played by the mother in her own elegy. Roland Barthes describes the aftermath of finding the Winter Garden photograph as the experience of a similar reversal: "From now on I could do no more than await my total, undialectical death."[50] Like Creeley, Barthes marks a different time that begins not from the moment of the mother's death, but from the moment of the mother's elegiac reanimation. As such, the aims of elegy consist, at least in part, in resurrecting a key witness to one's own demise at the moment that the death of the mother has confirmed its approach. Instead of reversing the progression of time in order to prevent the mother's death, Creeley's speaker takes her place there. The span of time for which the poem raises the mother back to life also marks the time during which the speaker can, in a fantasy-laden poetic bargain, enter into the otherwise inaccessible space of his own death. Instead of a poem whose mourning finds a substitutive satisfaction for the mother's body, "Mother's Photograph" seeks out, as if compelled to do so by the dead mother, a substitutive death. Elegy is still, as Culler has it, a genre of temporal manipulations. In Creeley's hands, however, these manipulations serve a different purpose and a different, more unsettling master.

Given that a capacity to prefigure the deaths of her mourners overtakes the work of maternal mourning, elegy is a genre that slips away. In the course of a poem whose syntax and prepositions make its ultimate destination undecidable, its presumably stable purpose as an elegy—whether consolation or condemnation—slips "out" of the speaker's grasp. Such a loss, of course, identifies an essential aspect of its subject; instead of a failed example of the genre, "Mother's Photograph" manages to perform a poetic repetition of a characteristic yet underrepresented gesture of loss, namely the losing of grief itself. The third paragraph of Emerson's "Experience" records just such a loss; there, speaking of the death of his son, Waldo, the mourning father "grieve[s] that grief can teach me nothing" and laments the "lubricity of all objects, which lets them slip through our fingers then when we clutch hardest" as "the most unhandsome part of our condition."[51] Stanley Cavell notes Emerson's pun on the failure to grasp and clutch as "unhandsome," adding that this technique speaks to "the writing taking shape under his hand and now in ours)."[52] "Mother's Photograph," in which, of all body parts, only a hand appears, is thus party to this recurring interest, to an insistence on the hand's—and perhaps thus the writer's, and then the reader's—failure to grasp, to transmit, and to hold what it wishes to "hold to" and to address. Paradoxically, the photograph we imagine the speaker holding in his hand and passing to the hand of his mother in order to ask "Could you see?" becomes the vehicle of an experience of being, in Winnicott's phrase, "insecurely held."[53] Her photograph is the means by which the mother's story of success becomes the account of her death as well as the speaker's. To hand a photograph, with one's living hand, to the hand of the dead also aims to consign it to an inaccessible realm of memory. "Mother's Photograph" seeks to sign away possession of the photograph—the image that is the speaker's only claim to her continued life as well as, in Barthes logic, the irreducible fact of her absolute death—to the mother herself. Whether she is, at the end of the poem, the child of the photograph, the fantasied living mother of the poem's address, or the body whose wholeness and deadness escapes the realm of the poem, this remains as uncertain as—as potential as—the poem's syntax. As for its reader, the poem's end returns us repeatedly to its beginning in an unending quest to settle its syntactic quandary. If Creeley's work of maternal mourning serves to question the status of elegiac writing, "Mother's Photograph" answers by endlessly reenacting both this unresolvable question and the "rather terrible" return of the dead *in* photographic writing (and *as* a return to the beginning of one's life with the mother) by which it had sought an answer. That is, if such a return of the dead had been sought in order to resolve the crisis of mourning, in Creeley's poetry what it revives, instead, is the crisis itself. Choosing neither womb nor tomb, neither the mother's life nor her death, the poem's dynamic rests in its ability to turn the mother's womb and tomb into the son's, as he finds not only the source of his own death but a surrogate motherhood in the death of the mother. As the losses of the poem mount, the central loss that the poem enacts and mourns in its radical redefinition of elegiac writing is the loss of elegy itself. The future of elegy, "Mother's Photograph" announces, is that of a genre that, dead itself, repeats, mourns, and perhaps haunts the loss of no external object so fiercely as itself.

Within this newly defined genre, however, a new space suggests its availability for the poetic reworking of language in which the accumulation of losses could be slowed. The "new house" in whose space the poem ends claims, perhaps, to compensate for the impossibility of joining the mother in the photograph by figuring not merely a tomb, but an alternative, poetic dwelling that the mother, in a deed that outlives her, will have made possible. That is, once photographic reading and writing have failed to accomplish the work of elegy and to produce the mother's body, the photograph exits the poem. Now, the space of the poem—rather than that of the photograph—figures as the only "new house" in which both the life and death of the mother and son could be, momentarily, shared. If the shattered temporality of "Mother's Photograph" can be said to have an organizing principle, the time of this elegiac poem is the time that the speaker needs to test the photograph as a potential space and time of dwelling, to recognize its failure, and to "get out of it" into another imagined space. Its "new house" dreams a potential poem in which mother and son, irreparably divided across a temporal chasm no longer bridgeable by elegy, can briefly dwell together. Rather than the work of mourning as it is traditionally configured or an embrace of the photograph as a technology that could "transform grief into mourning," "Mother's Photograph" transforms its mourning of the elegiac possibilities of the photograph into an exploration of new renderings of postphotographic poetic space.[54] Its words return to an investment in the poetic construction of containers for grief, but with a lingering consciousness, befitting the novelty of its "new" structure, that those constructions hold on to, rather than hand off, the images whose absolute certification of death admits of no consoling vision. Although the poem's title indicates the subject of the photograph, read otherwise it reminds us that "Mother's Photograph," like her voice, remains her possession and leaves the grieving speaker, in the grip of her death *and* in the grip of her photograph.

Usually, Creeley's poems use language beyond signification to seek something like consolation. Charles Altieri notes that a Creeley poem succeeds "less in what it says than in the sudden realization that the speaking has found linguistic means to bring that momentary peace."[55] "Mother's Photograph," on the other hand, grants itself, instead of any momentary closure, only an enclosure. The poem's power derives from the intersection, in this space, of a poetic will aligned with elegy and a genre revealed to be inhospitable to those poetic aims. Once the photographic meditation has made its dwelling simultaneously in an elegiac, anti-elegiac, self-elegizing, and no longer elegiac poem, it ends—the words "new house" are the final words of the poem—in a decidedly layered silence.

First, this silence is that of the photograph, which never speaks and which outlives the poem in its atemporal muteness despite all efforts of the speaker to "hand" it off. It is also the silence of a mother who cannot, for all the elegiac efforts to the contrary, be made to speak after her death; not only is her death irreversible, she is revived in the space of the poem only long enough to be replaced in death by her son and silenced by a speaker who fears that her answer will (again, as in "Mother's Voice") endanger him. It is also the silence of a speaker stunned at how the photographic poem has brought him to a new recognition of his own contingent life, continuing mortality, and approaching death.

Rachel Blau DuPlessis, among the relatively few commentators to take up Creeley's more recent work, notes its preoccupation with impending death.[56] But rather than calibrate the "late" of his oeuvre to Creeley's own advancing age, it is in response to his mother's death, which occurred when Creeley was not yet fifty, that a stage of his reading and writing we can properly call "photographic" begins. This stage explores the implications of a profound paradox, namely that by holding to the image of the mother Creeley simultaneously secures his own poetics and his own future death. In its own final vision, the speaker of "Mother's Photograph" would choose his own death in place of his mother's, even as he recognizes that such a substitution would deprive her of death's rest and leave her to her "sad condition." After his more formal elegies, which put the mother's remembered voice and words and memories inside the lyric, Creeley's turn to photographic technology produces, as Barthes might have predicted, catastrophic results. The photograph puts elegy to the test by refusing to permit that genre's characteristic manipulations of time. Instead, the photograph fixes the poem's speaker in its gaze. Within the space of the poem, the photograph turns a lens onto the speaker who aims to use it for his own purposes. In so doing, the photograph leaves behind a negative, an absolute death still to be developed, perhaps continually, from this moment forward, in the womb that Marder calls "the darkroom," that place where the speaker "must, in some sense, allow himself to reproduce the photograph in his own psyche."[57] The poem's brief duration is the time of the photograph's own flash, the moment in which a lyric camera shoots the speaker with this knowledge, silencing him and the backdrop of his poem all at once. It is through a mode of photographic and poetic reading that takes place under the watchful, single eye of a photographed and photographing mother that the mournful and self-elegizing strivings of Creeley's later poetry can begin to be—like the photograph itself—glimpsed, if not entirely grasped. Regarding Creeley's subsequent poems as afterimages of this attempt to hold the maternal image may suggest the means by which new poetic modes, ones that less violently and unhandsomely reconfigure the relationship of speech to its newly absent source, could be born.

Ted Berrigan's Reparations

"O my love, I will weep a less bitter truth,
   till other times, making a minor repair"[1]

In perhaps his most provocative statement on poetics, Ted Berrigan wrote, "some people prefer the interior monologue./I like to beat people up."[2] Compared to Stevens, Jarrell, and Creeley, Berrigan's poetry is harsh, brash, and loud. Where the previous three were hesitant as their poetry crossed the threshold of interpersonal engagement, Berrigan's use of collage method demanded the participation of others, both friends and enemies, in the making of poems. The uses to which Berrigan put collage changed significantly as his career developed, however; from aggression in his earliest work, *The Sonnets*, and open mockery of James Dickey in the long poem "A Boke," Berrigan's elegies for Frank O'Hara after the latter's death in 1966 show a poet looking not only for consolation, but for a way to make reparations. This conceptual vocabulary, drawn from Melanie Klein, suggests that reading Berrigan is similar to the work Berrigan himself undertook in the poems, that of integrating, in a single body, divergent impulses of aggression and reparation.

Ted Berrigan earned his place in the pantheon of American poetry by developing a distinctive method of poetic collage, and it's by means of collage that he indulged a capacity for violence and a tendency toward reparation. Like much of his poetics, Berrigan honed his collage procedure in conscious homage to a self-selected community of Modernist artists and contemporary writers. Visual artists like Marcel Duchamp and Tristan Tzara provided his first models, while William Burroughs and Brion Gysin's experiments with cut-up texts prepared the way.[3] Berrigan's first major book, *The Sonnets* (1964), contains fourteen-line poems constructed out of words and lines from Berrigan's own discarded poems as well as lines from poets Berrigan was reading at the time, a list that ranges from Arthur Rimbaud and Rainer Maria Rilke to his close friends Ron Padgett and Dick Gallup. *The Sonnets* rearranges and frequently repeats selected fragments to create what Libby Rifkin calls "reverb" throughout the sequence.[4] The fragment repertoire sustains a kind of collective ventriloquism, one in which the poet speaks with many voices at once. The method signaled admiration for the poets whose work Berrigan selected, but it also functioned as a mode of aggression. His refusal of meditative interiority—"some people prefer the interior monologue"—was, Berrigan thought, so explosive that it had "terrorist implications,"[5] a capacity to induce fear on a grand scale. In order to reinvent lyric interiority on his own terms, Berrigan took the liberty of invading—and symbolically destroying—the interior monologues of poetic strangers and friends.

This is to say that while Berrigan rejected the interior monologue, he did not disdain interiority per se. Critics have not often acknowledged this, and for good reason. Berrigan's poems read like a collective biography, and, as such, much of the commentary on Berrigan's poetry has been biographical, focused on his close affiliation with poets of the New York School's first and second generations, and on his role in unifying a lower Manhattan artistic scene during the 1960s and 1970s. While this work has been valuable for elucidating the ways midcentury poets challenged ideas about poetic self-sufficiency, one part of Berrigan's poetics that can be overlooked by focusing on poetic communities is the way in which it makes something internal and nonmonologic happen. By addressing poetic others using language that is quite literally interpersonal, Berrigan's poems effect personal affective transformations.

Another means of recovering Berrigan's peculiar interiority is by highlighting his relationship to Robert Creeley, whom he claimed to have been "plagiarizing … before I ever really got into John Ashbery."[6] If Berrigan learned his urban sensibility and sociability from his New York elders and contemporaries, he built a poetics of line and breath from Creeley, who was far from the New York School in his sensibility and sociability. While both poets place their work in a tradition that favors Pound over Stevens, both also demonstrate, along with Stevens, a profound investment in tracking the variations of poetic subjectivity as they happen from instant to instant, rather than in history's *longue durée*. The constant shifts that account for Berrigan's use of personal pronouns, for example, speak to a poet far more interested in the pole of individuality than is often recognized. And far more than a reveler, Berrigan like Creeley is a prominent midcentury mourner. Especially in his late work, lost others provide the occasion for poetic experiments that reflect on poetry's solitude. Where Creeley's elegies compare the elegiac efficacy of poetry and photography, Berrigan's question the viability and survival of other poets' words and names. The ambivalence apparent in Creeley's elegies for his mother is mirrored in Berrigan's elegies for Frank O'Hara. Berrigan mourns, but only after he has inflicted injury, putting poetry to use as, in Stevens's words, "a destructive force" against other poets. Only then does he work to repair old wounds and prove poetry's capacity to recuperate its own losses.

Berrigan's poems cultivate, then, an interiority constructed by bringing in what he called the "language which reels about everywhere else."[7] Read, selected, and rearranged, his fragments bear witness to a unique project of textual introjection,[8] a psychological activity akin to identification that consists in bringing into the ego "everything that is a source of pleasure" in the outside world.[9] By means of introjection, Berrigan can respond to the world, at times vehemently, using the words of that world. Berrigan was indeed a social poet, but beyond his active participation in the social world, the economy of introjection by which he found material for writing addresses the complex selfhood Berrigan fostered in close proximity to poetic rivals and friends. The psychoanalytic theorist best known for outlining this relationship between the inner world and the outer world is Melanie Klein, in whom literary theorists have developed an increased interest in the last three decades.[10] Klein's work outlines dynamics of mental life by which Berrigan's collage poetics takes shape. As with D.W. Winnicott, the flexibility and capaciousness of Kleinian concepts like the depressive position and reparation makes them useful for rereading, rather than simply containing, Berrigan's poems.

Melanie Klein: A poetics of the inner world

Although Klein maintained her allegiance to Freud throughout her life, her work makes a signature departure from her mentor's. Based on observations of the play of very small children, Klein argued that definitive aspects of adult mental life begin in the conflicts constitutive of infancy and early childhood, long before those of the Oedipal period. Debunking an idealized version of early childhood, she believed that the infantile experience of intolerable anxieties of annihilation and abandonment provides the template for later experiences of emotion. Her modification of Freud's theory of mind, one based in conflict, depicted mental life as "a continually shifting, kaleidoscopic stream of primitive, phantasmagoric images, fantasies, and terrors."[11] For her, the psyche "remains always unstable, fluid, constantly fending off psychotic anxieties."[12] A personality develops through the characteristic habits the mind builds in its attempts to manage this constitutive instability. More than Freud, for whom the overwhelming force of the drives underwrote a certain fungibility of "objects" in the outside world, Klein's work, without neglecting drive theory, insists on the foundational role played by relationships with other people.[13] She stipulated that such objects are not only real, external entities, but also fantasized, internal ones, where they represent a "mental process which generates a characteristic emotional state."[14] Long before any capacity for reality testing has developed, "the infant believes that his fantasies, both loving and hateful, have powerful actual impact on the objects of those fantasies."[15] Even more than interactions in the external world, it is the dynamics at work in the world of internal objects that determine and are determined by the affects, which take on an outsized role in Klein's work. To some extent, this adjusted focus, from impulses to affects, accounts for Klein's relevance to contemporary theory. As Eve Sedgwick, the literary theorist whose work first revived interest in Klein, noted, "Klein's psychoanalysis, by contrast to Freud's, is based in affect and offers a compelling account of the developments and transformations of affective life".[16] Klein can be especially valuable for thinking beyond Freud with respect to the affective transformations that characterize creativity, which can no longer be reduced to a sublimation of the sexual drive.

Klein's exchange of some of classical Freudian psychoanalysis' most rigid concepts for more capacious ones lends itself to a far less dogmatic and procrustean psychoanalytic literary. As opposed to discrete developmental stages pegged to biological age in classical Freudian psychoanalysis (if not so much in Freud's own work), Klein posited that emotional life took shape through positions, templates, or "organizations of experience" that were fluid and often transient, "lost and regained" throughout one's life.[17] Klein's understanding of her work's relationship to the creative process stems from her concepts of two positions that are first achieved in the child's first years, but which color experience throughout adult life. The name paranoid-schizoid position indicates the anxiety of invasion and annihilation by which it is motivated (paranoid) and the defense mechanism of splitting by which it aims to assuage these fears (schizoid). In order to contain and diminish the anxieties of being annihilated, and to preserve what remains of love, a whole object is split into two separate parts, one good and one bad. For the infant in the paranoid-schizoid position, the mother cannot be perceived as a whole, only as her immediately perceivable parts; she is alternately, in Klein's admittedly strange construction, the good, nurturing, and available breast and the bad, destructive, and abandoning one. While one part object can be loved, the other can be violently attacked. This organization of experience has the advantage of salvaging a strong and good part object from the violent attacks directed elsewhere, but it comes at the cost of feeling that the bad object's attacks are unmitigated.

In a contrast that may not be experienced as clearly as it is formulated, the depressive position describes an organization of experience in which the child begins to integrate both the good and bad aspects of the parent into a single whole image to be regarded ambivalently. This position is difficult to achieve because the survival of the good and loving part object seems precarious, susceptible to complete destruction by what has been understood as the bad part object. However, the depressive position marks a moment when love and hate begin to coexist as the child begins to build a relationship with a whole person. While aggression and caring exist during this phase, the characteristic affect of the depressive position is guilt. The child's recognition that it hates and harms the same object that it loves allows for this guilt to emerge out of vengeful anger. In response to guilt, Klein recognized in the child a desire for reparation, an attempt to make good the injuries inflicted during moments of hate and aggression. Klein developed her views on reparation after observing children's play. Directly following violent attacks of tearing, beating, and throwing, children treated toys and play objects with special care and compassion. In mental life, the reparations of the depressive position are a direct response to "distress at [one's] own aggressiveness."[18] They constitute attempts to "repair the effects" of "destructive phantasies" and to "restore … wholeness to the loved object" as a way of "negating the evil that has been done it."[19] Reparation is the way the child begins to express a new kind of love, one that is not "merely a sign of dependence upon a friendly and helpful person."[20]

The coordinates of the depressive position are significant, Klein theorized, because they describe not only an aspect of child development, but also one route by which creative activity in later life takes shape. In the 1929 essay "Infantile Anxiety Situations Reflected in a Work of Art and in the Creative Impulse," Klein argued that the affective positions characteristic of early development provide a template for understanding creative production in adult life. She describes creative economies that take structure from the symbolic reparations that follow murderously violent symbolic attacks. For a painter whose portraits first depicted the brutal effects of aging and then, after a long gap, idealized the mother's youth, "the desire to make reparation, to make good the injury psychologically done to the mother and also to restore her was at the bottom of the compelling urge to paint."[21] For a child depicted in a Ravel opera, rage-inspired mistreatment of toys, plants, and animals gives way, after a moment of guilt, to caring, tender handling of the immediate environment. In addition to glossing moments in works of art when a clear desire to "make good" becomes apparent, Klein insists that reparation happens at moments when love and hate interact. In contrast to the Freudian concept of sublimation, reparation is "a result of the confluence of the opposing instinctual drives rather than merely a displacement of an impulse on to some socially acceptable representative."[22] It may be especially useful for describing creative economies that highlight a tentative, precarious, and unstable transition from aggression to compassion. Because Berrigan's collage poetics consists of acts of symbolic cutting followed by incorporation and rearrangement, and because Berrigan described his method as violent and yet used it to make reparation for that violence, I consider the depressive position and reparation as especially appropriate concepts for reading his work.

Beginning in the mid-1990s, Eve Sedgwick brought renewed attention to Melanie Klein's work by characterizing the paradigmatic mode of contemporary critical theory as paranoid. She would propose a reparative alternative, a practice of reading and writing based less in using special insights into "epistemologies of enmity"[23] to achieve "conceptual economy or elegance"[24] than in an openness to surprise, something that has not been anticipated and outlined in advance. Building on Klein's concept of the reparative, then, Sedgwick has called for critics to practice "reparative reading," a form of attention interested in "the many ways selves and communities succeed in extracting sustenance from the objects of a culture—even of a culture whose avowed desire has been not to sustain them."[25] It's possible, then, to consider Berrigan's method reparative in two senses. Cutting fragments may be read not only as an act of damaging culture through aggression but as the work of "extract[ing] sustenance" from it where it would otherwise be impossible to access. Like Randall Jarrell, Ted Berrigan maintained a relationship with poetry that brought self-destruction along with it. Berrigan's acts of cutting are thus dually constituted, as acts of self-harm and as a means of healing. As a result, Berrigan made reparations for this particularly violent form of reparation.

Kleinian reparation, which contextualizes the anger, guilt, and ambivalence at work in creative activity by reference to an inner world of introjects, also provides a model for readings of poetic collage; by the same token, recent work in queer theory and feminism that uses Klein's work to promote "reparative reading" (a practice that may have its roots in Modernist bricolage) can be useful for reevaluating the aesthetic practices of midcentury poets.[26] In what follows, I suggest that Berrigan's work adds to Klein's own examples of creative economies that take their shape from the depressive position. Berrigan's poems careen back and forth between aggression and reparation, and as such their dominant affect can be a guilty, restless ambivalence. This chapter considers the ambivalence of Berrigan's collective interiority in poems he wrote in relationship to the work of a poet he did not like, James Dickey, and the work of a poet he revered, Frank O'Hara. First, however, it turns to Berrigan's signature achievement in poetic collage, *The Sonnets*.

The Sonnets

Berrigan referred to the process by which he made *The Sonnets* as "the method," but his descriptions are inconsistent. Joe Brainard reports being with Berrigan at the moment he invented the method, but provides no further details. Ron Padgett mentions several sources of Berrigan's fragments—lines drawn from Berrigan's own old poems; from those of his friends and acquaintances Padgett, Dick Gallup, Frank O'Hara, and John Ashbery; and from poets he was reading at the time such as Rimbaud, Rilke, and Stevens—and locates the site of the first sonnets' composition as "a rented room on 113th Street between Broadway and Amsterdam."[27] In later interviews, Berrigan insisted on the importance of the fact that he wrote all but the final poems of the sequence in the three months before the birth of his first son, David. Still, the techniques that gave birth to *The Sonnets*, as well as the source of the energy that fueled their production, remain largely unknown.

Berrigan's comments on his collage method point to the dual psychological poles of the practice. At times, Berrigan viewed the process of drawing material from other poets as one of creating new wholes rather than robbing or desecrating unfit ones. Alice Notley summarized Berrigan's view as follows: "to cut something up into pieces and make something else from them is not to break down the first thing ... The first entity is whole, the second is too."[28] But elsewhere, Berrigan maligned his friends' words and depicted his collage method as a sort of triumph over them. If the practice of taking words usually connotes appreciation, Berrigan claimed that his practice alone could confer value on lines that hadn't originally succeeded. On taking a line from Dick Gallup, Berrigan reported, "In Dick's poem it wasn't so good anyway. I mean, it had what's good about Dick's work in it ... And it's a poem he sort of threw out later. I mean, in fact it's a sort of ghastly poem that he threw out. But I took it and rearranged a few lines, moved the things around, changed a couple of things."[29] Berrigan's targeting of "ghastly" poems shows that collage often depends on an attack of the original object, but it also announces poetic work's redemptive capacity. Poetry can turn its bad objects into good ones by a process aimed at healing, rather than destroying. In some way, cut-up method finds Berrigan at his most nurturing; his work of rearranging creates a place for lines and thoughts that would otherwise be obliterated. All poetic making takes place at the threshold of destruction: "Put away your books! Who shall speak of us/when we are gone?"[30] Consistent with the tradition rather than opposed to it, Berrigan's collages serve the aim of poetry as Horace articulates it. They prevent the loss of names, and of words, that would otherwise be lost in the "long night of oblivion/because they lacked a sacred bard."[31]

Berrigan was not shy about associating his poetry with violence, and the impulse is especially strong in *The Sonnets*, in which he wrote, "Be watching for me when blood/flows down the streets."[32] The poems move at breakneck speed through personal recollection and esoteric reference, picking up momentum more from the discordance of juxtaposed fragments and their repetition than from any narrative coherence. In the process, they construct an image of poetic work akin to that of Ruskin. Poems "burn phosphorescent," their "innocence gleaned/annealed," as if "bouncing a red rubber ball in the veins."[33] But this incandescence and dynamism is tinged with violence. "Life's/my dream which is gunfire in my poem," he writes in Sonnet L, which marshals Calderón de la Barca for street warfare and closes with Berrigan's challenge to his quietist contemporaries: "Some people prefer 'the interior monologue'/I like to beat people up."[34] The sonnets will involve people and will do so whether they like it or not. Other poets fare poorly in the sequence: William Carlos Williams is "the hungry dead doctor" (35), and "Keats was a baiter of bears" (37). Echoing Wallace Stevens's claim that "poetry is a destructive force," at times Berrigan weaponizes the sonnet, transforming it momentarily from the poetic form most closely associated with the immortality of the addressee into a vehicle of interpersonal violence.

As *The Sonnets* proceeds however, the inseparability of Berrigan's aggressive and reparative impulses becomes clear. Sonnet LXXX exemplifies the commingling of brash resolve and tenderness that typifies many of the later sonnets. It opens as a group elegy—"Bearden is dead Gallup is dead Margie is dead"—and in its closing lines debuts a phrase that will repeat in subsequent poems after mentioning the names of the dead: "whose grief I would most assuage."[35] At the same time, the poem contains its share of anti-elegiac violence. The isolated phrases "I rage in a blue shirt" and "'He Shot Me' was once my favorite poem" hint that Berrigan's mourning is multivalent and that repeated, collaged fragments like these provide a stage from which ambivalence and anger can echo.[36] The words of others are used here to accomplish tonal shifts that prevent any single poem from delivering the kind of unmixed emotion associated with the sentimentality of the interior monologue. And as if to say that *The Sonnets* have exhausted the need to cut and also expunged Berrigan's record of having done so, Sonnet LXXXIV proclaims, "I never beat people up."[37] Despite the wounds they have inflicted, the sonnets claim healing powers. In so doing, they provide a template for later poetic experiments in which mockery joins identification and mournful consolation joins ambivalence to forge a poetry of conflicted collective interiority.

"A Boke"

No poem demonstrates the fundamental ambivalence at work in reparative affect more effectively than Berrigan's 1965 long poem, "A Boke," which rearranges lines from James Dickey's *New York Times* essay "Barnstorming for Poetry." Dickey's essay chronicles the poet's reading tour, and by quoting Dickey's words with telling modifications and insertions, "A Boke" mocks Dickey's travelogue relentlessly. It showcases Berrigan's wit in its most pleasurable guise, as he revels in just how easy it is to bring a writer low by raising his purple prose on high. Unlike most of the borrowing in *The Sonnets*, which signaled admiration for its sources, Berrigan's use of Dickey's lines is vicious, accusing the author of egregious grandstanding in the name of poetic diplomacy. Although the marked differences between Dickey and Berrigan become clear in the course of the poem, Berrigan's coterie audience would have been even more familiar with his distaste for award-winning academic poets with a flair for bombast. At the same time, and much like *The Sonnets*, "A Boke" leaves room for a surprising reparative gesture.

At face value, "A Boke" allows Berrigan several hundred lines of verse to beat someone up: "He learns to/time his words and lines to the/hammer-strokes, and before long/he is giving something."[38] With a closer look, the poem's relationship to its object appears more complicated. Berrigan had claimed that his social life was wide ranging among the competing schools of contemporary poetry: "I like to know all the groups, because that way is the most fun, and the most interesting."[39] He spoke fondly of poets like Conrad Aiken and Richard Wilbur whose affiliations and styles diverged from his own. "A Boke" goes beyond brutal mockery by using "Barnstorming for Poetry" as the skeleton of an *ars poetica* built upon meticulous devotion to the contours of Dickey's statements, if not complete fidelity to their letter or spirit. Berrigan's rearrangement in "A Boke" suggests that he found, in his reading of Dickey, a remarkable (if crude) resource for articulating a positive poetics of selfhood and community. While beating Dickey up, Berrigan pieces together a platform.

Berrigan's collage reading represents a form of antisocial sociability. Winnicott argued that "the antisocial act is a sign of hope that the individual will rediscover the good experience" that has been lost.[40] Berrigan was known not only for stealing lines, but for stealing and reselling books from stores all over New York City. But stealing and other "delinquent" acts may, from an object relations perspective, demonstrate a belief that resources for creativity can still be found in a world that has ceased to nurture them as it once did. In this light, Berrigan's collage reading—along with the other activities he used to sustain his reading—represents a form of antisocial sociability. In contrast to silence, or despair, Berrigan finds words wherever they are available, even or especially at moments when he cites authors and exclaims, "I hate books."[41]

Perhaps the best way to characterize Berrigan's role in this strange long poem, Berrigan's first, is to say that in writing it he is, in Christopher Bollas's formulation, being a character, experiencing himself by means of an object whose structure permits a particular "form of subjective transformation".[42] Berrigan's reading of "Barnstorming for Poetry" equally involves taking away from and investing in the external world. "A Boke" is unusual among Berrigan's poems not only because he draws from an unlikely source, but also because of how fully he relies on it. Unlike many of the sonnets, in which lines from other writers merely punctuate Berrigan's own words, Dickey's original text accounts for the vast majority of "A Boke." Rather than sustain a disjunctive syntax of the kind that propelled his earlier work, Berrigan is here willing to copy sentences almost wholesale. In other cases, Berrigan incorporates other writers' work; here he inhabits and is inhabited by it. Rather than a static relationship between objects, Bollas notes that "being a character" involves a constantly shifting dynamic in which one "bring[s] along with one's articulating idiom those inner presences— or spirits—that we all contain."[43] Berrigan claimed in "Red Shift" that he was "only pronouns." Although it is surprising for Berrigan to take James Dickey as an "inner presence," it is nevertheless essential to Berrigan's poetics to constantly inhabit others, both investing them with emotions and experiences that would otherwise remain unthought and becoming "substantially metamorphosed" by the objects themselves.[44] "A Boke" is the poetic result of a psychic process that stumbles upon good enough containers for otherwise inarticulable aspects of experience. In response, they become a suitable, permeable container of what has sustained them. As Berrigan asserts elsewhere, "'The Poems' are not a cage."[45]

On its own terms, Dickey's essay is peculiar. "Barnstorming for Poetry" chronicles a reading tour Dickey embarked upon before the publication of his third book of poems, *Helmet* (1964). The distinctive voice derives from its third-person narration, which is by turns grandiose and colloquial. As a featured reader drawing sizable crowds, the poet is exalted; boarding in hotels and dorm rooms, and responsible for his own travel, he has time to wax eloquent on the nature of the poet's task. In passage after passage, Dickey crescendos from restrained description to epiphany:

> At the college he is given a room in the cavernous building and told that he has an hour or two before dinner. He lies down on the bed, then gets up and paces back and forth. There is a skull on the table, and suddenly, at the sight of this *momento mori*, the great themes of poetry hit him squarely: the possibility of love and the inevitability of death. He has tried for years to formulate his relationship to these things and to say something about them. He takes out his two volumes of poetry and his manuscript of a third book, and, ever cognizant of his bodiless, staring audience and of the skull beneath his own skin, rearranges his evening's program around the themes of love and death.[46]

In addition to serving as a sort of travel journalism, with comments on Midwest landscapes and small college life, "Barnstorming" questions poetic selfhood and personality. Since "the self he has become on this trip bears but little relation to the self he left at home in the mind, say, of his wife," the poet can hardly coincide with, or be limited to, his work. As such, and although they are the reason for the trip, "Barnstorming" makes no mention of the content of Dickey's poems, favoring instead a close recounting of his raucous behavior and favorable reception at the various colleges and universities where he has read. After condescending slightly to the students and handlers he meets, in the essay's closing lines Dickey announces that he has found a part of himself in the characters he has encountered along the way. He has discovered, too, a new if fleeting "intensity" in the pace and expectations of the tour. "For better or for worse, he has been moving and speaking among his kind."[47] Dickey claims that the trip has been worthwhile not merely for himself, but for the cause of poetry in general.[48]

Berrigan regards "Barnstorming for Poetry" as an appalling piece of writing. In his hands, the narrator comes across as an absurd figure, by turns self-congratulatory and numbly mystical. In the words Berrigan adds or rearranges, his poetry is "incoherent babbling," his proper place "Literary Vaudeville," and his character utterly "psychotic." He is less convincing as a writer than as a buffoon, a Byronesque Don Juan unaware that his high opinion of himself has no basis in reality. Warping Dickey's phrases and collaging them allows Berrigan to cut into Dickey's self-regard. Dickey was well known for drinking to excess after his readings; Berrigan suggests that the poetry itself is painfully intoxicating: "At the outset of the/trip he had thought that/the songs themselves would be enough/ so had a terrible hangover the next day."[49] All four lines are Dickey's own, but Berrigan imported the fourth and inserted it as if it were continuous.

As the poem proceeds, however, it becomes less clear that Berrigan is mocking Dickey and not using Dickey's words to mock himself. Berrigan's entire poetics consists of intimations of transformation akin to Dickey's revelations in "Barnstorming." Once again, Berrigan had proclaimed, "I'm only pronouns, & I am all of them."[50] Dickey is prone to naïve, affected rhetoric concerning the art, but so is Berrigan, as he seems to recognize. Nothing in Dickey's essay is as sentimental as in Berrigan's, "I am in love with poetry. Every way I turn/this, my weakness, smites me."[51] The poem takes on a dazed tone as Berrigan recognizes that he, like Dickey, is threatened by the "particular favors" of his vocation:

> There are no buses or trains until after time confers her
> particular favors on a stranger she
> will never see again, one who last night
> grew more emotional, more harried, more impulsive.[52]

Berrigan was fond of adjectival triads when he came to self-description. He expected himself to be "feminine marvelous and tough" and proclaimed "at heart we are infinite, we are/ethereal, we are weird".[53] Berrigan had good reason to mock Dickey's travelogue, since he was guilty of composing his own. "The Chicago Report," written three years later, is a blustery reading tour travelogue that sounds remarkably like "Barnstorming." Once again, bus travel provides the occasion for bravado and terror:

> The bus stops in Hicksville, the 300th stop, for one minute, and I tell Henry to get the candy bars. He returns chagrined. The bus driver said nobody gets off. I say, wait here. I go to the front of the bus, the door is shut. I press a few forbidden buttons, the door opens. I saunter off like Broderick Crawford, and the driver outside avoids my eyes. I buy fifty candy bars. I get back on.[54]

In Dickey's piece, the poet fears leaving behind his audience. For Berrigan, though, it's the departure from his close friends, "the Irish good-bye scene," that leaves him "more emotional, more harried, more impulsive": "Then, into the bus station. Inside, it's horrible. I shudder, and begin to feel a little sick, a little lost, a little scared, a little crazy."[55] For both poets, the motion and commotion of touring is akin to madness. By way of differentiation, it might be said that Dickey sought to avoid madness by ending his tour, while Berrigan never stopped going around cities in search of it.

"A Boke" exemplifies the reparative underpinnings of Berrigan's method. The poem inhabits Dickey's words for the purpose of mocking them and of redeeming them. They are bombastic already; for Berrigan, they have the potential to represent a state of poetry-induced madness. "A Boke" links two poets whose practice of "barnstorming" in the service of poetry exposed them to its dangers. But for Berrigan, the danger is not of losing himself, but of taking on the other, and it is a danger that must be accepted as part of the poet's essential task. "A Boke" highlights the tensions between authenticity and artifice that constitute every attempt to speak about poetic vocation. Is it really possible, he asks, to speak anew about poetry without leaving a record of one's reading? Doesn't poetic vocation demand an admission that all words were once, and perhaps very recently, someone else's?

"A Boke" does, in some sense, honor Dickey's words by using them in the service of Berrigan's own *ars poetica*. By casting one of his longest discussions of poetics as a mock-heroic collage, Berrigan demands an interpersonal poetics in which love and hate do not so much oppose each other as interact continuously. Berrigan argues that the poet sustains himself not only by maintaining his good objects but by redeeming his bad ones, even if the process leads to madness. It would, in any case, be a madness the poet shares with the inner presences he's brought along. In Berrigan's reading, "Barnstorming" is, or can be, an essay about leaving behind the interior monologue in favor of a vision of interiority that is, no matter how compromised, forged collectively. Sonnet LXXII closes on a phrase that condenses the apostrophic yearning of his entire oeuvre: "and O, I am not alone."[56]

Such collectivity is constitutive of collage procedure according to Aaron Kunin, a poet and theorist I will consider in Chapter 6. For him, collage is not about theft or appropriation, but about "letting go, becoming another person, in the same way that we become other people when we read books."[57] Berrigan gestures at a similar conception of collage in the final lines of "A Boke." Reflecting back on the process of writing a poem, Berrigan writes of his persona, "He has definitely been/another person."[58] Rather than focus on the act of rearranging lines from others, Berrigan here speaks to the moments just before the act of taking, moments in which the poet inhabits the work of an other, in a sense becoming "another person," in order to find the materials of collage. It's the process of becoming another writer in the time of reading to which the rearranged poem points most urgently; cutting has only been the means for representing an end that places the poet's vocation squarely within the process of transformation. This kind of writing is reparative because it selects and combines disparate vocabularies precisely in order to commemorate the ambivalent intimacies that reading makes possible.[59] As such, the collage method permitted Berrigan not only to become other people, but to communicate to others in a new way, one that beats up the interior monologue *and* finds it worthy of repair and reuse.

Frank O'Hara

On a personal level, Ted Berrigan was not close to Frank O'Hara. Berrigan had read O'Hara's poems while still in Tulsa, and shortly after his arrival in New York began to idolize him. Brad Gooch, O'Hara's biographer, reports that Berrigan "used to stand on Avenue A staring up patiently at O'Hara's apartment before they even met."[60] Although they met in the spring of 1962, they hardly formed the kind of friendship—one characterized by nonstop conversation, collaboration, and drug use—that Berrigan sustained with Ron Padgett, Joe Brainard, and Dick Gallup. As Bill Berkson put it, Berrigan "never really became pals with Frank."[61] Poetically, however, Berrigan regarded O'Hara as a mentor and model. The elder poet's language would liberate him from the self-diagnosed sentimentality of *A Lily for My Love*, Berrigan's first, self-published collection, and would usher him into language that circulated—around a group of friends, around New York City, and, for Berrigan, around fixed or newly mobilized fragments of text.

Berrigan's friends and commentators have devoted significant energy to fending off accusations that his work is merely derivative of Frank O'Hara's. Certainly, critics devoted to establishing O'Hara's legacy have often dismissed Berrigan's work in this way.[62] But both sides miss some of the point: Berrigan's work is unique precisely because it risks being derivative, becomes derivative, and then responds creatively to this condition.[63] Once, after a scolding from Kenneth Koch, Berrigan admitted that he had reached a point in his writing when he felt that O'Hara was "a very bad influence … like I was getting too close."[64] But as his elegies for O'Hara will reveal, Berrigan's fear of getting too close to O'Hara produced some of his most interesting work, precisely because, while O'Hara did not use collage method, Berrigan's encounters with him almost always do. (Just after writing his most emphatic version of his mantra, "I LIKE TO BEAT PEOPLE UP!!!" in Sonnet LXXIII, he quotes O'Hara's tranquil line, "Grace to be born and live."[65])

As such, rather than the influence of Frank O'Hara's poetry, it's the uses to which Berrigan put O'Hara's own words and proper name that account for some of the most original aspects of his poetics. With O'Hara as with Dickey, Berrigan doesn't so much imitate as introject; while he had drawn on O'Hara's words and name in *The Sonnets*, O'Hara's early and sudden death in 1966 gave Berrigan an even more urgent reason to make O'Hara one of his inner presences. Berrigan dedicated *Many Happy Returns*, his first book after O'Hara's death, to Frank O'Hara and Anne Kepler. In 1974, he would assume an editorial role, collecting eleven of O'Hara's later poems for publication in a small pamphlet under the Berrigan-esque title, *The End of the Far West*.[66] It's my contention that much of Berrigan's work after 1966 functions as an extended elegy for Berrigan's dead, among whom O'Hara figures most prominently. Since "for Klein, the work of the depressive position is the work of mourning," Berrigan's own mourning permits a closer look at the threshold of aggression, guilt, ambivalence, and love upon which much of his poetics rests.[67]

Elegy is, nevertheless, a strange term to use in connection with Ted Berrigan, and doing so reveals several sites of tension in his poetics. First, the poles of address—subject and object—that operate in Berrigan's mourning are deliberately obscured by a poet who proclaimed, "I'm only pronouns, & I am all of them." For all of the times Berrigan names friends and enemies specifically, he also relies on a nonspecific, apostrophic "you," and frequently invokes "people," whether to beat them up or hail them as heroes. Instead of specifying a single lost or mourned object, these addresses posit a broader category of external objects whose potential loss would be catastrophic. (This technique calls to mind John Ashbery's line, "I prefer you in the plural.") In poems and personal letters, Berrigan also alternated between first-person singular and plural pronouns.[68] Their interchangeability announces that singular poetic identity inheres only in the incorporated plurality of extrinsic texts, the poet plus the sources of his words. This constellation poses a problem for the affects associated with elegy. In a poetics that constantly exchanges its "selves" for others, who mourns whom? What capacities for feeling does a pluralized self demonstrate in its addresses to the plural dead? How might fragments, detached from their original contexts, convey feelings associated with the detachments of loss?

At the same time, Berrigan recognized that mourning played a major role in his poetics, and his understanding of the process is uniquely Freudian. In normal mourning, "Reality-testing has shown that the loved object no longer exists, and it proceeds to demand that all libido shall be withdrawn from its attachments to that object."[69] A passage from "Things to Do in Providence" echoes the psychoanalytic claim that libido must be "withdrawn from its attachment"[70] to a loved object: "The heart stops briefly when someone dies,/a quick pain as you hear the news, & someone passes/from your outside life to inside."[71] Berrigan used the same phrase to describe the context for one of his most famous poems, the group elegy "People who died":

> The person had simply passed from my outside life to my inside life. And then one day sitting in my room I realized that this had happened to me many times in my life, but that when I was young I'd kept myself in a sort of trance so that I wouldn't have any feelings I wouldn't be able to handle, so I hadn't allowed myself to feel this sort of thing too strongly. So I decided to go back and get the times that it had happened, and I had hoped that it would come out to be around fourteen lines.[72]

The lines point to Berrigan's recognition that no matter when death has occurred, the time of mourning is always now. Berrigan's elegies for O'Hara are preoccupied with precisely this problem. They inspect the process of incorporation as it happens to see when and whether it is complete, and concern themselves with knowing whether the newly incorporated object is too close or too far away. One is just longer and one is just shorter than fourteen lines.

Before proceeding, a note on Melanie Klein's contributions to the psychoanalytic understanding of mourning is necessary. The incorporation at work in mourning plays a specific and significant role in Melanie Klein's work. Freud and Karl Abraham recognized that the psychological processes at work in mourning and melancholia related back to those of the oral stage of development, when the child's identifications with external objects are made by a process of devouring and incorporating their attributes. Klein, following this line of thought, argued that the loss of external objects has a corresponding effect on their internal counterparts. That is, in actuality, "the loss of the object is an internal event."[73] In her pivotal essay on the subject, "Mourning and Its Relation to Manic-Depressive States," Klein wrote that "the poignancy of the actual loss of a loved person is, in my view, greatly increased by the mourner's unconscious phantasies of having lost his *internal* 'good' objects as well."[74] Berrigan's elegies for Frank O'Hara take place at the intersection of two moments of mournful ambivalence: the first caused by a poetics on the brink of the depressive position, and the second caused by the loss of an external object. Elegy allows Berrigan to continue the work of showing concern toward wounded objects, although now the wounds have become fatal. In my reading, Berrigan took O'Hara's death as a threat with several faces. It jeopardized the survival of O'Hara's name and the survival of the fragments that Berrigan held within himself for poetic use. It represented a loss that, unlike many others, Berrigan's poetry could not contain. And the elegies bear witness not only to the intensity of Berrigan's grief, but to the dawning recognition that his acts of collage contributed, if only symbolically, to O'Hara's death. In response, Berrigan's poems must heal the wounds inflicted through collage and "derive pleasure" from any contact he can still sustain with O'Hara by poetic means. What is most striking about the poems is that they make elegiac use of the collage method for which they atone and that the person who must struggle to survive this method is Berrigan himself.

The poem "Frank O'Hara," published in Berrigan's 1975 book, *Red Wagon*, finds Berrigan responding to O'Hara's death and to the fact that he is still in the process of moving from "your outside life to the inside." The poem concerns the process of setting up a lasting internal image of O'Hara that could effectively replace the living poet. As such, it is especially interested in the distance that separates Berrigan and O'Hara. After his death, what intimacy with him is still possible, or even desirable? What does Berrigan still need from O'Hara, and, conversely, what does O'Hara need from Berrigan?

Frank O'Hara
Winter in the country, Southampton, pale horse
as the soot rises, then settles, over the pictures
The birds that were singing this morning have shut up
I thought I saw a couple, kissing, but Larry said no
It's a strange bird. He should know. & I think now
"Grandmother divided by monkey equals outer space." Ron
put me in that picture. In another picture, a good-
looking poet is thinking it over; nevertheless, he will
never speak of that it. But, his face is open, his eyes
are clear, and, leaning lightly on an elbow, fist below
his ear, he will never be less than perfectly frank,
listening, completely interested in whatever there may
be to hear. Attentive to me alone here. Between friends,
nothing would seem stranger to me than true intimacy.
What seems genuine, truly real, is thinking of you, how
that makes me feel. You are dead. And you'll never
write again about the country, that's true.

But the people in the sky really love
to have dinner & to take a walk with you.[75]

The first three lines of this modified ekphrastic poem outline a grim landscape. The summer of O'Hara's death has turned to winter; his city has been replaced by the country, and a deathly "pale horse" emerges, as so much does in Berrigan's poem, without any obvious link to the surrounding scene. In the conventional elegy, birds would sing mournfully; Berrigan puns on the fact that they were, recently, "singing this morning," but now they are completely silent. "Frank O'Hara" signals that it picks up the work of mourning where most elegies leave off.

Within this silent, deathly space, "Frank O'Hara" uses its preoccupations with distance and thought to contain O'Hara's death. Line four features a figure that will repeat later in the poem, that of an apparent double that turns out instead to be something single and "strange." Having already drawn attention to the process in "Things to Do in Providence," Berrigan now focuses more closely on the process of internalizing a dead other, of watching what was once two become only one. He does so impassively, chatting with Larry all the while. Variations on "thought" or "thinking" appear four times in the poem, drawing the poem's landscape inward from Southampton to a mind that is nevertheless expansive: it can produce "outer space" by simple division. In this expansive inner space, a "picture" of O'Hara can be maintained and contained, kept "attentive to me alone here," but also kept at bay. Berrigan's use of the line "between friends, nothing would seem stranger to me than true intimacy" is calculated, since it is a fragment Berrigan used in *The Sonnets* and later poems such as "Á la Recherche du Temps Perdu." In order to shield himself from contact with the dead, Berrigan draws on the defensive gesture he has relied on throughout his career. At the moment it claims friendship with O'Hara, the poem uses a fragment, calling on the force of multiple poems to prevent anything like "true intimacy."

The poem's closing lines continue the barrage. Although Freud wrote of the inherent difficulty in mourning, that one never willingly abandons a libidinal position, "Frank O'Hara" seems to welcome the process. A nonintimate encounter with the dead O'Hara, one that involves "thinking" rather than speaking or touching, is "genuine, truly real." And at the moment it experiences this vitality of thought most fully, and as it speaks eloquently of true feeling, it reasserts the self-evident truth: "You are dead. And you'll never/write again." The last two lines of "Frank O'Hara" are also collaged fragments, but this time from Berrigan's translation of Jean Cocteau's demeaning elegy for Guillaume

Apollinaire. As if to claim that his own method bested that of the man who invented the term "collage," Berrigan delighted in claiming, in *The Sonnets*, "Guillaume Apollinaire is dead."[76] By its conclusion, "Frank O'Hara" is hardly an elegy; it's a celebration.

The 1982 poem "Give Them Back, Who Never Were," which was published posthumously in *A Certain Slant of Sunlight*, finds Berrigan in altogether different territory. The poem's title reworks William Penn's poem, "We seem to give them back to thee, o God who gavest them to us"; for Berrigan, however, death isn't a willing return of others to God, but rather the occasion to demand God to return them to us, even at the moment that death makes any claims to their prior existence untenable. Unlike the traditional elegy, which plays with the dialectical alternation between life and death, these dead "never were." From its opening confrontation through a breathless list, "Give Them Back" is quintessentially Berrigan, but the poem recognizes its mode as the articulation of an impotent wish: how can those who never were be given back? How can they even, in accordance with Berrigan's paradigm of mourning, pass from one's outside life to inside?

> Give Them Back, Who Never Were
> I am lonesome after mine own kind—the
> hussy Irish barmaid; the Yankee drunk who was once
> a horsecart Dr.'s son, & who still is, for that matter;
> The shining Catholic schoolboy face, in serious glasses,
> with proper trim of hair, bent over a text by Peire Vidal,
> & already you can see a rakish quality of intellect there;
> Geraldine Weicker, who played Nurse in MY HEART'S IN
> THE HIGHLANDS, on pills, & who eventually married whom? The
> fat kid from Oregon, who grew up to be our only real poet;
> & the jaunty Jamaica, Queens, stick-figure, ex US Navy, former
> French Negro poet, to whom Frank O'Hara once wrote an Ode,
> or meant to, before everything died, Fire Island, New
> York, Summer, 1966.[77]

"Give Them Back" does not identify itself immediately as an elegy. The poem proceeds by describing living poets and friends from Berrigan's life. The descriptions are deliberately truncated, the attributes barely sufficient for identification. The reader's longing to name these blurred characters both mimics the speaker's "longing" and ushers in the more properly elegiac part of the poem. In the last three lines of the poem, Berrigan suggests that it has been impossible to fully individuate these persons because of Frank O'Hara's death, a death that took "everything" along with it.

The possibility of the poem's characters ever having existed, along with Berrigan's capacity for writing about them, is overwhelmed, retroactively, by O'Hara's death. If Berrigan had wanted to write an ode for them, just as O'Hara "meant to" write an ode for Lorenzo Thomas, his ability to do so has been compromised by a death that cannot be contained. O'Hara's death is murderous. Berrigan's achievement, in the space of this poem, is to group together people whom he cannot address at length, and to write a short ode to the living before the poem shades into elegy. At the precise moment that "Give Them Back" uses the word "ode," asserting its genre, O'Hara's inescapable death overwhelms it and brings the poem to a close. Alice Notley calls the poem "a beautiful instance of the identity merge" in which "every poet or person is the same one."[78] A miniature Berriganian *ars poetica*, "Give Them Back" traces its disregard for boundaries (a key aspect of Berrigan's method) to O'Hara's death, despite the fact that his poetic vocation and method clearly *precede* it. "Give Them Back" suggests that much of Berrigan's writing takes place in the shadow of elegy, in the recognition that writing to and about people, often using their own words, can always be overwhelmed by death, by the possibility that they will never write again and that they will never have existed at all.

Berrigan's inversion of elegy eventually sounds an even more elegiac note. Rather than claim that O'Hara's death changed everything that came after it, the poem, which only announces that death in its final lines, suggests that the death evacuates history. If O'Hara can no longer write poems, like the planned ode for a French Negro poet, the figures he would have apostrophized do not merely lack poetic significance: their names no longer exist. Such figures as "the fat kid from Oregon, who grew up to be our only real poet" are indeed lost in Horace's long night. Although the poem is a powerful elegy for O'Hara, it also speaks to Berrigan's understanding of poetry as a medium. Here, he can recover only part of the purpose of O'Hara's poetics—can only represent a fragment of it. Poetry is always engaged in the effort of shoring fragments against a ruin that has already happened.

In a final turn of the screw, Berrigan makes reparations for the violence of his method by joining, rather than simply elegizing, his dead. Perhaps the "everything" that died in 1966 includes Berrigan, who can hardly survive O'Hara's loss. As such, "Give Them Back" becomes a prime example of yet another form of merger, that of elegy into self-elegy. It's the recognition that Berrigan died along with O'Hara that suggests he is lonesome for the (then) still-living figures, from John Ashbery to Philip Whalen to Lorenzo Thomas, whom he remembers in the space of the poem. The force of the elegy comes in its assertion that O'Hara cannot be properly mourned. He cannot be incorporated, cannot "pass/from your outside life to your inside,"[79] because his death leaves no survivors. It is as if to say that since his death, Berrigan has written from beyond the grave. To cut from O'Hara's writing after O'Hara's death is to write in the words of the dead, something Berrigan recognizes as profoundly different from cutting fragments from the living. It's no longer "your outside life" that you're pillaging, but your own inner world.

I insist on calling this work reparative because it recognizes and articulates the indebtedness of this poetics not just to others' writing, but to others' lives. Unlike his collage poems, "Give Them Back" aims to incorporate or reincorporate others as wholes, rather than as textual parts. Named and described rather than cut into, O'Hara survives in the space of a poem that announces his death as unmournable. When "everything dies," the only survivor is, of course, the poem, and it's Berrigan's "posthumous," elegiac gift to use every means at his disposal to ensure O'Hara's poetic survival, even when O'Hara's death jeopardizes his own.[80]

Eve Sedgwick explains that reparative reading is the exploration of "the many ways selves and communities succeed in extracting sustenance from the objects of a culture—even of a culture whose avowed desire has been not to sustain them."[81] Berrigan is a reparative reader of the very texts he so violently cut from himself, Frank O'Hara, and other writers. By elegizing and self-elegizing, Berrigan makes amends for the sadistic violence of his method; he recognizes that he depends on the wholeness and suffers from the loss of the very objects he attacks. By drawing upon this violent method even in this work of mourning, he signals the fact that poetic making always situates itself squarely between the violent erasure of some names and the recuperative rescue of others.

Ted Berrigan depended completely on poetry. As Alice Notley wrote, the couple sustained a "continuous involvement with poetry" such that "everything we did or said became part of it."[82] Berrigan wrote and spoke often about his death in the years preceding it and acknowledged what many of his friends recognized, that he hastened it by his attachment to the habits that supported his poetry. In "Last Poem," which Notley notes was written four years before Berrigan's death, the poet imagines himself writing from beyond the grave and admits, bluntly, that "the pills kept me going, until now."[83] Collage may figure most prominently among the deleterious habits, in the sense that Berrigan's introjection of others jeopardized the integrity of his own body and mind. As Anne Waldman writes of Berrigan's final years, "It was as if he were too many people for his aging body."[84]

It's in this permeability between poem and self that the contagion of Berrigan's affect—his aggression, his tenderness, and his ambivalence—reveals itself most clearly. Charles Bernstein writes that "Berrigan's writing poses the startling fact of writing's lethal and consuming importance in requiring the yielding of body and mind to its inexorable priority."[85] By sacrificing his physical body to writing, Berrigan calls to mind Arthur Rimbaud. In a way, it's not coincidental that Berrigan's sonnets incorporate fragments from his own translations of Rimbaud, of whom Blanchot wrote, "while still alive he had poetry cut out of him."[86] Unlike Rimbaud, however, who left poetry behind, Berrigan cut his own body out of poetry with each voice he brought in, and did so until his final days. Berrigan's poetry, then, represents an encounter with poetic selves that was not only violent *and* reparative, but violent because reparative, precisely because his reparations did violence to the self. Berrigan attempted to incorporate names and persons as whole objects, and as he did so the "I" upon which he continued to rely swelled to bursting. An "abject dependence" on an "irreplaceable ... whole object" defines the extreme difficulty of the depressive position.[87] All of Berrigan's oeuvre, from "I hate books" to "I am in love with poetry," and from the most violent attacks on objects to the most caring elegiac reparations, represents an attempt to articulate the potential creative productivity of abject dependence on an art form that could, he came to recognize, both give and take itself away. As with Wallace Stevens and Randall Jarrell, Berrigan's approach toward relationships, his hovering at the edge of more intimate interpersonal engagement, is what makes his work most interesting. Far from containing his aggression and reparation in self-sufficient poems, Berrigan attempted elaborate renovation of existing poetic rooms. "Is there room in the room that you room in," Sonnet I asks, and in making room for himself and inviting others into his space Berrigan's collages reveal the circulations of an affective environment unlike any other.

6

Aaron Kunin's Line of Shame

As the arena of this study's concern moves into the twenty-first century with readings of recent books by Aaron Kunin and Claudia Rankine, it is worth noting that both poets, who have been linked to the avant-garde, question poetry's relationship to the historical, poetic, and temporal past. Although situated within a poetic avant-garde, Rankine's poems nevertheless focus on new ways of representing how the past accumulates in what would otherwise be illegible experiences of frustration, anger, and rage in the present. Kunin's poetry, as we shall see, considers the affect of shame as a possible corrective to a long history of poems acting with less justifiable restraint on the lives and feelings of their readers. Inasmuch as rage and shame in the present depend for their power on the existence of relationships in the past, and inasmuch as these powerful affects change the ability of the feeling subject to envision the future, these chapters draw attention to the ways that affect's ineluctable, often overwhelming presentness may also represent the regimes of time—past and future—that lie outside it.

Without excluding the genre entirely, both twenty-first-century chapters also look to poetry beyond the lyric. As several commentators have pointed out, the richness of Claudia Rankine's *Citizen: An American Lyric* is shown in the simple fact that it was the first book ever to be selected as a finalist for the National Book Critics Circle Award in two categories—poetry and criticism. And Kunin, who regards scholarly writing and poetic production as equally important tools, derives the necessity for and the precise coordinates of a concept of poetic shame from twentieth-century poetry criticism, literary theory, and psychology. As such, I turn to Kunin's own literary criticism alongside his poetry in this chapter in order to consider how and why poems can—and perhaps should—generate shame.[1] Following on the heels of a century in which the very existence of the genre of lyric was deeply contested, both Kunin and Rankine's interventions suggest that it may be in the very withdrawal of lyric from the foreground of poetic production that its most intense affects can be witnessed.

By blending a complex conceptual apparatus with theoretical references derived from affect theory, gender studies, and art and literary history, Aaron Kunin's 2005 collection, *Folding Ruler Star*, quickly established itself as among the most difficult volumes of recent poetry. Taking its title from a set of photographs by the German artist Sigmar Polke, its line measure and mise-en-scéne from a combination of Milton and Oulipo, and theoretical cues from the psychologist Silvan Tomkins, whose work is best known through Eve Sedgwick and Adam Frank's anthology, *Shame and Its Sisters*, the scope of *Folding Ruler Star* is as vast as its vision is intricate. The poems depict miniature dramas of punishment and blocked communication that unfold between the fragile, limited, and rigidly zoned parts of the terrorized human body and an array of personified objects haunting domestic tableaus. These constellations of human and inhuman pain unfold in a line of five syllables, and each poem stares into a mirror, a poem of the same title on the facing page, though what it sees is hardly human: "kindly no human/face shines out of a/folding ruler star."[2] *Folding Ruler Star* is the book-length answer to a question Kunin asks in *Grace Period*, a collection of his journals and notebooks: "What do I really understand about shame?"[3] I have claimed, in preceding chapters, that anxiety and melancholy affect poetic form; Kunin's poems argue that an even less tolerable affect's formal and conceptual constraints offer an essential corrective to historical poetic practice.

In a review of Kunin's second collection, *The Sore Throat & Other Poems*, Stephen Burt acknowledged "complete bafflement" at the poems of *Folding Ruler Star*.[4] And indeed, the density of the volume's program, the multiplicity of the inputs and intertexts that contribute to its conceptual apparatus, and the strangeness of the doubled poems' *tableau vivants* of punishment and shame seem calculated to scramble the supposed unity of subjective experience. As a poem illustratively titled "Access Denied" has it, "he worked/in accordance with/ secret principles."[5] However, I will argue that Kunin's formal and conceptual interventions—his use of a five-syllable line and a mirror poem, the prominent speaking and feeling roles granted to furniture and machines—distort the face of lyric poetry for a reason. They offer an alternative to what Kunin calls, in a 2009 *PMLA* article, poetry's "preservation fantasy," a relationship to futurity and immortality of which, in Kunin's analysis, poetry ought to be ashamed.[6]

In what follows, I first explore Kunin's arguments that conventional poetry, inasmuch as it "proposes a violent intervention in the given world," one that would "suspend" both "mortality and temporality," (93) is ethically problematic. Then, I'll introduce *Folding Ruler Star*'s experimentation as one attempt at enacting a different sort of poetic logic, one that activates "a shame response" to existing poetry's dangerous "experimentation" and that uses shame-producing formal and conceptual constraints to reconceive of poetry's purpose. Finally, I'll touch on the ways that shame, at times, exceeds the human dimension of affect and permits a discussion of poetry's relationship to artificial intelligence (AI). *Folding Ruler Star* is a brief and physically unassuming book; its ambition, however, mirrors its privileged affect in that it exceeds self-containment to forge new and surprising social bonds.

In the distinct, forceful, and unadorned (but not indecorous) tone his criticism shares with his poetry, Aaron Kunin defines the "preservation fantasy" as poetic thought related to "the humanist imperative to preserve cultural artifacts … in their original form."[7] Such preservation is generally accepted as "an absolute good," not only in Kunin's privileged examples—Horace, Spenser, Shakespeare, Milton—but in the academy as a whole. It's Kunin's claim that this fantasy, as conventional as every reader of Shakespeare knows it to be, has serious, and not simply "theoretical" consequences.

Kunin finds the authoritative statement of the preservation fantasy in Allen Grossman's poetics. Grossman names the poetic "commonplace" that "the kind of success which poetry facilitates is called 'immortality.'"[8] He traces the commonplace to two sources in Horace's *Odes*, one of which claims, *non omnis moriar*, "I shall not altogether die"[9] and another that adds "there were many heroes before Agamemnon."[10] The first creates what Kunin calls a "quasihuman" space, a rare gap between life and death in which a part of the human (but which part?) can survive.[11] The second line suggests that one answer to the question "which part?" is "the proper name."[12] The poems in which Kunin is most interested, however, are sonnets by Spenser, Shakespeare, and Milton that propose solutions to various problems the preservation fantasy encounters. Spenser's *Amoretti* sonnets demonstrate the (limited, but detectable) resistance that poetic addressees put up to their preservation: in the course of a sonnet that claims to preserve the name of Elizabeth Boyle, the proper name never appears.[13] In Shakespeare's *Sonnets*, various naïve sexual theories are proposed to ensure the survival of the young man through reproduction before they are rejected in favor of a (well-known and) purely poetic solution, found in Sonnet 18: "As long as men can breathe or eyes can see/So long lives this, and this gives life to thee." Kunin reads the repeated "this" not only as "this book" or "this poem," but as "a magic word," one that again "creates the middle space between life and death" where a fantasy of preservation "initiated by the act of writing" can be "fulfilled by the act of reading."[14] For Kunin, the fantasied, transitional space created by this "not altogether" death presents several additional problems. At what cost would such preservation be enacted and proven to have been accomplished? By a reading of Milton's sonnet-like poem, "On Shakespeare," Kunin suggests that preservation is extraordinarily costly; the immortality of the addressee is exchanged for that of the poet and, later, for that of the reader: the poet's immortality can be enjoyed neither in bodily nor in traditional symbolic forms, and, perhaps most importantly, reading preservationist poems denies readers their own lives. Kunin translates Milton's lines, "Then thou our fancy of itself bereaving/Dost make us Marble with too much conceiving," as a death warrant for the reader, who "becomes possessed by [Shakespeare]" and "follow[s] a script written by him."[15]

If this line alone does not make a dramatic point, this readerly problem takes more drastic form elsewhere in Shakespeare, where we discover that the central problem of the preservationist fantasy is just how often it is yoked to an apocalyptic one. Sonnet 11, Kunin shows, figures mostly as "an exercise in imagining the destruction of all culture and all life," since "everyone else has to die to prove that the young man is indesctructible"[16]: "Let those whom nature hath not made for store … barrenly perish. Look whom she best endowed … " Darkly paradoxical, the fantasy of securing immortality for one person accomplishes nothing quite so well as enforcing its literal opposite on the world at large: "Shakespeare does not need a tomb for his bones because he has turned the entire human population into tombs."[17] Kunin's indictment of the preservation fantasy does not merely describe a trope. Rather, Kunin speaks to the "sense in which poems are a form of research on human subjects," affecting the fantasies and fates readers accept when we, by reading, become part of the experiment.[18] Because the preservation fantasy crosses increasingly troubling ethical boundaries in the process of responding to successive challenges to the efficacy of its program, Kunin calls for a kind of poetry more serious about seeking approval for the kinds of experiments it conducts.

According to Kunin, the poetic means for fantasying preservation, one we might otherwise accept as innocuous, or only historical, indulges a darker fantasy of holocaust at its core. That is, if at first glance the humanist theory, which aims to preserve a part of the person beyond death in immortal fame, seems sincerely concerned with lyric's role in society, its apocalyptic fallout upsets such illusions. The preservation fantasy's endgame suggests that poetics itself has something to be ashamed of.

***

It is against this backdrop, and in a similarly startling way, that Kunin's poems in *Folding Ruler Star* foreground shame. As an affect that is asocial by definition, occasioning a withdrawal from attachments that are necessary to being able to experience the affect at all, shame may nevertheless hold out one possibility for poetry to forge a more ethical relationship to the social. Kunin derives his concept of shame from the American psychologist Silvan Tomkins, who regards it as the most distressing of all negative affects, but one that is unique for connecting those who experience it to those who cause it. In their introduction of Tomkins's work, Eve Sedgwick and Adam Frank conclude that "the pulsations of cathexis around shame, of all things, are what either enable or disenable so basic a function as the ability to be interested in the world."[19] Silvan Tomkins shows how it is that shame can be constitutive of reduced communication and of unique forms of attachments to others, and why Kunin takes it as an affect that can reorient poetry.

According to Tomkins, there are a discreet number of intrinsically positive or negative innate affects, which, although "programmed" or structured subcortically by "internal working models" or "scripts," are always and only conscious. Two of the affects in Tomkins's system are positive, one is neutral, and six are negative, of which the most intricate and interesting is shame, the one which "strike[s] deepest into the heart of man."[20] *Folding Ruler Star* uses Tomkins's definition of the physical response characteristic of the affect of shame as its epigraph:

> The shame response is an act which reduces facial communication. It stands in the same relation to looking and smiling as silence stands to speech and as disgust, nausea, and vomiting stand to hunger and eating. By dropping his eyes, his eyelids, his head, and sometimes the whole upper part of his body, the individual calls a halt to looking at another person, particularly the other person's face, and to the other person's looking at him, particularly at his face.

Unlike most descriptions of poetic mediation, which emphasize poetry's capacity for facilitating communication, Kunin writes under the sign of "reduced facial communication." What is poetically possible—and impossible—under these conditions? First, poetry generated under the sign of the shame response can no longer, or not so simply, fetishize physical beauty: the cataloging technique of blazon, for example, is impossible for the bowed head. Affected by shame, the faces of addressors and addressees are poetically invisible to each other. What do poems look at when they address themselves to other persons without looking at them? What do they consume when they don't, with Herbert's speaker in "Love (III)," "sit and eat"?

Kunin's poems capitalize on shame's inextricable relationship to the social. Crucially for Kunin (and for queer theorists who devote significant thought to "Gay Shame" as a response to the homogenizing impulse of "Gay Pride"), shame is not only negative. Unlike the other negative affect, disgust, which represents a complete rejection and separation from an object, shame's "facial communication reduction" represents an "incompletely reduced" bond with an object of desire. The excitement and enjoyment of the attachment to that other are still, in the moment of shame, minimally intact, allowing shame to communicate its withdrawal from the one who shames. In some cases, the shame response may even be contagious, so that the one who shames may, in recognizing the reduction of enjoyment or excitement he or she has caused as well as the reduction of communicative possibility he or she has instantiated, become himself or herself ashamed.

In response to a poetics in which readers are overwhelmed by demands on their eyes, their attention, and their lives, Kunin needs poems to communicate less, in a more limited sphere, and to in this way to be less demanding of the preservation and reproduction of persons beyond the poem. For this, he finds fertile ground in shame. Rather than measure the success of the poem by the extent to which it immortalizes its addressee, Kunin develops a poetic line that takes the measure of objects as poetic speech withdraws from them. Although several formal and conceptual characteristics of *Folding Ruler Star* contribute to the book's upregulation of shame, I focus here on Kunin's five-syllable line, which takes the pentameter Blank Verse line of Milton and Shakespeare as its antecedent in such a way as to foreground an attachment to these poets and their meter that produces shame.

This understanding of line, like that of the poetics of preservation, derives from Allen Grossman, who writes that "line-forms, and verse forms in general, are fundamentally discussable as mediations of relationships, as rules and orders of polities."[21] Blank Verse, in all its forms, came to depict the speech characteristic of "persons in social situations."[22] To Ezra Pound, Blank Verse arose as a critique of medieval Christian poetic procedure in which rhyme signified the infinity of the person in relation to divine infinity. Nevertheless, a certain kind of personhood constitutes this social sphere: "only 'gentle' persons speak Blank Verse" in Shakespeare, and thus only these persons can be considered "well-formed"; for Milton, "to liberate verse from rhyme is ... to liberate from bondage, to set up the human form divine."[23] In his own poems, Kunin uses what he will call an "almost ... iambic pentameter line" to stay in a relationship to his predecessors while simultaneously withdrawing from them. As Sedgwick and Frank note, the most interesting aspect of shame is that it "is characterized by its failure ever to renounce its object cathexis, its relation to the desire for pleasure as well as the need to avoid pain."[24] Kunin's project distinguishes itself from the ground-clearing manifestoes of many avant-garde movements by acknowledging that its critique is predicated on desire for and attachment to a poetics that it also resists.

Folding Ruler Star is composed in a five-syllable line that cuts the pentameter line in half in order to disrupt a social vision perpetuated by traditional poetic technique. I propose three ways of reading Kunin's line as a line of shame. First, Kunin's lines are shamed by the pentameter line, to whose expectations they cannot measure up. The social order upheld and reproduced by the pentameter line—one of gentility, civility, and reciprocity—casts shame on the scenes of punishment, deprivation, cruelty, dissatisfaction, and silence in Kunin's poems. In accordance with the shame response, the poems are reduced, their communication cryptic and ciphered. The line of five is a line cut short by the social conditions with which pentameter is complicit. The three lines of "The Shame Tree" cry out in response to an unrecorded punishment, but these words of supplication can only increase its degradation:

aspirin tonight
no contempt please no
contempt tonight please[25]

From another vantage, though, Kunin's lines are not merely shamed by the pentameter line but, having been shamed, demonstrate the wide array of possibilities for poetic communication in this state. The line of five, extending across the page as if toward a desired end of ten syllables, finds, when it is truncated, that its enjoyment of the social vision proclaimed by the pentameter line—with the social conditions it represents—is also radically, if incompletely, reduced, but not that it has relinquished curiosity for other aspects of desire and the world. It's in the capacities for other poetries opened up by this nonpreservationist reduction that Kunin's poems thrive. When the line stops at five syllables, its head bowed in shame, it rejects the embalmed lyric faces immortalized by previous poems and discovers, as in the volume's title poem, faces that previous poems have overlooked:

draw a circle in
the mirror (inside
and outside are not
places (half the size

of your face a hinged
ruler is a good
enough mother[26]

A poetics of shame is not, then, a poetics of failure. The odd, asymmetrical, uneven, and shame-producing social encounters represented in Kunin's poems exceed the capacity of the line of ten's even syllables and its divinely mediated, hierarchically sanctioned fantasy of equitable social life. Moreover, as we've seen already, they have no desire to measure up to a lyric form that includes the kind of experimentation to which poems of the preservationist fantasy expose their addressees and readers. And if one consequence of the preservation fantasy is that readers' lives are threatened, Kunin notices the homogenization of sexual desire under such a regime and uses *Folding Ruler Star* to imagine, from within shame, alternate configurations. As "Petting Impersonal" has it (and in one of the most clear statements of purpose the book contains), "these poems express my/dissatisfaction/with sexual life."[27] The word dissatisfaction has a particular resonance in this case, since it hints at the queerness of any sexuality that excuses itself from satisfaction as well as from pride at the simple fact of difference. As David M. Halperin and Valerie Traub note in their introduction to *Gay Shame*, using Kunin's word, "gay pride has generated considerable dissatisfactions of its own among some of the very people it has aimed, or claimed, to benefit."[28] I take Kunin's experiment in poetic shame as one example of a refusal to foreclose the potential of a negative affect even or especially when its immediate surround calls for assimilation into its opposite.[29]

Finally, Kunin's five-syllable line can be regarded as a radical form of anacrusis, or decapitation, in which the first syllables of a line are cut without altering the line's status as metrically sufficient. "Almost is a good/enough iambic/pentameter line," the title poem ends.[30] Good enough because these syllables survive as a part of the whole, but as a surviving part they are more ethically sound than the names or the bodies of addressees and readers. And good enough, for Kunin, because this decapitation permits the poems to engage with a perceptual world that iambic pentameter fails to notice, one far too distanced from the lyric beloved and too close to the face of the speaker. The opening lines of "Food Syntax" demonstrate the way that Kunin's lines are affected by their shame to see a world only visible to one who looks down:

my hands seek out new
textures (he often
imagined stabbing

himself in the eye)
for example with
a pen (scooping them
out with a grapefruit
spoon or otherwise
de-eyeing himself
etctetera) I
am always happy
because I have a
razor hidden in
my face[31]

Rather than list the parts of the face of the beloved within metaphors, Kunin's speaker mutilates his own face and declares himself "always happy." At least, the poem seems to argue, the power to lose one's life in a poem is maintained by and limited to the speaker, rather than cast on to the reader at the cost of poetic immortality.

The decapitation that accompanies Kunin's line, one that he announces with the phrase, "reading a book/is cutting off the head," demonstrates an ethic that has always been a part of reading. Inasmuch as a reader must always lower his or her eyes to encounter the lines in a poem, a shame response—alongside its generativity for socialization—is always potentially available to poetic reading. When the reader of Kunin's poem lowers her eyes, however, it's into lines that have already, in deference and acknowledgment of poetry's shameful history, receded. Kunin's syllables suggest what poetic reading should have been all along, not a triumphalist narrative or fantasy of preservation with its unethical sequellae, but a reminder of the vulnerabilities of the body (and the person bound within it) to time and death. Furthermore, while Shakespeare's sonnets enclose the reader in a script from which she cannot escape, Kunin's decapitations release—or eject— the reader from the poem, a space she has already been decapitated in order to enter. Rather than excise what Shakespeare calls the "harsh, featureless, and rude," Kunin's poems decapitate the beautiful and champion the shameful in the belief that, as he writes in *The Sore Throat*, "the part of yourself that you're most ashamed of is interesting and can be used as material for art."[32]

By nevertheless maintaining, consistent with the workings of shame, an "incompletely reduced enjoyment" of the pentameter line, these syllables demonstrate the zero degree of residual, complicit attachment to a system of poetic conventions revealed to be almost certainly unjustifiable and potentially apocalyptic. Again, if "almost is a good/enough iambic/pentameter line," then the ethos as well as the phrasing is Winnicott's: the supposedly "better" than "good enough mother" merely terrorizes her child through neglect or impingement, just as the pentameter line fails to immortalize its addressee and still entombs the possessed reader. For Kunin, to use poetic lines at all is to admit complicity with a kind of "experimentation on human subjects"; as we shall see, the aim of *Folding Ruler Star* is to find ways of putting inhuman objects, including machines, to work for poetic research.

Eve Sedgwick and Adam Frank recognize an alignment between the shame response and reading as one key to the contemporary engagement with affect:

> If, as Tomkins describes it, the lowering of the eyelids, the lowering of the eyes, the hanging of the head is the attitude of shame, it may also be that of reading— reading maps, magazines, novels, comics, and heavy volumes of psychology, if not billboards and traffic signs. We ... know the force field-creating power of this attitude, the kind of skin that sheer textual attention can weave around a reading body.[33]

Just as the book was figured as a "security blanket" into which the reader "withdraws," Sedgwick and Frank speak of "textual attention" as such a textile; but rather than a Winnicottian holding environment in which affective attunement promises healthy development, Sedgwick, Frank, and Kunin pick up on the way that reading allows for a withdrawal that may be induced as much by shame as by its necessary condition, desire. Kunin makes the connection explicit in "Five Security Zones," a poem that notes the pain that ironically results from too strong an attempt to avoid pain: "the pain of self-exposure/until (avoidance becomes painful)."[34] The poem's ending connects this phenomenon to reading:

> at
> which your shield becomes
> a burden (your shield)
> reading a book is
> cutting off the head[35]

If the shamed person can turn, in his or her downward glance of "reduced facial communication," to the book as to a source of consolation, Kunin shows that the shield of the book is also a sword. If shame makes communication difficult, reading makes it impossible. Tomkins suggests one reason that reading a book like *Folding Ruler Star* may be especially dangerous for the reader:

> A second major source of shame, in addition to barriers of excitement or joy, is the shame response of the other. If another individual with whom I am identified

or in whom I am interested or with whom I have experienced enjoyment lowers his eyes or head to me as an object of his interest or enjoyment, then my own positive affect can be sufficiently reduced to evoke my shame.[36]

If *Folding Ruler Star* is a book that lowers its head in shame, whether this shame responds to my interest or expected enjoyment of the book, so may I, the reader, lower my head in shame, doubling (as does a mirror) the difficulty of reading.

Vanessa Place and Rob Fitterman argue that conceptual writing "is dependent on its reader for completion."[37] *Folding Ruler Star* notes that such completion does not enlighten or illumine the reader, as though he or she had accomplished an interpretation. Rather, the book's completion is predicated on the reader's violent incompletion, a violation of the zones of his or her body. Rather than confer immortality, as the "preservation fantasy" would assert, these poems perform mortality. But because the "preservation fantasy" is already, for Kunin, "a violent intervention in the given world that would suspend two of the limiting conditions on human life, mortality and temporality," even decapitating the reader, which challenges the technology of preservation, may be a more ethical end for poems.[38]

***

Rather than a human face, Kunin chooses an apple to serve as a transitional object in *Folding Ruler Star*, a substitute for the human face and for a human reader upon whom the reading of poems would be an unethical experiment. In a book that notes its debt to *Paradise Lost* in its opening sentences, apples allude to the biblical temptation of Eve as well as to the connotations they pick up throughout the book. In the loose retelling of the biblical story in "Girl and Reptile," the passing of an apple from the girl to her "little brother" mimics Eve's handing of the apple to Adam.[39] In Kunin's poem, however, the only thing apple-like about the apple is that it can be eaten, cored, and peeled. It is more like a knife than an apple, and its damaging influence shines through in "Girl and Reptile": "(her tongue/wiping the shredded/inside of her cheek)."[40] When it returns in "Zipdown Day," the apple is just the vehicle of a metaphor ("the/room seemed larger (like//an apple dully/shining)"[41] and seems intended mainly to allow the fruit to reassert its ubiquity. And indeed this reminder pays off, because the apple comes back in the penultimate stanza of *Folding Ruler Star*:

the machine (they can't
blush cry or love but

> it's precisely in
> blushing crying and
> loving that they are
> most machine-like) like
> an apple that did
> not ripen (astral
> physiognomy)
> kindly no human
> face smiles out of a
> folding ruler star[42]

The edible apple that causes shame at the book's beginning progresses backward from being cored and peeled to shining dully to finally being unripe. It is in this final (although chronologically prior) state that the apple helps evoke the most important quality of a folding ruler star, that its face is "astral" and not human. The nonfacial aspect shared by "the machine," the unripe apple, and the folding ruler star links the biblical to the contemporary source of shame and suggests a third faceless term as a possible solution. Part simple machine (folding ruler), part celestial body (star), part cultural artifact (the photograph bearing its name), and part loved object (bamboo pole loves folding ruler star), *Folding Ruler Star* becomes a book of poems by the experimental process of communicating across multiple zones of noncommunication. Kunin affixes a voice to multiple sites or zones of pain, and by making them speak a regulated, if not regular or normal speech, he demonstrates the possibility that an affect other than shame might arise from an overwhelming situation of "total affect shame-bind."[43] That affect or action is embodied in the strange adverb that opens the last stanza. From the inhuman light of the TV that shone with two faces and two memories in the collection's opening poem, Kunin's poetic labors have brought us to a place where the face has finally been successfully masked and protected from the incessant mirroring that threatens it. If a folding ruler star is any kind of face, it is an astral one, and one that thus recalls Shakespeare's lines in *Romeo and Juliet*, lines of mourning that reenact the violence of death in a ritual of mourning that alone could be adequate to reorient the gaze to its proper object:

> And when he shall die, cut him out in little stars, and he shall make the face of heav'n so bright, that all the world will be in love with night, and pay no worship to the garish sun.[44]

Despite the collection's explicit affinity with Silvan Tomkins, whose affect theory is articulated as a radical revision to Freudian drive theory, Kunin draws on one of Winnicott's most popular concepts in deriving his own book's *felix culpa*. In order to get out of the shame bind, it would seem, Kunin needs to have recourse to a psychoanalytic way of thinking. Winnicott's "good enough mother" is adept at bringing her child from dependence to independence by a progressively less immediate attention to the child's needs. Without being perfect at any point, the "good enough mother" is, most importantly, able to allow her child to experience frustrations only when he or she is capable of integrating these frustrations into an experience of the world that includes the existence of "not-me" objects. To return to the first two stanzas of "Folding Ruler Star" (1) is to find Winnicott's term brought to yet another intricately designed scene characterized by a voice that commands and a parenthetical voice that, in this poem, annotates and elaborates.

> draw a circle in
> the mirror (inside
> and outside are not
> places) half the size
> of your face a hinged
> ruler is a good
> enough mother (out
> of sympathy) for
> measuring the bridge
> between parent and
> child[45]

Just as the five-syllable line is half the length of the pentameter, the circle in the mirror, which is "half the size/of your face," is the right size for a "folding ruler star" to circumscribe. Although a face cannot fit inside the circle on the mirror, the hinged ruler that is these poems is "good enough" as an adaptive mother and as an instrument for what can be spoken about shame. The final poem of the collection emphasizes that the exclusion of the face has been necessary for the work that the folding ruler star can do with its noncommunicative affect. It is not until the final lines of the book that we read this:

> kindly no human
> face shines out of a
> folding ruler star[46]

What can poems do with things that exclude the human face? How can poems "express my/dissatisfaction/with sexual life"[47] and yet describe sexual life and measure the affect that "lives in the face" at the same time? *Folding Ruler Star* does both. Shame is the key word for both of these endeavors, because it is, as Kunin shows, the affect that allows a measurement of the object as it recedes, and because in the disappearing or removing that it causes, it shows both the strength of sexual desire and the inevitable knots in which its pursuit entangles us.

Kunin's poems exemplify a different poetic logic than preservationist poems for the peculiar lengths they go to avoid "research on human subjects."[48] While machines will figure more prominently in Kunin's second volume of poems, *Folding Ruler Star* substitutes inhuman apparatuses for human persons not only to indicate the reduced scope of vision characteristic of shame, but also to explore how dramas that might otherwise invoke humans, and especially readers, can unfold on a different scale.[49] Kunin's objects—in *Folding Ruler Star* they are mostly domestic, personal objects and furniture—do not so much interact with humans, then, as act in their stead, meting out punishments, moving in response to stimuli, and even feeling. In "Facesitting," for example, the "human" face belongs to a doll, and objects, from "a hand/held instrument of/gratification" to a "mirror" and a "knife," proliferate in order to obscure and finally to do violence to the doll's face.[50] Poems like "Facesitting," in which cryptic dramas of "arousal" and "gratification"[51] unfold among objects, contrast sharply with poems like "Petting Impersonal," in which a person is the subject of experimentation. In both the poem and the essay, the word "experiment" indicates an unethical incursion of poetic reading into human life.

> they decided to
> torture him as an
> experiment and
> the result was that
> they got aroused (the
> results they obtained
> were inconclusive)
> these poems express my
> dissatisfaction
> with sexual life[52]

The speaker's dissatisfaction "results" from the barrenness of a forced, nonconsensual interaction that produces feelings of arousal only to record them as "results." The poem produces no shame, and thus only dissatisfaction, because no relationship of desire binds the experimenters to their subject. Without this precondition, all petting is impersonal, and the poem, if it is a machine, is a dysfunctional one. A certain degree of consent is a necessary precondition for shame to enter the affective space of a poem. In contrast to Shakespeare's solution, in which "the young man is finally preserved as a keepsake without his consent,"[53] Kunin's poems manage both to maintain a space of consent and to eject readers violently from the space of the poem.

***

In a trenchant analysis of recent developments in AI and their relationship to Silvan Tomkins's affect theory, Elizabeth Wilson argues that overlooking shame may account for the failures of certain machines that nevertheless responded to stimuli with something like feeling. According to Wilson, shame is directly linked to AI, whose "enthusiastic projects are predestined for disappointment, or more specifically for the incomplete reduction of interest, enjoyment, and surprise."[54] In the case of the Kismet robot developed by MIT to model a human infant's development by interaction and integration with its environment, this disappointment and shame is directly linked to the exclusion of shame itself. The Kismet robot could express six major emotions on its face, but not shame. Wilson considers how "the shaming elements of Tomkins' theory would have brought more emotive life, more skilled sociality to this artificial agent,"[55] especially since, according to Tomkins, shame is linked as much to the positive affects as to the negative ones:

> shared shame [is] a prime instrument for strengthening the sense of mutuality and community whether it be between parent and child, friend and friend, or citizen and citizen. When one is ashamed of the other, that other is not only forced into shame but he is also reminded that the other is sufficiently concerned positively as well as negatively to feel ashamed of and for the other.[56]

Kunin's "Petting Impersonal," like the Kismet robot, demonstrates the shame characteristic of experiments that exclude shame, while "Facesitting," which foregrounds the affect's play among inhuman objects, features an exceptionally lively social backdrop. And no humans or readers were tortured, or even harmed, in its reading. In fact, despite the conceptual requirement that readers complete the work, the reader isn't necessary to *Folding Ruler Star* at all. As Ben Lerner argues, "That's the anxiety *Folding Ruler Star* produces: these poems don't need me, thinks the reader, and, precisely for that reason, they will survive me."[57]

If the mirroring withdrawnness characteristic of the shame response is everywhere present in *Folding Ruler Star*, it may nevertheless be that these shared withdrawals carry their own reminders that positive concern is their necessary condition. Perhaps, given the constraints on meaning and feeling in our contemporary world, shame is the best or only way to communicate this reminder that such concern exists and may also make the removal of shame binds (affective as well as poetic) possible.

If, as Elizabeth Wilson reminds us, "shame itself can be one of the things that is most acutely shaming: 'one is as ashamed of being ashamed as of anything else,'"[58] it is evidence of a particular form of poetic courage that Aaron Kunin takes on the affect in *Folding Ruler Star*. Instead of being so ashamed by shame to silence it, as Wilson suggests the Kismet programmers did,[59] Kunin trots out the affect in the hope that its recognition and writing can reprogram our response to shame and make us more likely to recognize its intimate relationship with the positive affects. In this way, shame can be a sign not only of weakness, nor of its own multiplication, but of its dependence on the ability to experience desire, love, interest, and surprise.

> One of the paradoxical consequences of the linkage of positive affect and shame is that the same positive affect which ties the self to the object also ties the self to shame. To the extent to which socialization involves a preponderance of positive affect, the individual is made to feel vulnerable to shame and unwilling to renounce either himself or others.[60]

In closing, I wish to show that poems by both Wallace Stevens and Robert Creeley bear on this peculiar relationship between the most painful of negative affects and the facilitation of social life upon which poetry justifies its aesthetic work. Creeley's "The Warning" casts a strikingly violent image in order to describe the interdependence of what, in Tomkins' vocabulary, we might call positive and negative affects.

> For love—I would
> split open your head and put
> a candle in
> behind the eyes.
> Love is dead in us
> if we forget
> the virtues of an amulet
> and quick surprise.[61]

Creeley's vision is frightening because it demands, at the risk of love's own survival, that we rewrite an act of violence as a "quick surprise." What's odd is that the ability to define violence as surprise both depends on the prior existence of love, because "love is dead in us" if we have forgotten how to do so, and claims to make love possible, inasmuch as the speaker would claim to "split open/ your head" on behalf of love, or "for love." For Creeley, the ability to provoke or strengthen love by drastic measures depends on a reserve of love without which splitting the head is, after all, just that. In this reading, the speaker, and author of violence, deserves the recriminations and shame that follow from actions that presumed intimacy in its absence. The two scripts of the poem—one to be run if love is still alive, and the other if it is dead—produce divergent outputs, but the fact that both are inscribed in the poem's logic suggests that Creeley's poems, like Kunin's, depend on their reader for completion and accept this dependence at the risk of being shamed, humiliated, and excoriated if approached by a certain reader. To Creeley's violence of splitting open the head, Kunin's "quick surprise" is a volume of poems that risk shaming their readers in order to remind them that shame is ubiquitous, that it expresses "dissatisfaction," that we are always vulnerable to it, and, finally, that it can happen only in the presence of the very genuine interest and concern for others that can dissolve its binds.

Wallace Stevens quotes and rewrites the early William Carlos Williams poem, "El Hombre," in a poem from *Harmonium* called "Nuances on a Theme by Williams":

> It is a strange courage
> you give me, ancient star.
> Shine alone in the sunrise
> to which you lend no part!
> I.
> Shine alone, shine nakedly, shine like bronze,
> that reflects neither my face nor any inner part
> of my being, shine like fire, that mirrors nothing.
> II.
> Lend no part to any humanity that suffuses
> you in its own light.
> Be not chimera of morning,
> Half-man, half-star.
> Be not an intelligence,
> Like a widow's bird
> Or an old horse.[62]

Against what Stevens takes as Williams's pathetic fallacy, the speaker of "Nuances" commands the star to "Lend no part to any humanity that suffuses/you in its own light," to "reflect neither my face nor any inner part/of my being," and to "shine like fire, that mirrors nothing." Kunin's own lines, "Kindly no human/face shines out of a/folding ruler star," birth a heavenly body that would be inhuman, reflect no shape, and mirror nothing (except perhaps itself), but moreover, would manage to do this not as the result of the command of a chagrined speaker, but out of some unexplained kindness. In this way, Kunin's poems hold on to a strange courage, even as they nuance an ancient story—"man's first disobedience and the fruit thereof"—for our post-Miltonic poetic age.

I have tried to show that *Folding Ruler Star*, by foregrounding shame, by maintaining a reduced relationship to poetic tradition by means of a formal constraint that represents shame, and by pioneering a poetics that would perform a more ethical kind of "experimentation on human subjects," relies on a negative affect to make a new sort of valuable, socializing poetic work possible. At the end of "Shakespeare's Preservation Fantasy," Kunin asks just what a "desirable response to a collection of poems" would be, given that the response Milton's "On Shakespeare" seems to require, "wishing to die," is less than optimal.[63] The closing poem of *Folding Ruler Star* is a found poem transcribed from a page inserted into a library book. The poem records, in all caps, the conservation treatment for a badly damaged volume: "DRY CLEANED/DISINFECTED/ BOOK REPAIR (HINGE REPAIR)."[64] The fact this poem exceeds the five-syllable line elsewhere prescribed in *Folding Ruler Star* suggests that what follows on the heels of shame is a labor of preservation more concerned with reparation than with immortality.

This Feeling of Time: Claudia Rankine's *Citizen*

Reviewers and awards committees have, in their assessments of Claudia Rankine's *Citizen* (2014), been emphatic, if not unanimously positive, about its uniqueness among books that address race and racism in America. They have focused on several of its defining characteristics: its reception as a work of both poetry and criticism; its use, in its opening sections, of the second-person pronoun to create a single persona drawn from the accounts of racist incidents experienced by multiple persons; its incorporation of images, mostly of works of art by contemporary African-American artists; its choice, in many poems, to depict the impact of racist incidents on a self-consciously middle-class or upper middle-class speaker; and its focus on the recent and highly publicized police killings of black men. In each of these ways, *Citizen* charts new territory in US poetry. In this chapter, I consider an aspect of the volume that has not yet received sufficient attention: its recognition and formal management of affects of anger and melancholy that, because they accumulate over time, are illegible in the present. How can poetry bear witness to affects that time itself cannot contain?

Citizen's inventions in poetic content and form extend the possibilities for representing minoritarian affect in the lyric. Most of the preceding chapters have explored single feelings synchronically. From Wallace Stevens's anxiety to Aaron Kunin's shame, I have examined feelings in relation to the poetic techniques by which they can be fleetingly represented and out of which these poets fashion a new, more permeable kind of poetic container. Claudia Rankine's poems, however, explore feelings that can only be understood, because they can only be felt, diachronically, as the result of a process of accumulation over time. *Citizen* represents such feelings across multiple poems that not only account for these feelings' persistence, but also, perhaps, for their illegibility to others. In order to account for the anger, melancholy, and, to some extent, the pleasure experienced in widely varying intensities and at unexpected times, Rankine's forms make what James Baldwin calls a "precarious adjustment" to lyric convention. In order to represent the accumulation of feeling associated with what Lauren Berlant, a key interlocutor in this chapter, calls the "everyday trauma" of racist "infractions," *Citizen* constructs alternative poetic temporalities. These poems bear witness to the failure of chronological time to diminish the experience of accumulating affects; they also distend time in order to represent the continuity of affective experience through repeated exposures to trauma. This poetics demonstrates traumatic events' foreclosure, limitation, or distortion of the capacity to respond in the moment as well as the creative pathways by which response emerges, when it does.

By means of their temporal manipulations, the poems of *Citizen* fail to close, allowing intensities of feeling to spill over into or be leached away from other poems, where they accumulate or explode. "I don't know how to end what doesn't have an ending,"[1] Rankine writes, and the individual poems recognize that the consequences of racial infractions do not end when the events themselves do, that an event's beginning and ending may be difficult to determine. This strategy makes the deferred effects of racist infractions on the bodies and minds of those who experienced them—effects that manifest in ways that are often misread as immature and unjustified—newly legible by poetic means. Foregrounding the presumed illegibility of such affects is one of the book's preoccupations. Discussing white responses to manifestations of black affect allows Rankine to posit that the expression of these feelings, which white audiences find illegible because they appear after a period of latency and return, is constitutive of contemporary black citizenship, a kind of belonging characterized not so much by rights held in common as by a common, constant exposure to everyday trauma.[2]

Unexpectedly, the affect that opens *Citizen*'s exploration of everyday racial trauma is happiness. The volume's epigraph dares readers to overlook this affect in the poems that follow, and suggests that if race is its explicit concern, the positive affect, while it may be easier to miss, still plays a significant role: "If they don't see the happiness in the picture, at least they'll see the black." *Citizen*'s happiness is, however, easy to miss. While smiles and laughter punctuate several poems,[3] the atmosphere of the book matches that of Rankine's previous books, which have explored new poetic forms for representing depression and isolation. Perhaps the point is that the happiness is easy to overlook, since it hardly appears as such in the book. Modifying Freud's assertion that affect can be unconscious, Lauren Berlant argues that "The affective world that a bodily performance fronts is enigmatic, and felt states might be anything—menacing, fearful, detached, deadened, distracted, shallow, genuinely light, and/or numb, for example."[4] Rather than claim that happiness is absent from *Citizen*, then, its epigraph encourages readers to find the affective structure of happiness fronting as, perhaps, rage and melancholy. It defines happiness as the potential for something beautiful to emerge from a situation in which further injury is perhaps more likely. Like anger and dread, happiness is a feeling that holds time present, past, and future, in tension. Time exposes the subject of traumatic infractions to additional injury and its potentially intolerable consequences. But time is also the condition of possibility of happiness, which can only emerge in situations characterized by ongoing, rather than by finality and completeness. Placing "happiness" in a subordinate, conditional, negative clause that nevertheless demands attention at the opening of the book points toward the simultaneously precarious and tenacious place of the affect in *Citizen*. In this way, happiness highlights, rather than obscures, the possibility that the accumulation of traumas in the wounded body will burst into a rage that is irrevocable, that forecloses the possibility of happiness once and for all. This continuous deferral of accumulation's threat is its most potent aspect: because it can always explode, even when it hasn't yet, it can always, like happiness, fail to be recognized.

In keeping with previous chapters' investment in the affects' transformation of poetics, then, I consider how Rankine's awareness of the accumulation of negative affects upsets a still-persistent notion of lyric containment. Because *Citizen* is concerned with the nature of poetry's own investment in the public sphere, the negative affects of anger and melancholy serve as a lens by which to consider the ways poetry gives language to everyday life at a moment when trauma itself is ordinary.

Most of my account of trauma will be been concerned with what Lauren Berlant identifies as "everyday trauma," and, indeed, Claudia Rankine explicitly aligns herself with Berlant in arguing that the accumulating affects of these episodes correspond to a kind of trauma marked not by an essential break with subjectivity but by that subjectivity's continuation by other, perhaps new means. And while Berlant opposes "everyday trauma" to the kinds of "unclaimed experiences" that Cathy Caruth emphasizes, Caruth's emphasis on latency in the temporality of trauma is helpful for linking the manipulations of time specific to the poems of *Citizen* to the poetic strategies that make these manipulations visible.

In her reading of Freud's *Moses and Monotheism*, Caruth concludes that the time of latency, "the period during which the effects of the experience are not apparent," is one of the characteristics common to traumatic experience.[5] As a result of latency, a time during which the original experience cannot actually be claimed as experience, the recurrence of the traumatic event is also in some sense an entirely new occurrence, a departure rather than any simple return.[6] Paradoxically then, an unconscious continuity with the first event and a conscious discontinuity from it mark the effect of latency. Caruth links trauma to literary language by insisting that trauma is "the story of a wound that cries out, that addresses us in the attempt to tell us of a reality or truth that is not otherwise available."[7] The structure of *Citizen* is such that this wound speaks not only from the poems, but from the spaces between individual poems where affects accumulate during a period of latency. Considering these spaces as zones of latency reminds us that affective injuries are possible outside of infractions themselves, or rather that the time of an infraction extends far beyond the event and its narration. This temporality makes the explosiveness of events of "explosive rage" intelligible inasmuch as they have an origin in an experience that can, because it was not consciously experienced, barely be identified as such.

Two poems in the beginning of *Citizen*'s third section serve to introduce several of Rankine's central concerns. In the first, which is accompanied by an image of the Rutgers women's basketball team that commentator Don Imus maligned in 2007, a friend greets the poem's "you" with the same racial slur Imus had used. The poem follows this moment of injury with a refrain familiar to the poems of *Citizen*: "what did you say?" These four words serve as a fulcrum between past and future. Their past tense turns back to the site of injury; their interrogative mood extends the time of the injury, its explanation, and its aftermath into the future. The poem's "you" then considers, before deciding to consider no longer, three different possibilities for explaining the friend's use of the slur, "You are late, you nappy-headed ho." The friend cannot respond to the question "what did you say?," so the speaker takes up this work for her:

> Maybe the content of her statement is irrelevant and she only means to signal the stereotype of "black people time" by employing what she perceives to be "black people language." Maybe she is jealous of whoever kept you and wants to suggest you are nothing or everything to her. Maybe she wants to have a belated conversation about Don Imus and the women's basketball team he insulted with this language. You don't know.[8]

The injury to the speaker's feelings has already occupied the first portion of the poem; now, during the time it takes to consider possible explanations, the speaker's anger grows, perhaps in direct proportion to her inability and then indifference to attempting a response: "You don't know what response she expects from you nor do you care."[9] While the friend "keeps insisting" that her greeting was "a joke," the speaker maintains a silence in which she undertakes not an explanation but an analysis of the injury she has just sustained. The poem's last two sentences read:

> For all your previous understandings, suddenly incoherence feels violent. You both experience this cut, which she keeps insisting is a joke, a joke stuck in her throat, and like any other injury, you watch it rupture along its suddenly exposed suture.[10]

The poem reveals in its first and last lines that this friendship already has distance and injury built into it. We know from the poem's opening that this friend lives "in a distant neighborhood" and that the speaker is on the way to meet her. In the poem's last line, the "suddenly exposed suture" suggests that previous injuries have been stitched together at the same site. Even as the poem began, we were in a space of an injury that has been accumulating "at a cellular level"[11] and that contributes to the response, or nonresponse, that takes place here. The fact that the poem ends here, without any closure, is once again indicative of the impossibility of containing the affects associated with racial slurs in the poetic time it takes to report their occurrence. The poem ends, that is, before any possibility of optimism can emerge from a "joke stuck in her throat." Taking the time to let poetic or chronological time "function as a power wash" will have to be deferred. As *Citizen* proceeds to the next poem, which will also feature the refrain "What did you say?", this first injury does not heal; in fact, the healing of prior injuries only signals more clearly the site of the current rupture. The news in this poem is the decidedly pessimistic report that susceptibility to threat is most concentrated in the sites that have already been wounded. Accordingly, the news of *Citizen* is that each poem is obligated to record not merely wounds, but their reopenings.

For Rankine, feeling's injuries are among the most pernicious. Each one contains the possibility, and perhaps the greater likelihood, of recurrence in the same site. It may even be the case that moving through the process of healing such an injury increases this threat. Recognizing this logic, the poem leaves an "exposed suture" for the next page to reckon with. Rankine considers not the moment when one's feelings are injurious, but when one sees them as such and begins to dread them. The next poem ["When you arrive"] opens, yet again, with the word "when," marking its temporality as continuous with that of the poem that precedes it. Rather than a phrase like "One day," which would shift the poem to align with chronological time and acknowledge that the following events happen on a different day, "when" precludes any determination of the distance between the two events. The second could precede the first, or could even be occurring to two different persons simultaneously. When it identifies "a woman you work with" as the speaker of offending words, this person is hardly differentiable from the previous poem's "friend."

> When a woman you work with calls you by the name of another woman you work with, it is too much of a cliché not to laugh out loud with the friend beside you who says, oh no she didn't.[12]

In this case, while "cliché" could refer to the first woman's mistake, it also refers to the "friend's" use of the phrase, "oh no she didn't," which, while not a slur, appropriates black vernacular to address the poem's speaker at the moment she has been injured.[13] Because most of the rest of the poem handles the initial injury, this slight cannot even be addressed. Until, perhaps, the poem's final stanza, which, in its single line, asks, "What did you say?" As if recalling not the naming but the friend's attempt to defuse it, the poem ends with words that, in the previous poem, preceded an attempt at explanation or understanding. Here, as a result of a continuously accumulating injury, an answer to these words cannot even be attempted. It's not only the exhaustion the speaker experiences after multiple infractions from a single coworker that leaves these words unanswered; the possibility that an additional injury will be committed in the time it takes to provide or solicit an answer leaves the closing words black and, in words of Zora Neale Hurston's that Rankine returns to, "against a sharp white background."

Accumulation: Failures of response

"Yes, and the body has memory."[14] The effects of racist infractions bypass consciousness and take up residence in the body. And once an event has "turned your flesh into its cupboard,"[15] it secures a permanent place denied to conscious memory. Lauren Berlant's *Cruel Optimism* shaped Rankine's thinking about the poetic techniques that would permit *Citizen* to represent the impact of such a literal incorporation of injury. In Rankine's words:

> [*Cruel Optimism*] talks about the ways in which … it's a mistake to think of trauma as a true break, but instead as something that happens and accumulates in small ways over time and … in thinking about this book and thinking formally about how to put it together it seemed to me that to think about these kinds of infractions … it was important to come up with a form that allowed the moments to accumulate.[16]

Because the effects and affects of everyday trauma cannot be confined to a single moment, because the feelings associated with experiencing, surviving, and responding to the situations Rankine describes cannot be contained by the time of their narration, the simultaneous projects of living in the present and envisioning a future are threatened by a force that remains mostly invisible, until it returns. In *Citizen*, racially marked subjects experience and respond to situations that happen repeatedly but start to feel the same. *Citizen* reports from an "enigmatic" affective world specific to a kind of recurring experience in which not just an event, but the ongoing history of one's feelings of anger and melancholy in response to the event is what hurts, threatens, and increases the risk of injury. Writing about Eve Sedgwick, Berlant invokes situations characterized by "a condition of possibility that also justifies the risk of having to survive, once again, disappointment and depression."[17] In *Citizen*, however, the inevitability of such repeated exposure to everyday trauma promises an unceasing accumulation of anger. Here, the mixed feelings of anger and the dread of anger raise the possibility that taking on the risks of moving forward is not so easily justified. Rather than protect the self from further injury, these feelings, in their foreclosure of so many futures, are themselves injurious.

The feelings Rankine will show to be threatening as a result of their accumulation cannot, at times, even be acknowledged. *Citizen* insists that minoritarian affects accumulate because they begin as invisible or illegible feelings, inchoate and unfelt because the situations in which they are first provoked admit no response or rebuttal. (Later, when they manifest more visibly, they will be maligned as immature or "insane, crass, crazy."[18]) In order to make the first instances of such feelings legible, to account for the role that a certain history of accumulation will play in their manifestation, Rankine represents disruptions that take place within ordinary experiences as significant events, which they have become precisely because they permit no resolution or response. As such, the poems are always already untimely—they represent something that will only be acknowledged later, at which point they will return with all the affective force the circumstances of their occurrence tried to contain.

A series of four poems in the first section of *Citizen* introduces the logic of accumulation. The first shows that feelings accumulate because, in order to manage them in places where they are not welcome, they must be suppressed. The poem's speaker weathers a racist infraction: "he tells you his dean is making him hire a person of color when there are so many great writers out there."[19] She mutes any response to it and considers the impact of previous infractions on the present moment:

As usual you drive straight through the moment with the expected backing
off of what was previously said. It is not only that confrontation is headache-
producing; it is also that you have a destination that doesn't include acting like
this moment isn't inhabitable, hasn't happened before, and the before isn't part
of the now as the night darkens and the time shortens between where we are and
where we are going.[20]

The four negatives in the poem's last sentence dramatize the labyrinthine
considerations that the speaker must face in "the now" that immediately follows
an infraction. The first three—doesn't, isn't, hasn't—represent the disappointment
of anticipating a place in which the only acceptable response is unfortunately
familiar. Once again, at this destination, the speaker will have to acknowledge
that such infractions are, in fact, inhabitable, that they can be tolerated precisely
because so many destinations foreclose any other response. In fact, so many
destinations of this sort exist that to react in any other way—to acknowledge
that something about the experience is uncontainable—would feel inauthentic,
like "acting." The worst part of this situation is that any connection with similar
events in the past, something that might make them intelligible, must also be
suppressed: they remain part of a "before" that "isn't part of the now."

As the following poems in the series demonstrate, time reserves the right
to inflame the effect of trauma. Rather than clear the mind or divert it, as time
progresses, the space that traumatic infractions fill only increases. The next poem
begins "when you arrive in your driveway," perhaps just after returning from
the night's destination, perhaps on an entirely different occasion. "You fear the
night is being locked in and coded on a cellular level and want time to function
as a power wash."[21] The poem explains, however, that the attempt to avoid the
accumulation of affects in the face of their necessary suppression, a "trying to
dodge the buildup of erasure," is rarely successful. In fact, "a medical term—John
Henryism" exists to describe its failure, the physiological drain reserved "for
people exposed to stresses stemming from racism."[22] The poem ends without
dispelling this fear or affirming the speaker's hope that "sitting in silence" will
help her avoid these physiological effects. Instead of wrapping up, the poem
acknowledges a diagnosis that awaits in the future. Despite the speaker's "want,"
the poem ends with a "hope," an acknowledgment that the effects of the action
taken in the poem, of "sitting in silence," can only be measured in a future that it
is momentarily impossible to envision.[23] The poem aims to find the kind of time
in which something besides threat and decay could result. *Citizen* asks whether
poems are containers for that kind of time, recognizes that they are not, and
devotes itself to exploring the possibilities that remain in the midst of this failure.

The third and fourth poems of the series end abruptly, leaving the infractions they describe unresolved. In the first, an airline passenger cannot respond to a racial infraction because she must now share a row with the woman who committed it. In the second, an infraction happens at the beginning of lunch; the poem ends when "the salads arrive."[24] In these situations, no possibility of response is permitted, but neither is any explanation of that impossibility provided. By now, this impossibility has become familiar. The poems' endings, which are hardly conclusions, suggest that the poems cannot contain the situations they describe. Their time extends far beyond the space and time of the poems that record them. And as such, they form part of the "before" to which other, later events will bear a striking similarity, even when it cannot be acknowledged.

The final poem of the series also reveals the role that disruptions of poetic self-containment play in Rankine's poetics of affective accumulation. Barbara Johnson defines intertextuality as "the multitude of ways a text has of not being self-contained," and Rankine adds that "the entrance of the black body works like that in the American landscape."[25] In her poems, black bodies are subjected to disruption precisely because they are already identified with or accused of disruption. "[A woman you do not know]" concerns the failure of the speaker's alma mater to admit a legacy student, the son of the woman with whom the speaker is eating lunch. Because the student's generational ties to the university should give him pride of place there, the woman scorns programs she calls "affirmative action or minority something."[26] In claiming prior historical rights to educational institutions, the interlocutor suggests that minority bodies are interlopers, and violators not only of her own desires ("She wanted her son to go there"), but of the proper regulations of the institutions themselves. The poem reveals that several disruptions precede the black body's supposedly disruptive "entrance." The interlocutor's remark is the actual disruption, the one that introduces and defines the black body as disruptive. Here, her remark disrupts the situation in which the speaker finds herself, having lunch with a stranger for reasons the speaker doesn't know: "This exchange, in effect, ends your lunch. The salads arrive."[27] Beyond the disruption of the lunch, the poem acknowledges the disruption of the speaker's ability to align internal experience and external circumstances. The lunch will continue despite its "effective" end, just as the feelings provoked by the disruptions will continue beyond the words of the poem, which also ends on the word "arrive." In the temporality of such disruptive infractions, the possibility for further relationships and additional poetic language is foreclosed without, however, closing the event within which they have been presented.[28] As such, the poem allows affective experiences to be signaled but not discussed, to be both salient and silent.

By allowing poems to close without closing off the impact of the events they describe, *Citizen* represents the continuity of affective experience that underlies and links discrete events. As Lauren Berlant reveals, "the director's cut of *Citizen*" featured a forward slash line at the end of each poem, enjambing it to the next, thus knitting the volume's short prose poems, longer lyrics, and "scripts" for multimedia production into a single lyric.[29] The volume's claims to continuity prevent moments of melancholy and rage from being read apart from the ongoing plots that contributed to them and the imagined futures to which they contribute and by which they are conditioned. On the other hand, the individual poems' failures to close are a reminder that the discontinuity, the inability of each experience to be washed away, moved on from, or separated out (and *Citizen* abounds with calls from friends to do just these impossible things, to "move forward" and "let it go")[30] is what bleeds into the next poem, leaving not only a residue but a continuing threat. If *Citizen* moves to make a certain aspect of black feeling legible, it does so in order to strategize about the affective risks of the visibility that attend any such project and, finally, about what may remain intractably illegible.

Response and rebuttal: You, yes, and

Citizen departs from lyric conventions of apostrophe in order to represent the difficulty and the beauty that the addressees of racist infractions experience and create when they can, if sometimes only minimally, respond. That is, *Citizen* presents its poetic speakers as primarily responders, already addressed by trauma-inducing speech and yet determined, by means of the poem, to continue speaking on their own terms when speech is possible. The book builds on an ontology that figures blackness as a condition of being, as Glissant believed, "born into the world,"[31] and as such a state of being always engaged in response and resistance. If Fred Moten writes, "The history of blackness is testament to the fact that objects can and do resist"[32] Rankine's addendum is that objects resist by responding lyrically, and that they do so even though it's in the ways response can be stymied that some of the most pernicious effects of racism can be shown. As a result of this form of resistance, one surprising precursor to the poems in *Citizen* is Sir Walter Ralegh's "The Nymph's Reply to the Shepherd," where a feminine response to the aggressive seduction of a masculine speaker reestablishes the poem as a site of defense and poetic address as a technique suited to rebuttal, a speech that emerges not only out of silence but in response to address.[33] The speaker of Ralegh's poem responds to the masculine addressor with a litany of the reasons she cannot return his love, but the most chilling of these refers to the story of Philomela:

> Time drives the flocks from field to fold,
> When Rivers rage and Rocks grow cold,
> And *Philomel* becometh dumb,
> The rest complains of cares to come.

The fact that the power of speech has, in previous instances, been violently eliminated fuels this speaker's response, which consists of a reminder that past aggression imprints itself on the possibility of relationships to be forged in the present. At a moment when response in the present is demanded by the pattern of the past, Rankine's personae also turn back to the histories that contextualize the content of their speech, referring consistently to the fact that because what happens happens "usually," it is conditioned by both the past and the future.[34]

The pronoun "you" establishes a unique phrase-universe in *Citizen*.[35] In many poems, an unnamed speaker addresses someone and narrates this person's experience of a race-related infraction, as in, once again, "A woman you do not know wants to join you for lunch."[36] While the addressor takes responsibility for narration, within the renarration the addressee sometimes becomes an addressor too, and does so in order to respond to the infraction with words or thoughts of her own. As such, the pronoun creates the minimal space in which speech can emanate from a position of response. "You," which is the pronoun of accusation and infraction, here becomes, against all odds, a site of reparation. If at times Rankine uses the pronoun to represent the violence that makes the addressee's response necessary, here it serves as a reminder that benevolent address exists.[37]

Most often, however, to be in the place of address is to be vulnerable. To return to the beginning of *Citizen*'s sixth poem, the speaker is an addressee, a "you," before any other words have been spoken:

> You are in the dark, in the car, watching the black-tarred street being swallowed by speed; he tells you his dean is making him hire a person of color when there are so many great writers out there.[38]

The poem is preoccupied with the fact that the poem's addressee, labeled "you," must spend time formulating a response, not to the poem's speaker but to a speaker who has come from outside the poem to disrupt the intimate space established in its opening words. The poem's second paragraph begins this response, as the poem's speaker presents the addressee's thinking in the present tense: "You think maybe this is an experiment and you are being tested."[39] The ability to respond outwardly—even with the familiar "what did you say?"—is not immediately available to the poem's addressee. By the poem's third paragraph, though, the "you" has begun a response, which, even though it is internal, sets in motion a chain of responses that become more outwardly focused in the course of the volume.[40] For now, it's an unvoiced address: "Why do you feel comfortable saying this to me?" By the end of the poem, the pronoun "you" has become, unpredictably, a "we," as the fact of the response permits a new, if still crisis-inflected, conjunction of subjects: "the night darkens and the time shortens between where we are now and where we are going."[41] Later in the collection, addressees will be able to respond more vehemently, and the poems will reflect on this new availability.

Rankine's poetics of response is a response-and-then-call in which the call announces an ongoing threat, which in this poem is the fact that no further response can yet be spoken during the time of the poem: "You have a destination that doesn't include acting like this moment isn't inhabitable, hasn't happened before, and the before isn't part of the now."[42] For Rankine, the first duty of a poetics of response is a recognition that its power to address is limited by the situations that necessitated response in the first place. The structures that demand response often leave no space for it; the energy of the speaker must be devoted, then, to finding the remaining options: "gathering energy has become its own task."[43]

Nevertheless, Rankine's poems show how infractions can be, again in Berlant's words, "opening[s] to all sorts of consequences" rather than a link in a "chain reaction."[44] In so doing, they demonstrate one way in which the book works against the kind of logic it posits as most harmful, a logic by which everyday trauma is illegible both in its daily iterations and in its eventual explosiveness. *Citizen* repeats the phrase, "yes, and" in situations that present no such alternative or opening.

In the opening pages of *Citizen*, a speaker recalls a conversation with a friend "comparing the merits of sentences constructed implicitly with 'yes, and' rather than 'yes, but.'"[45] She goes on:

> You and your friend decided that "yes, and" attested to a life with no turn-off, no alternative routes: you pull yourself to standing, soon enough the blouse is rinsed, it's another week, the blouse is beneath your sweater, against your skin, and you smell good.[46]

Individual poems, like the next one in *Citizen*, come to rely on the phrase "yes, and": "The trees, their bark, their leaves, even the dead ones, are more vibrant wet. Yes, and it's raining."[47] Nevertheless, the book's work of accumulation situates *Citizen* within the logic of "yes, but." This is the logic of response and rebuttal that, even when it can only acknowledge that it has been smothered, never repeats the received wisdom, ignorance, small-mindedness, and fear of the initial address, but transforms it and "assumes an original form."[48] Using their status as addressees to represent the experience of everyday trauma and its potential reparation in the intimate speech act of renarration, the voices populating *Citizen* speak to the inevitable risks and possible rewards of living on in a present characterized equally as foreclosed and radically open to "alternative routes" of the kind Berlant suggests in *Cruel Optimism*:

> The protagonists are ... people who live on in unstable and shattered ordinaries and who are building a new nervous system around them no longer based on foreclosure but in the optimism of learning from one's precarity. People develop worlds for their new intuitions, habits of ordinariness, and genres of affect management in recognition of the unfinished business of the historical moment they are living on in, where they live the rhythm of the habit called personality that can never quite settle into a shape.[49]

Despite the implicit affinity I have suggested between this vision of uncruel optimism and *Citizen*, Rankine is explicitly ambivalent about affirming that lives touched by racism can be accounted for by this logic of "yes, but." Within individual poems, uncontainable affects manifest as regulators of time, even as, in the poems, affect's subordination to time drives the poems' incompleteness. In the pages that follow, I trace the ways *Citizen* wrestles with this vision.

On the one hand, a show of resilience in the face of continued exposure to racist infractions may merely postpone the moment when a life is revealed to be "a life with no turnoffs."[50] The possibility that this is the case imbues every moment of black life in *Citizen*, where a constant struggle with the risks of visibility, recognition, and legibility plays out in the midst of repeated and continued exposure to infractions. How can any optimism nurtured by this affective environment not be cruel?

On the other hand, *Citizen* is interested, as is Berlant, in building "a new nervous system," and it does so by relying on poetic time to represent uncontainable or illegible affects. *Citizen* extends the time of everyday trauma both backward and forward, linking events that *will* contribute to a future situation to those that respond explosively to events buried in the past. By so doing, Rankine bears witness not only to the almost intolerable rage that prefigures a "rebuttal," but also to the formations of new families, new modes for interrupting everyday life, and new literary genres that exist between the restrictions of "yes, and" and the optimism of "yes, but."

Returning to "[A man knocked over her son]" reveals an example of the quick transformation of rage into something new. The words "yes, and" figure prominently in the content of the poem, which concerns etiquette. The speaker has just recounted that a white man's failure to apologize for his actions has led another woman to respond:

> He's okay, but the son of a bitch kept walking … She says she grabbed the stranger's arm and told him to apologize: I told him to look at the boy and apologize. *Yes, and* you want it to stop, you want the child pushed to the ground to be seen.[51]

By switching from the "I" who was narrating the story to *Citizen*'s more common "you," the poem signals the resumption, in the present tense, of a familiar drama. If the woman's response in the poem is to speak, to demand an apology, the poem's speaker addresses the woman with "Yes, and" in order to acknowledge the fear that infractions require their objects to live "a life with no turnoffs." In fact, as the poem's own ongoing reveals, it's only as a result of this angry response, the grabbing of the stranger's arm, that something new can emerge in the poem's final paragraph: "The beautiful thing is that a group of men began to stand behind me like a fleet of bodyguards, she says, like newly found uncles and brothers."[52] The poem awaits the emergence of the beautiful from a specific form of response, even as the response provokes the speaker's doubts and fears. The closing lines of the poem link a *performance* of "yes, but"—a means of resisting the logic of "no turnoffs"—to the speaker's "yes, and," and in so doing they make the poem's final word an assertion of the possibility of escaping deterministic and co-opted responses. The fact that the end of the poem recounts a moment in which something merely begins—"the men began to stand behind me"— suggests that the poem's incompleteness is necessary for its rebuttal to the logic of "yes, and." The continued use of the present tense, as in the reminder that "she says" this story that is itself now in the past, reiterates that what is still happening never recedes from view, even when what has happened is traumatic. The tension that remains at the end of the poem is, on the one hand, an acknowledgment that response opens onto the risk of additional threat, violence, and undoing, and, on the other, a way of recognizing what else—a certain kind of beauty—is also possible. Standing against lyric self-containment may be a way of indicating how what cannot be contained can be, sometimes, an opening onto positive affect. It's this possibility that my next section explores.

Rage as response: Serena Williams and Zinedine Zidane

Rankine draws her two chief examples of the kind of anger that culminates in "explosive behavior" from the world of sports. The first, an essay that makes up section II of *Citizen*, concerns the tennis star Serena Williams, and chronicles decisive moments in a career of "frustrations" and "disappointments" owing to both on-court and off-court infractions. From umpires and interviewers to other players, what Williams weathers drains or diminishes what Rankine calls her "resilience," the ability, often attributed to her by commentators, to carry on through setbacks without drawing attention to them. This "daily diminishment," Rankine explains, "is a low flame, a constant drip"[53] and contributes to a reserve of memory held within a body that eventually cannot contain its history. The price of what Rankine calls "black excellence,"[54] especially when it is played out "against a sharp white background,"[55] is revealed to be a susceptibility to racist infractions compounded by the fact that these dramas play out in public, where they can be denounced more quickly as "immature and classless."[56] Another cost of the accumulation of everyday anger is a susceptibility to moments of "explosive" rage. The poem-essay on Serena Williams interrogates the history that precedes moments of explosive rage, and the injuries to the self that result from this expression of anger.

For Williams, the decisive moment in the expression of anger came in 2009. Williams reacted to a decisive foot fault call with an expletive-laced threat that Rankine describes, at first, as "crazy" and "offensive."[57] The essay's intervention, however, is to insist that Williams is not reacting to the call, or not to this call only. Rather, she responds to a history of calls that includes a 2004 US Open match in which umpire Mariana Alves called a series of Williams's serves out. At the end of the match, Williams "was able to hold it together" but asked, "Shall I go on?"[58] By recognizing the risk that inheres in continuing to go forward, Williams seems to foresee the 2009 incident in which she would not hold everything together, but would instead scream, "I swear to God I'm fucking going to take this fucking ball and shove it down your fucking throat, you hear that? I swear to God!" A significant portion of the pain that characterizes the early incident is the knowledge that its conclusion is deferred and, as a result, intensified.

Before Rankine recounts the punishment meted out to Williams for this "moment of manumission," she remarks that, for a certain viewer, "it is difficult not to applaud [Williams] for reacting immediately to being thrown against a sharp white background."[59] Reading Williams's words against the long history of Williams's career permits this applause: "all the injustice she has played through all the years of her illustrious career flashes before her and she decides finally to respond to all of it with a string of invectives."[60] The words Williams says in 2009 are spoken "belatedly"[61] when seen alongside the instances of racist infractions that she has faced without reacting over the years. And the expression of rage is a way of making a call, like the ones that have been made against Williams. It is a way of saying that "randomly the rules everyone else gets to play by no longer apply to you."[62] Rage is made legible in *Citizen* because it can be recognized in its expression or metabolism as a decisive *response* to a history that challenges chronological temporality by returning, again and again, with increasing affective force, to a body that can no longer contain it. It is more than legible, and even laudable, if it points up the way that racism creates a different set of rules for one group of people:

> In any case, it is difficult not to think that if Serena lost context by abandoning all rules of civility, it could be because her body, trapped in a racial imaginary, trapped in disbelief—code for being black in America—is being governed not by the tennis match she is participating in but by a collapsed relationship that had promised to play by the rules.[63]

In this way, explosive rage is a way of circumventing the trap of racism, of finding a way to overcome the containment it imposes in favor of an uncontained, if unsanctioned relationship to the "rules everyone else gets to play by."

Rage is not legible to everyone who witnesses it, however. Williams was punished severely for her reaction: she suffered a point penalty which cost her the match, a severe fine, and a long probation. Even worse, "witnessing the expression of this more ordinary and daily anger might make the witness believe that a person is 'insane,'"[64] and Williams was regarded as "insane, crass, crazy" for her behavior in this and other situations. The affective injuries to which rage exposes those who express it are severe. Rage exposes them to extreme disappointment, "in the sense that no amount of visibility will alter the ways in which one is perceived," and to "loneliness."[65] Much like Silvan Tomkins's "total affect shame bind," exposure to anger leaves few routes open that do not lead to yet more anger or to the conversion of anger into other negative affects like mourning. Even the kind of "good behavior" associated with resilience may actually be a sign of dissociation. In Williams's case, they "support [her] claim that she has had to split herself off from herself and create different personae."[66] Rage, itself a compound, compounds the affective difficulties those who express it face. This poem-essay functions as an explosion in the midst of *Citizen*. After a series of poems exploring infractions to which the speaker cannot respond, the paragraphs of the essay explore the explosive response of Serena Williams as if to both promise and infinitely defer a similar explosion at the heart of the book.

The second text Rankine uses to explore responses of explosive rage is a collage text, called a "situation script," on the subject of Zinedine Zidane's "coup de foudre" in the 2006 World Cup final. The form of the poem is unique. "Black-Blanc-Beur" splices strips of images between quotations from a canon of authors that includes James Baldwin, Frantz Fanon, Frederick Douglass, and Maurice Blanchot. Within these texts, which consider both the buildup of and explosive response to racism, Rankine repeats the insults hurled at Zidane during the World Cup final. The images, in sets of six, feature a sequence of still frames that record the seconds prior to Zidane's head-butt of Italian player Marco Materazzi. The poem reads this action as a decisive "response" to racist insults, and it finds beauty to be one possible terminus for the temporality of the affective structure of ordinary trauma.

Lauren Berlant shows that the defining structure of everyday trauma is the "situation"—"a state of things in which something that will perhaps matter is unfolding amid the usual activity of life."[67] Rankine's "scripts for situation video," completed in collaboration with John Lucas, depict racist situations that "will perhaps matter" because they are endlessly repeated. "Stop-and-Frisk," for example, punctuates individual accounts of racial profiling with variations on the sentences, "there is only one guy who is always the guy fitting the description … you are not that guy."[68] By representing several men as "that guy," the poem both performs the logic of racial profiling, in which every black man can "fit the description," and protests against it. It shows how this logic, which continually fails to identify its suspects, defines the experience of an entire demographic, all of whose members are thus linked.

Like the essay on Serena Williams, "Black-Blanc-Beur" completes the temporal logic of poems from the opening sections of *Citizen*. Those poems recorded the micro-aggressions and everyday traumas that contribute to later responses of explosive rage, while here a moment of "explosive rage" fulfills the earlier poems' promise that affective accumulation cannot be contained. Rather than the earlier poems' abrupt endings, the scripts for situation video slow down poetic time to show that culminating events have a lineage that begins in such micro-aggressions. "Black-Blanc-Beur" tracks the still frames of the situation in eight six-frame segments that begin at the moment when Materazzi insults Zidane. By proceeding slowly, interrupted by a collage of quotations, the time of the poem is an ongoing but delimited moment in which a "situation" unfolds. Zidane's own words, printed in bold, show that this moment takes place in the time of ritual, a habit called upon for sustenance in the midst of continual insults: "Every day I think about where I came from and I am still proud to be who I am."[69] Here, quite apart from his explosive rebuttal, Zidane models a response to infractions that is effective because it can, in its daily repetition, keep pace with their multiplicity and accumulation.

Rankine allows us to read Zidane's rebuttal not merely as explosive but as considered, a dramatic response to a long affective history. The poem gives Zidane's much-maligned (and severely punished) response duration by punctuating each set of images with quotations that place Zidane in canon of writers, thinkers, and activists. Situating Zidane's "original response" in this context demonstrates the potential for literary forms to represent otherwise illegible moments of black affective life. The closing quotation in the script raises Zidane's response to an even higher level. Drawn from James Baldwin's "The Fire Next Time," the final words read: "This endless struggle to achieve and reveal and confirm a human identity, human authority, contains, for all its horror, something very beautiful."[70] The quotation does not claim that aesthetic reparations for racist violence are sufficient, but it acknowledges that beauty is one potential outcome, though continued exposure to risk is another, of going on in the present.

Everyday traumatic time

As previous chapters have explored, temporal manipulations like Rankine's are a hallmark of the genre of lyric. Even more primarily, lyric convention assumes that an absent addressee remains sufficiently present, or will once again be sufficiently present, to the scene of address in order to respond (and assent) to its addresses. The silence out of which the poetic voice speaks and into which it recedes depends on the illusion that time only progresses within the space of lyric and that it does so according to the rules—metrical or otherwise—that the poem itself regulates. In fact, it is the poem's imposition of its own nonchronological time that accounts for its brevity and constitutes its essential intervention: one thing a poem can do, after all, is mark an alternative to time.

The opening line of Shakespeare's Sonnet 73, for example, refers to a "time of year" outside of the poem but does so in order to establish the speaker of the poem as the reliable container of time: "That time of year thou mayst in me behold." As the poem proceeds, its present tense contrasts first what has already passed and then what is about to come. From phrases such as "where late the sweet birds sang" and "after sunset," in which the poem's present faces toward the past, the sonnet turns, in its closing couplet, to a present that is oriented toward an ominous future: "This thou perceivest, which makes thy love more strong,/To love that well which thou must leave ere long." The poem achieves closure by placing the moment of "leaving," which the entire poem has anticipated, in its final words. It achieves its aim—a plea for the lover to love him "well" and even "more strong"—by performing the passage within a poetic present from a vibrant past to a fatal near future. Shakespeare's poem shows how, traditionally, lyric poems command—open and then close—their own self-contained temporalities.

Because the poems in *Citizen* deliberately open with references to the passage of time but conclude before the situations—and the affects they have provoked—are complete, they call out to the time that passes between them. These poems respond to events that happen within chronological time but cannot, despite their alternative temporality, contain the fact that additional events happen. If a poem aims to inhabit a singular time, Rankine's poems are singular for admitting that the time of everyday trauma is iterable. When yet another event occurs, traumatic time returns, as do, in *Citizen*, the poetic conventions by which it had been represented. As a result, Rankine's poems emphasize that the poem's "now of writing" bears a strange relationship to chronological time: it both responds to what happens in time and suggests that traumatic time accompanies its seemingly relentless progress.

The temporality at work in Rankine's poems both resembles and differs subtly from the temporal distortions most often associated with trauma theory. Rankine's poems explore a traumatic time that differs subtly from the time of "unclaimed experience." Pushing back against a model of trauma in which "trauma detaches the subject from the historical present, sentencing its subjects to a terrifying suffusion of the past," Berlant argues that "trauma, after all, does not make experiencing the historical present impossible but possible."[71] For both Rankine and Berlant, the subject can claim the experience of "everyday trauma" as it happens *and* be flooded or overwhelmed by it later.[72] Thus, it may be in the otherwise unrecognized categories of anticipation, dread, or uncertainty about the aftereffects of this event that a significant portion of the injury that "everyday trauma" can inflict becomes apparent. Rankine's poems explore this paradox—of a trauma that is both experienced *and* able to return—by responding (or depicting the impossibility of response) during the experience of trauma and leaving room for the accumulation of affects that cannot be contained there.[73]

Feeling's injury

It is fitting to close this chapter, and this book, by turning away from chronology and toward James Baldwin, one of Rankine's key interlocutors and theorists of everyday trauma *avant la lettre*. Baldwin's words, as we have seen, close "Black-Blanc-Beur," but his presence can be felt throughout the book, which explores, as Baldwin had done, affective injuries that are not just untimely but potentially injurious in their untimeliness. James Baldwin's essay "Notes of a Native Son," from which the closing words of "Black-Blanc-Beur" are drawn, suggests that the time of injuries related to recurring incidents of racism includes the time of latency, the period between an instance of racial trauma and its return, either to mind, in memory, or to the body in an another, similar experience. Rankine draws on Baldwin's essay in order to highlight both the continued threat and the continued potential for happiness with which surviving racial trauma is imbued. In this space of survival, one waits for happiness at the cost of sustaining potentially injurious feelings.

"Notes of a Native Son," like *Citizen*, concerns hatred and mourning. Every black person, Baldwin writes, is susceptible to a self-damaging hatred as a result of the power, complacency, and "gratuitous humiliation" he experiences at the hands of whites.[74] Baldwin acknowledges that in the face of this potentially self-destroying hatred, and in order to move beyond it, one must make "perpetual qualifications."[75] The work of adjustment, however, is not without its own dangers. Paradoxically, it is in continuously moving on (*Citizen* will refer to this work as "letting it go"),[76] going beyond hatred, and in metabolizing it that one exposes oneself to its effects, accumulations, aftereffects, and residual injuries. Furthermore, it is the illegibility of this susceptibility and of what it can lead to—the impossibility for others to read rage as an accretion or accumulation, and instead to condemn it as childishness or the failure of discipline—that constitutes an additional injury.[77]

As in Rankine's poems, the progression in Baldwin from composure to rage is shown to be the result of continued exposure to infractions over multiple episodes rather than the result of a single episode. Baldwin prefaces the scene he will describe by explaining that he "contracted" the affective consequences of racism while living, for the first time, in close proximity to Southerners.[78] There, as a result of segregated lunch counters, he "contracted some dread, chronic disease, the unfailing symptom of which is a kind of blind fever, a pounding in the skull and fire in the bowels."[79] The effect of this fever is to make him more susceptible to acting on the hatred he now carries. One night, this hatred comes to a head.

When Baldwin is first told, in the course of a night, "we don't serve Negroes here," he writes that "this reply failed to discompose me."[80] After the initial encounter, however, Baldwin leaves the restaurant and recalls that "something happened to me which had the force of an optical illusion, or a nightmare."[81] Surrounded by whites on the street, he was overcome by a desire to "crush these white faces which were crushing me."[82] In the next restaurant, he responds to the same boilerplate words, "we don't serve Negroes here," very differently, by throwing a mug of water at the offending waitress. Once he narrowly escapes the situation, Baldwin recounts being astounded by the force and threat of his own hatred, which is so strong that "I had been ready to commit murder."[83] It is Baldwin's conclusion that the real threat, the most lethal threat, is from his own feelings: "my life, my *real* life, was in danger, and not from anything other people might do but from the hatred I carried in my own heart."[84] The susceptibility to hatred, which grows during a period of latency and exposes the impossibility of fully experiencing everyday trauma, stands as one of everyday trauma's greatest threats.

More specifically, the relationship between black and white Americans powers the inner workings of a mitigated hatred that damages its bearer far worse than its objects. The relationship "prohibits anything as uncomplicated and satisfactory as pure hatred" such that "In order to really hate white people, one has to blot out so much of the mind—and the heart—that this hatred itself becomes an exhausting and self-destructive pose."[85] Despite this recognition, "love" does not "come easily."[86] Black Americans are caught in a bind created by a prohibition of pure hatred and of love. The affective labor left for Baldwin to do is unsupported and unrecognized by the environment in which it must be sustained. As he puts it later in the essay, "One is absolutely forced to make perpetual qualifications and one's own reactions are always canceling each other out."[87] The fact that these affects persist commits the one who carries them to a labor for which there is no compensation.

Baldwin's essay closes by recognizing, again, the toll on the individual's feelings that the responsibility to remain free of hatred demands. Upon realizing that, after the death of his father, whose own life had been marred by bitterness and hatred, "it now had been laid to my charge to keep my own heart free of hatred and despair," Baldwin adds: "this intimation made my heart heavy."[88] Baldwin realizes that the greatest threat is posed by the transmission of his father's bitterness to him: "it frightened me … to see how powerful and overflowing this bitterness could be and to realize that this bitterness now was mine … the bitterness which had helped to kill my father could also kill me."[89] By tracking the movement from rage to melancholy, Baldwin shows that the pathways available to the person who experiences rage are often limited to continually accumulating rage and rage turned inward in depressive melancholy. Like Baldwin, Rankine explores the way that everyday trauma and its associated affects drastically limit the range of affective experiences available to those who must survive it. *Citizen*'s closing sections explore the physical and legal limitations imposed on black bodies as a result of racial profiling, police violence, and discrimination; its opening sections highlight the less visible impact of racial infractions on the mind and heart.

Conclusion

Everyday trauma enforces a continuous exposure to the violence of one's feelings as they develop in response to the ongoing effects of one's prior experiences of feeling. Yes, but the struggle to go on manages to use its constitutive duration, its endurance, to do something traditional poems cannot—to move beyond poetic containers by way of response in order to make "something very beautiful." Ann Cvetkovich argues that thinking feeling's relationship to citizenship may lead outside definitions of the citizen based primarily in the rational person subjected to state sovereignty.[90] *Citizen* redefines the word and links it to a process, rather than a single experience, of feeling. According to Cathy Caruth, "trauma may lead … to the encounter with another, through the very possibility and surprise of listening to another's wound."[91] Rankine creates the conditions for this sort of encounter, but emphasizes that engaging in this act is risky. The poems of *Citizen* enter the "precarious public sphere" to emphasize that black affective citizenship is an act of resistance, one founded on surviving, again and again, both the injury of everyday trauma and the hope of happiness that it fails to contain.[92]

No reader can successfully hold *Citizen*, just as no single subject anchors these poems' explorations of affects that accumulate both individually and collectively. The logic of affective accumulation works to historicize and contextualize affects to which some readers are symptomatically blind, but it also demonstrates the multiple routes affects can take as they are transmitted to others. While some readers react to *Citizen* with rage of their own, many respond to its collective rage with a desire to form new communities around the book itself. Its popularity among college summer reading programs, book clubs, and in classrooms (my own included) bespeaks its timeliness, which is all the more surprising because the book remains unequivocally committed to what is untimely, namely the emergence of something new from a past that only some can regard as past at all. Like Wallace Stevens's "Planet on the Table," *Citizen* confronts the reader with the facts that necessitated its making; unlike its predecessor, Rankine's planet welcomes the permeability of its atmosphere and invites readers to partake of its stunning failures to hold.

Notes

Introduction

1   Reading that relies too heavily on the emotions bears a close relationship to the pathetic fallacy, the figure applied, most often pejoratively, to writing that attributes emotions and feelings to unfeeling objects. In John Ruskin's identification of the trope, he notes, however, that "the temperament which admits the pathetic fallacy … is a more or less noble state, according to the force of the emotion which has induced it." He goes on to note that even poets of the "first" order are susceptible to the unbalanced response characteristic of the pathetic fallacy because "there are always some subjects which ought to throw him off his balance; some, by which his poor human capacity of thought should be conquered, and brought into the inaccurate and vague state of perception" (John Ruskin, *Modern Painters* (New York: Wiley & Halstead, 1857–1860), *HathiTrust Digital Library*, April 4, 2012, 151).

2   An extreme version of this latter pole would invoke Ruth Leys, who suggests that any affective turn is mistaken in thinking that literature or other works of art provoke meaningful feelings and not simply interpretable meanings. "The fact that a novel or painting makes me feel or think a certain way may be a significant aspect of my response to the work, but, simply as my response, it has no standing as an interpretation of it" (Ruth Leys, "The Turn to Affect: A Critique," *Critical Inquiry* 37.3 (2011): 451n31).

3   In recent literary studies, both Jonathan Flatley and Charles Altieri have provided extensive glosses of the concepts and their use, and each adds that the multiplicity of definitions makes their attention to detail both necessary and complex. Flatley, who relies mostly on Tomkins and holds Freud accountable as a theorist who "never really developed a coherent account of the affects," distinguishes between emotion and affect by emphasizing the "relational" quality of the latter and the "expressive" quality of the former: "Where emotion suggests something that happens inside and tends toward outward expression, affect indicates something relational and transformative. One has emotions; one is affected *by* people or things" (Jonathan Flatley, *Affective Mapping: Melancholy and the Politics of Modernism* (Cambridge, MA: Harvard University Press, 2008), 12).

Altieri's account, which depends mostly on a critique of cognitivism that derives from philosophical psychology and takes its cues from William James, uses "affect" as its "umbrella term" to describe "the entire range of states that are bounded on one side by pure sensation and on the other by thoughts that have no visible or tangible impact on our bodies. Affects are immediate modes of sensual responsiveness to the world characterized by an accompanying imaginative dimension" (Charles Altieri, *The Particulars of Rapture* (Ithaca, NY: Cornell University Press, 2003), 2). While Flatley lists four terms, adding mood and structure of feeling to affect and emotion, Altieri calls on feelings, moods, emotions, and passions to describe variations of affects.

4   According to this definition, in which affects refer to the overwhelming of self that we often accord to the sublime, it is impossible to simply list "the affects," though some theorists working in a slightly different tradition (notably Tomkins) aim to do so. Nevertheless, anxiety is, for my study, the affect par excellence inasmuch as Winnicott defines it as experience of which its sufferer is unaware: "It seems to me that the word 'anxious' is applicable when an individual is in the grips of physical experience (be it excitement, anger, fear, or anything else) which he can neither avoid nor understand; that is to say, he is unaware of the greater proportion of the reason for what is happening" (D.W. Winnicott, "Birth Memories, Birth Trauma, and Anxiety," *Through Paediatrics to Psychoanalysis* (London: Karnac, 1984), 181).

5   In contrast to Altieri, who uses "affect" as an umbrella term to collect the denotations of feeling, mood, emotion, and passion (Altieri, *The Particulars of Rapture*, 2).

6   Jahan Ramazani, *A Transnational Poetics* (Chicago: University of Chicago Press, 2009).

7   "Unpleasure is always the expression of a higher degree of tension" (Sigmund Freud, "On Narcissism," in *The Standard Edition of the Complete Psychological Works of Sigmund Freud*, Vol. XIV (London: Hogarth Press, 1953, Web. *PEP Archive* www.pep-web.org), 85) and "unpleasurable feelings are connected with an increase and pleasurable feelings with a decrease of stimulus" (Sigmund Freud, "Instincts and Their Vicissitudes," SE XIV, 120–121). Freud would, in *Beyond the Pleasure Principle*, substantially revise the theory of drives that obtains in both of these essays. It is important to note, however, that he had already recognized that some component instincts of sexual instinct involve a heightening of tension in the service of pleasure, as best exemplified by the heightening of tension that allows for the pleasure of sexual climax. If, in *Beyond the Pleasure Principle*, Freud argues that heightening of tension serves the life instincts, it is still the case that this heightening is most often experienced in its immediacy as unpleasurable. Freud, "On Narcissism," 67–102; Freud, "Instincts and Their Vicissitudes," 109–140; Sigmund Freud, *Beyond the Pleasure Principle*, SE XVIII, 1–64.

8   Recent literary criticism has attended, in mostly separate accounts, to both positive and negative affects. Sianne Ngai's *Ugly Feelings* stands as a significant exception to the rule of poetry's absence in studies that incline toward affect. However, some of her most pointed comments on US poetry, which reference Bruce Andrews' *I Don't Have Any Paper So Shut Up*, identify a poetics of disgust that challenges the

"flatness or ongoingness" of most of the "ugly feelings" taken up in the rest of the book and signals that a genealogy of the unspeakably intense affects still needs to be formulated (Sianne Ngai, *Ugly Feelings* (Cambridge, MA: Harvard University Press, 2007)).

My conclusion signals a movement in the direction of neutral affects, the lack of affect, and, finally, the positive affects in contemporary poetry. Despite the different registers of our chosen affects, this project shares a methodological inheritance with Michael Snediker's *Queer Optimism*. Snediker turns to a Winnicottian conceptual vocabulary as part of a re-evaluation of what he characterizes as the prevailing melancholy of queer theory and privileges poems as "striking ... experiments in the very forms of affect and personhood I seek to rescue from short shrift" (Michael Snediker, *Queer Optimism* (Minneapolis, MN: University of Minnesota Press, 2007), 31).

9   D.W. Winnicott, "String: A Technique of Communication," in *The Maturational Processes and the Facilitating Environment* (London: Hogarth, 1965), 153–157.

10 Andre Green, *The Fabric of Affect in the Psychoanalytic Discourse*, Trans. Alan Sheridan (New York: Routledge, 1999), 15.

11 Sigmund Freud, *Inhibitions, Symptoms, and Anxiety* SE XX 133; Jean Laplanche and J.B. Pontalis, *The Language of Psychoanalysis*, Trans. Donald Nicholson-Smith (London: Hogarth Press, 1973), 14.

12 Recent books by Maggie Nelson and Alison Bechdel, among others, have renewed attention to Winnicott's work. Nelson in particular calls attention to this revival of interest and suggests that the answer to the question, "Why Winnicott Now?," lies in the style of his writing, whose seeming simplicity runs against the grain of most psychoanalytic writing. Maggie Nelson, *The Argonauts* (Minneapolis, MN: Graywolf Press, 2016), 19, 45; Alison Bechdel, *Are You My Mother?: A Comic Drama* (New York: Mariner, 2013).

13 As André Green paraphrases Winnicott's understanding of this dynamic in the infant-mother relationship: "... between the mother who is physically holding the baby and the baby there is a layer which we have to acknowledge, which is an aspect of herself and at the same time an aspect of her baby. It is mad to hold this view and yet the view must be maintained" (Andre Green, "The Bifurcation of Contemporary Psychoanalysis," in *Between Winnicott and Lacan: A Clinical Engagement*, Ed. Lewis A. Kirshner (London: Taylor & Francis, 2011), 46).

14 Teresa Brennan's work is most notable in this regard. Teresa Brennan, *The Transmission of Affect* (Ithaca, NY: Cornell University Press, 2004). See also Leo Bersani and Adam Phillips, *Intimacies* (Chicago: University of Chicago Press, 2010), 48–50.

15 Claire Nouvet, "The Inarticulate Affect: Lyotard and Psychoanalytic Testimony," *Discourse* 25.1 (2003): 245.

16 The phrase "psycho-analytic explorations" is the title of the volume containing
    Winnicott's posthumously published papers. For Winnicott's remarks on the
    metaphysical poets as a particular example of a regard for intermediate space, see
    the "Introduction" to *Playing and Reality*.

17 D.W. Winnicott, "The Location of Cultural Experience," in *Playing and Reality*
    (New York: Routledge, 2005), 135.

18 D.W. Winnicott, "Communication between Infant and Mother, and Mother and
    Infant, Compared and Contrasted," in *Babies and Their Mothers* (Reading, MA:
    Addison-Wesley, 1987), 89–103. Winnicott's biographer emphasizes his lifelong
    affinity for poetry. Although he was first trained as a pediatrician and later as a
    child psychoanalyst, Winnicott wrote poetry throughout his life and found solace
    in reading it. Rodman notes his particular love for Stevens's near-contemporary,
    Rainer Maria Rilke (Robert F. Rodman, *Winnicott: Life and Work* (Cambridge, MA:
    Perseus, 2003), 96).

19 Cf. Rodman, *Winnicott*, 165. Winnicott spoke similarly about not reading Ferenczi
    so as to "protect his original thinking" (ibid., 109).

20 Bersani and Phillips, *Intimacies*, vii.

21 Adam Phillips, "Depression," in *On Flirtation* (Cambridge, MA: Harvard University
    Press, 1996), 226.

22 The most famous example of this commitment to patients as teachers in their
    own right comes in the humorous dedication page of the posthumously published
    volume, *Playing and Reality*. The inscription reads, "To my patients who have paid
    to teach me."

23 While Freud claims that any therapy claiming to be psychoanalytic must recognize
    the concepts of transference and resistance (cf., in particular, Sigmund Freud,
    "On the History of the Psycho-Analytic Movement," SE XIV, 60, 66), Winnicott
    argues that resistance derives just as much from the analyst as from the patient.
    Because "Interpretation outside the ripeness of the material is indoctrination and
    produces compliance ... A corollary is that resistance arises out of interpretations
    given outside the area of the overlap of the patient's and the analyst's playing
    together" (D.W. Winnicott, "Playing: A Theoretical Statement," *Playing and Reality*
    (2005): 51).

24 As I will discuss at more length in Chapter 2, Winnicott, like Freud, uses an
    understanding of pathological phenomena to describe psychological and
    metapsychological experience. In contrast, however, Winnicott employs the
    concept of "health" quite liberally. Masud Khan explains that Winnicott identified
    "representatives of ... dissociation in healthy persons and in healthy living (private
    self reserved for intimacies, and public self adapted for socialization)." (Masud
    R. Khan, "Introduction," in *Maturational Processes and the Facilitating Environment*
    (London: Hogarth Press, 1965), 9.)

25 Geoffrey Hartman, in a brief dismissal of the relevance of Winnicott's theory of
    play and of "transitional space" to literary studies, turns to Schiller's "aesthetic
    state," Victor Turner's concept of "marginality," and Johan Huizinga's *Homo Ludens*
    to argue that Winnicott's theory, by positing a phase of development that follows
    transitional phenomena, misses the fact that the "mystery of aesthetic education
    is in the understanding it gives of liminal or transitional states as such" (Geoffrey
    Hartman, *Criticism in the Wilderness*, 2nd ed. (New Haven: Yale University Press,
    2007), 262–263). Had Hartman read Winnicott's, "The Location of Cultural
    Experience," he would have recognized that his views and Winnicott's are closer
    than he claims. For Winnicott, the transitional space of play is the precursor of
    "cultural experience," a place of "infinite variability" tied both to the cultural
    tradition of the past and to the possibility of original contributions to a "cultural
    pool." The space in which this "potential space" occurs must be defined because
    it exists neither in inner psychic reality nor in externally objective reality but
    between the two, and as such it has to do with the space between "separateness"
    and "union" (Winnicott, "The Location of Cultural Experience," 130). As Schwartz
    has it, the account of aesthetics given in "Location" represents "Winnicott's most
    eloquent statement of his revision of the Freudian worldview" (M.M. Schwartz,
    "Introduction: D.W. Winnicott's Cultural Space," *Psychoanalytic Review* 79 (1992):
    169–174. *PEP Archive*. March 30, 2011, 172).
26 Wallace Stevens, *The Collected Poems of Wallace Stevens* (New York: Vintage,
    1990), 358.
27 Eve Kosofsky Sedgwick and Adam Frank, *Shame and Its Sisters: A Silvan Tomkins
    Reader* (Durham, NC: Duke University Press, 1995), 22.
28 Ibid. 23
29 Lauren Berlant, *Cruel Optimism* (Durham, NC: Duke University Press, 2011), 4.
30 Ibid., 6
31 Ibid., 1–2.
32 Allen Grossman, *The Sighted Singer* (Baltimore, MD: Johns Hopkins University
    Press, 1991), x.
33 Maurice Blanchot, *The Writing of the Disaster*, Trans. Ann Smock (Lincoln, NE:
    University of Nebraska Press, 1986), 10.
34 Freud, "The Unconscious," 179.
35 Oren Izenberg, "Confiance au monde; Or, The Poetry of Ease," *Nonsite.org*.
    February 12, 2012, Web. http://nonsite.org/article/confiance-au-monde-or-the-
    poetry-of-ease.
36 Tracing a trajectory of British poetry that is true in *The Poetry of Mourning* for US
    poets as well, Ramazani remarks that "For [Geoffrey] Hill as already for Hardy,
    every elegy is an elegy for elegy—a poem that mourns the diminished efficacy
    and legitimacy of poetic mourning" (Jahan Ramazani, *The Poetry of Mourning*
    (Chicago: University of Chicago Press, 1994), 8).

37 Pound's "Coda" calls into question the positive affects—what Silvan Tomkins might call their "excitement/interest"—that attach to poems confident of their own effectiveness in achieving traditional elegiac results: "O My songs, / Why do you look so eagerly and so curiously into / people's faces, / Will you find your lost dead among them?" (103).

38 Ralph Waldo Emerson, *Essays and Lectures*, Ed. Joel Porte (New York: Library of America, 1983), 473.

39 Wallace Stevens, *The Letters of Wallace Stevens*, Ed. Holly Stevens (New York: Knopf, 1966), 507.

40 See, most notably, *Gay Shame*, which brings together papers first presented at the landmark 2003 conference of the same name at the University of Michigan. David Halperin and Valerie Traub, Ed. *Gay Shame* (Chicago: University of Chicago Press, 2010).

41 Claudia Rankine, *Citizen* (Minneapolis, MN: Graywolf, 2014), 143.

42 Jean- François Lyotard, *The Differend*, Trans. Georges van den Abbeele (Minneapolis, MN: University of Minnesota Press, 1989).

43 For three examples of poems that identify themselves with small containers, see Shakespeare's sonnet LV, Allen Grossman's "Stanzas on Pots," and Dorothea Lasky's "Porn."

44 Berlant, *Cruel Optimism*, 2.

45 John Ashbery, *Rivers and Mountains* (New York: Ecco, 1977), 26.

Chapter 1

1 Wallace Stevens, *Opus Posthumous: Poems, Plays, Prose*, Ed. Milton J. Bates (New York: Vintage, 1990), 189.

2 Wallace Stevens, *Collected Poetry and Prose*, Ed. Frank Kermode and Joan Richardson (New York: Library of America, 1997), 476.

3 Stevens, *The Collected Poems of Wallace Stevens*, 239.

4 Ibid., 374.

5 Stevens's confidence was a matter of importance to even his earliest reviewers. Harriet Monroe's sympathetic review of *Harmonium* praises it, exclaiming, "The black despairs of lesser men visit him not at all," while Marianne Moore's counterpoint places such confidence on the side of "a deliberate bearishness—a shadow of acrimonious, unprovoked contumely" (Steven Gould Axelrod and Helen Deese, "Wallace Stevens: The Critical Reception," in *Critical Essays on Wallace Stevens*, Ed. Steven Gould Axelrod and Helen Deese (Boston, MA: G.K. Hall, 1988), 4).

6 By way of introduction, see, for example, "Of Modern Poetry," in which the poem is figured as "an instrument … wholly / Containing the mind, below which it cannot

descend, / Beyond which it has no will to rise" (Stevens, *The Collected Poems of Wallace Stevens*, 240). Other poems that explicitly concern the poem's ability to hold or contain include "The Owl in the Sarcophagus," "Stars at Tallapoosa," "So and So Reclining on Her Couch," and "Les Plus Belles Pages."

7   Stevens used the phrase "materia poetica" as the title for another collection of aphorisms on poetry and speaks there of prose as the "well" from which poetry draws its inventions and interventions into reality. While I use the phrase to refer to a more abstract "materia," that of affective quantities, that make up a significant part of Stevens's poetic making ("Poetry is great only as it exploits great ideas or what is often the same thing great feelings" (Stevens, *Opus Posthumous*, 200)), Graham Foust notes that the term applies equally well to money, in that Stevens considered the physical embodiments of his poems in books and manuscripts (what Foust calls, punning, "the materials of his working life") as objects of value and exchange in their own right. (Graham Foust, "Wallace Stevens's Manuscript as if in the Dump," *Jacket 2* 14 (2001): Web. http://jacketmagazine.com/14/foust-on-stevens.html.)

8   Frederic Jameson, "Wallace Stevens," *New Orleans Review* 11.1 (1984): 11.

9   Stevens, *The Collected Poems of Wallace Stevens*, 532.

10 D.W. Winnicott "Knowing and Learning," in *Babies and Their Mothers* (Reading, MA: Addison-Wesley, 1987), 18.

11 Stevens, *The Collected Poems of Wallace Stevens*, 532–533.

12 Cf. Gregory Brazeal, "Wallace Stevens' Philosophical Evasions," *Wallace Stevens Journal* 31.1 (Spring 2007): 14–26; Helen Vendler, "The Qualified Assertions of Wallace Stevens," in *The Act of the Mind*, Ed. Roy Harvey Pearce and J. Hillis Miller (Baltimore: Johns Hopkins University Press, 1965), 163–178.

13 Stevens, *The Collected Poems of Wallace Stevens*, 384.

14 Freud, *Beyond the Pleasure Principle*, 12.

15 For another reading of "Anecdote" that emphasizes what is hidden by the poem over what it "airs," see Emig, who calls the poem a "modernist reminder of the destruction that underlies history" (Rainer Emig, "Dominion, Order, Loss: Approaching Wallace Stevens' Poetry through Psychoanalysis and Phenomenology," *Wallace Stevens Journal* 24.1 (Spring 2000): 73).

16 Stevens, *The Collected Poems of Wallace Stevens*, 76.

17 Stevens, *The Collected Poems of Wallace Stevens*, 192–193.

18 Ibid., 192, 193.

19 Ibid., 193.

20 Though I have chosen to bring out the implications of anxiety related to holding, "destruction" and "hate" are also significant, and related concepts in Winnicott's oeuvre. While anxiety about holding is one response of the holder to a threatening object, Winnicott writes that this is one major reason that "mothers hate their babies," a fact he urges skeptical readers to accept in "Hate in

the Countertransference." On the other side of this equation, that the held object *must* be threatening becomes a major aspect of Winnicott's late theory of "object use," a stage beyond simply relating that requires the "destruction" (in fantasy) and survival (in reality) of the loved (and holding) object in order for the child to develop a capacity for creativity, object constancy, and love (cf. D.W. Winnicott, "The Use of an Object and Relating through Identifications," in *Psycho-Analytic Explorations*, Ed. Clare Winnicott, Ray Shepherd, and Madeleine Davis (London: Karnac, 2010), 218–227).

21 Though I do not dwell here on Winnicott's allegiance to and divergence from Freudian metapsychology, it is worth noting one similarity with regard to anxiety. Both realized that the phenomenon of anxiety could not be isolated from larger problems, but that if it was to be understood, it would only be as an integral part of the functioning of other psychic structures in what Freud calls the "mental apparatus" (Freud, "Inhibitions," 129).

22 For one example of why the former method would be mistaken, note that Winnicott formulates his most famous concept, that of the "transitional object"— the plaything or blanket that soothes a child and is his or her first creation and possession—with reference to anxiety. He notes that the child first turns to such an object as a "defense against anxiety" (D.W. Winnicott, "Transitional Objects and Transitional Phenomena," in *Playing and Reality* (London: Tavistock, 1971), 5).

23 The difference between Freud and Winnicott in terms of theory and technique begins to become clear here. While for Freud the "royal road" of dreams leads to a knowledge of unconscious conflicts and the conflictual remnants of infantile, usually Oedipal sexuality, for Winnicott an understanding of the pre-Oedipal "holding environment" supplies the most significant knowledge for psychoanalytic treatment. In terms of cure, Freud's oft-quoted aim of restoring patients to an ability to experience "ordinary unhappiness" bears at least a degree of stylistic difference from Winnicott's less jaundiced rhetoric of health and "creative living." D.W. Winnicott, "The Location of Cultural Experience," *Playing and Reality*, 135.

24 For this definition, the *OED* gives as one example a line from the memoirs of R. Cumberland: "I had a holding on Lord Halifax, founded on my father's merits."

25 D.W. Winnicott, "Theory of the Parent-Infant Relationship," in *Maturational Processes and the Facilitating Environment* (London: Hogarth, 1965), 48.

26 Holding, Winnicott writes, "Takes account of the infant's skin sensitivity—touch, temperature, auditory sensitivity, visual sensitivity, sensitivity to falling (action of gravity) and of the infant's lack of knowledge of the existence of anything other than the self. It includes the whole routine of care throughout the day and night, and it is not the same with any two infants because it is part of the infant, and no two infants are alike." Winnicott, "Theory of the Parent-Infant Relationship," 48–49.

27 To note how the concept of holding distinguishes Winnicott is not to ignore the many ways in which it links him to his predecessors and contemporaries. Not only

did Winnicott credit his wife, Clare, for the term "holding," as we will see later, his most detailed statement on holding comes with a rare, extended discussion of Freud.

28 Critical attention to Winnicott's idiosyncratic use of language manifests in guidebooks like Jan Abram's *The Language of Winnicott*. Perhaps no other analyst outside of Freud and Lacan has received as much attention for this aspect of his psychoanalytic writing.

29 Winnicott, "Theory of the Parent-Infant Relationship," 42.

30 (Winnicott, "Knowing and Learning," 18.) For a critique of Winnicott's image of the mother, see Susan Rubin Suleiman's "Writing and Motherhood," which references Nancy Chodorow's remarks on the clinician's general blindness to the difficulty of what they nevertheless describe as normal mothering (Susan Rubin Suleiman, "Writing and Motherhood," in *The (M)other Tongue: Essays in Feminist Psychoanalytic Interpretation*, Ed. Shirley Nelson Garner, Claire Kahane, and Madelon Sprengnether (Ithaca, NY: Cornell University Press, 1986), 355; Nancy Chodorow, *The Reproduction of Mothering: Psychoanalysis and the Sociology of Gender* (Berkeley, CA: University of California Press, 1978), 84–85. Claire Kahane also criticizes the reductive gender schema at work in Winnicott's concept of the transitional object. (Claire Kahane, "Gender and Voice in Transitional Phenomena," in *Transitional Objects and Potential Spaces: Literary Uses of D.W. Winnicott*, Ed. Peter Rudnytsky (New York: Columbia University Press, 1993), 278–291.)

31 Elissa Marder, *The Mother in the Age of Mechanical Reproduction* (New York: Fordham University Press, 2012).

32 Winnicott, "Theory of the Parent-Infant Relationship," 49.

33 Ibid., 49.

34 D.W. Winnicott, "Anxiety Associated with Insecurity," in *D.W. Winnicott: Collected Papers* (London: Karnac, 1984), 98.

35 Ibid., 54.

36 Ibid., 47.

37 Ibid., 44.

38 Ibid., 47.

39 Winnicott, "Knowing and Learning," 18.

40 Jan Abram, *The Language of Winnicott* (London: Karnac, 2007), 198.

41 Ibid., 198.

42 Winnicott, "Theory of the Parent-Infant Relationship," 74.

43 D.W. Winnicott, "Psychiatric Disorder in Terms of Infant Maturational Processes," in *The Maturational Processes and the Facilitating Environment* (London: Hogarth Press, 1965), 240.

44 Stevens, *The Collected Poems of Wallace Stevens*, 357–358.

45 Roman Jakobson, *Language in Literature*, Ed. Krystyna Pomorska and Stephen Rudy (Cambridge: Harvard University Press, 1987), 354.

46 Barbara Johnson, "Apostrophe, Animation, and Abortion," *Diacritics* 16.1 (Spring 1986): 31.

47 Stevens, *The Letters of Wallace Stevens*, 507.

48 Ibid., 507.

49 Ibid.

50 Ibid.

51 As the last lines of "Man and Bottle" have it, "The poem lashes more fiercely than the wind, / As the mind, to find what will suffice, destroys / Romantic tenements of rose and ice" (Stevens, *The Collected Poems of Wallace Stevens*, 100). In "Repetitions of a Young Captain," another poem that depicts a storm destroying a theater, "The wind beat in the roof and half the walls" (Stevens, *The Collected Poems of Wallace Stevens*, 306). Stevens's attention to the vicissitudes of weather was so precise that there are, of course, many qualities of wind described in the poems from breezes to hurricanes. One is struck, however, by a disproportionate number of powerful and/ or violent winds.

52 Stevens, *The Collected Poems of Wallace Stevens*, 96.

53 Marjorie Perloff notes that Georges Perec's motto, "Never use the word 'etcetera,'" stands as "an injunction that might be the epigraph for a manual on the poetics of constraint" (*Radical*, 141). Only by showing everything, and then showing how such a complete showing actually reveals very little, serves the constrained writer's purpose—revealing how language itself shows everything, its resources and originality, only when it seems constrained to the point of producing nothing. While Stevens was by no means writing under the sorts of constraints adopted by members of OULIPO, Perec's positing of the concealing function of "etcetera" bolsters our sense that by allowing the "et cetera," and thus not coming to the end of the description of the "spectacle," Stevens's speaker only further enmeshes himself in its chaos. If constrained writing proceeds through order to a positive chaos, Stevens's "Chaos," in its attempt to forestall chaos, opens the floodgates.

54 Helen Vendler, *Wallace Stevens: Words Chosen Out of Desire* (Cambridge, MA: Harvard University Press, 1986), 16.

55 Winnicott, "Knowing and Learning," 18.

56 Vendler, *Wallace Stevens*, 15.

Chapter 2

1 Stevens, *Collected Poetry and Prose*, 22.

2 Ibid., 908.

3 Ibid., 661.

4 Ibid., 901.

5   For a longer list of critics who placed Stevens firmly in the camp of dandyism, sparking a counter-response in the criticism of defenses of Stevens, see Jacqueline Vaught Brogan, *Stevens and Simile: A Theory of Language* (Princeton: Princeton University Press, 1986), 7n13.

6   Consider the evocation of incomplete or continuing movements of the body as well as the mind in titles such as "Ploughing on Sunday," "The Pleasures of Merely Circulating," and "Notes toward a Supreme Fiction." Stevens's deployment of and commentary on the figure of metaphor deserves fuller treatment than I give it here, but several commentators have noted Stevens's awareness of the term's Greek root, *metaphorein*, to transfer.

7   "[I]n neurotic anxiety the ego is making a similar attempt at flight from the demand by its libido, that it is treating this internal danger as though it were an external one" (SE XVI:405).

8   For a careful treatment of the relationship between Stevens and Freud, and in particular Stevens's reading of Freud's late work, *The Future of an Illusion*, see Raina Kostova, "The Dangerous Voice of the Realist: Wallace Stevens's Extended Critique of Freud's The Future of an Illusion," *The Wallace Stevens Journal* 34.2 (2010): 222–240.

9   Adam Phillips, *Winnicott* (New York: Penguin, 2007), 58.

10   Winnicott, "Transitional Objects and Transitional Phenomena," 13.

11   Thus, for Freud, if an individual does not resolve Oedipal phase conflicts of genital organization, they will "persist in an unconscious state in the id and will later manifest [their] pathogenic effect" in a failure to choose romantic objects that are sufficiently different from those modeled by parental figures (SE XIX: 177).

12   Gina Masucci Mackenzie and Daniel T. O'Hara, "Beyond Romance: Wallace Stevens with D.W. Winnicott on the Objects of Insight," *The Wallace Stevens Journal* 34.2 (2010): 244.

13   Stevens used the phrase as a title for the section of his journals he published in *View* in 1940, but when Harold Bloom commented that "*materia poetica* and poetry [are] the same thing for Stevens," he licensed it for broader use among critics, who have employed the phrase to hint at the diverse topics Stevens's drew together for his poems, as well as to discuss the Stevens's concept of a kind of workmanship between reality and imagination.

14   D.W. Winnicott, "Communicating and Not Communicating Leading to a Study of Certain Opposites," in *The Maturational Processes and the Facilitating Environment* (London: Hogarth Press, 1965), 180.

15   Ibid., 184.

16   For a helpful gloss of some of the enticements and some of the obstacles presented by Winnicott's vocabulary, cf. Ogden, who writes that its paradoxical constructions and lack of jargon account both for its "popular appeal" and its "insulat[ion] … from systematic exploration, modification, and extension" (Thomas H. Ogden, "On

Potential Space," *International Journal of Psychoanalysis* 66 (1985): 129–141, *PEP Archive*, November 23, 2012, 130).

17 I take the "not-communicating" of Stevens's poems as a strategy helpful for elaborating the relationship of poetic language to its nonpoetic counterpart, the discourse of social life. Without suggesting that the social world subsumes poetic language, that this language is only a means to a social end, or that such ends could be easily translated from poetic texts, I do intend to suggest a distinction between poetic language and social discourse by which the former, motivated by communicative crisis, works to make the latter once again possible. By reading "not-communicating" strategies as evidence that Stevens recognizes and responds to obstacles of communication by means of a (provisional) inward turn, I take it that he elaborates upon his theory that "the poem is a café (restoration)" (Stevens, *Collected Poetry and Prose*, 909), a stay against confusion, and a place to create the world in the mind—all, however, in preparation to face the world that is not in the mind alone but among persons. Take, as an example of Stevens's desire for as-of-yet unintelligible speech to eventually find its proper addressee the last poem of *Harmonium*, "To the Roaring Wind":

What syllable are you seeking,
Vocalissimus,
In the distances of sleep?
Speak it. (Stevens, *Collected Poetry and Prose*, 77)

Stevens, too, felt addressed by a command to "Speak it," as the recent studies on Stevens's involvement in current events plainly show. The fact that Stevens's poems do not always form and voice their syllables promptly upon receiving such a command suggests that the often chaotic motion between silent selfhood and garrulous publicity remains a definitive attribute of Stevensian poetic space. For seminal accounts of poetic interpretation grounded in the continuity of poetic investment in the social, see Grossman, *The Sighted Singer*, and Oren Izenberg, *Being Numerous: Poetry and the Ground of Social Life* (Princeton, NJ: Princeton University Press, 2011).

18 D.W. Winnicott, "Ego Distortion in Terms of True and False Self," in *The Maturational Processes and the Facilitating Environment* (London: Hogarth Press, 1965), 148.

19 Winnicott, "Communicating and Not Communicating Leading to a Study of Certain Opposites," 184.

20 Ibid., 187.

21 Mark Halliday, *Stevens and the Interpersonal* (Princeton, NJ: Princeton University Press, 1991), 174n1.

22 Gerald Bruns, "Stevens without Epistemology," in *Wallace Stevens: The Poetics of Modernism*, Ed. Albert Gelpi (Cambridge: Cambridge University Press, 1985), 35.

23   Ibid., 26.

24   Harold Bloom, *Modern Critical Views* (New York: Chelsea House, 1985), 5.

25   Helen Vendler, "The Hunting of Wallace Stevens," in *The Music of What Happens*
     (Cambridge, MA: Harvard University Press, 1988), 74–75. Bart Eeckhout notes
     that some of the charges accruing to Stevens on account of his interiority might
     be better attributed to the nature of the lyric (20). Although I do not have time to
     speak in depth to Stevens's peculiar relationship to the interiority constitutive of
     the lyric, my reading of Stevens's revisions of Keats in his "Autumn Refrain" and
     "Waving Adieu, Adieu, Adieu" will touch on this relationship.

26   Jacqueline Vaught Brogan, *The Violence within the Violence Without* (Athens:
     University of Georgia Press, 2003), 2.

27   Ibid., 2.

28   Alan Filreis, *Wallace Stevens and the Actual World* (Princeton: Princeton University
     Press, 1991), xviii. For a similar statement, see James Longenbach, *Wallace Stevens:
     The Plain Sense of Things* (New York: Oxford, 1991), 279.

29   Stevens, *Collected Poetry and Prose*, 262.

30   This constructivist approach to selfhood, a founding tenet of psychoanalysis,
     is an essential feature of Winnicott's theory of communication. Notably, in
     Winnicott's examples, such a founding moment often concerns an act of writing.
     He describes one patient's childhood experience of "establishing a private self
     that is not communicating" by keeping a diary her mother could not access
     ("Communicating," 186). Another patient contrasted her writing of poems with
     autobiographic writing. The former, Winnicott reports, "she does not publish … or
     even show to anybody" (ibid., 187).

31   Winnicott, "Communicating and Not Communicating Leading to a Study of
     Certain Opposites," 184.

32   Ibid., 187.

33   Stevens, *Collected Poetry and Prose*, 902.

34   Helen Vendler, *On Extended Wings* (Cambridge, MA: Harvard University Press,
     1969), 39.

35   Stevens, *Collected Poetry and Prose*, 36.

36   Ibid., 28, 29.

37   Mary Watson, "Wallace Stevens and the Maternal Art of Poetry," *Wallace Stevens
     Journal* 22.1 (1988): 77.

38   Stevens, *Collected Poetry and Prose*, 23.

39   Because my interest is in the way Stevens turns from the outside world to the inside
     world, and how he proposed to manage the two in tandem, I leave aside the rest
     of "Comedian," which builds on the foundation of interiority established in its
     opening cantos.

40   Stevens, *Collected Poetry and Prose*, 22.

41   Ibid., 22, 23.

42 Ibid., 22.

43 Ibid.

44 Ibid., 14.

45 Ibid.

46 "Contact" is, of course, no alien concept to Williams, as it figured as the title of the little magazine he edited from December 1920 to July 1923, and again for three issues in 1932. But if for Williams contact denoted the result of an external object's becoming knowable as (according to the "Manifesto" of *Contact*) "personal realization" came to bear upon it, Stevens suggests that the unknowability of both self and object drives the energy of the encounter they nevertheless sustain. To cultivate respect for individual difference in the realm of contact forms the central tenet of "Re-statement of Romance," in which the two lovers experience, rather than the self-erasing merger characteristic of the Shakespearean dyad (cf. "The Phoenix and Turtle," where "number … in love was slain"), an experience of solitude "far beyond the casual solitudes" (Stevens, *The Collected Poems of Wallace Stevens*, 146).

47 Stevens, *Collected Poetry and Prose*, 22.

48 Ibid., 22.

49 Ibid.

50 Ibid.

51 Ibid., 70.

52 Ibid., 23.

53 Winnicott, "Communicating and Not Communicating Leading to a Study of Certain Opposites," 184.

54 Stevens, *The Collected Poems of Wallace Stevens*, 24.

55 Cf. Emily Sun, "Facing Keats with Winnicott: On a New Therapeutics of Poetry," *Studies in Romanticism* 46.1 (2007): 57–75; Toshiaki Komura, "Modern Elegy and the Fiction and Creation of Loss: Wallace Stevens's 'The Owl in the Sarcophagus,'" *ELH* 77.1 (2010): 45–70.

56 Cf. Phillips, *Winnicott*, 139.

57 Jakobson, *Language in Literature*, 69, 66.

58 Rachel Cole, "Rethinking the Value of Lyric Closure: Giorgio Agamben, Wallace Stevens, and the Ethics of Satisfaction," *PMLA* 126.2 (2011): 394.

59 Stevens, *Collected Poetry and Prose*, 50.

60 "Ki-ki-ri-ki" and "rou-cou" are, of course, anything but pure sound. The second term may derive from the French verb, *roucoler*, to warble. Nevertheless, the steps that mediate between a conventional American English onomatopoeic notation such as "chirp, chirp" and the French-derived term (which is not, of course, lexical French) suggest a modification of intelligible, social speech serving to advance the poem's narrative of failed seduction to a private or at least more private register in which the reported address of "ki-ki-ri-ki," which goes unanswered, signifies a

retroactively withdrawn voicing of desire. If the call receives no answer, the speaker seems to say, then it was not intended as a call in the first place, but rather as a metaphorical substitution for a call that would, in fact, "bring rou-cou."

61 Cole, "Rethinking the Value of Lyric Closure," 394.

62 Stevens, *Collected Poetry and Prose*, 129.

63 Ibid., 129.

64 For a more complete description of this aspect of elegy, see Jonathan Culler, "Apostrophe," *Diacritics* 7.4 (1977): 67.

65 Stevens, *Collected Poetry and Prose*, 129.

66 I draw this observation by analogy from Freud's discussion, in Chapter 1 of *The Interpretation of Dreams*, of a class of dreams that derive from "internal organic somatic stimuli." These sounds have that source within the body and can, for "an excellent sleeper" like Freud himself, prove more capable of contributing to dream material than external stimuli (SE IV: 33, 229).

67 "[I]n many medieval and Renaissance texts, Philomela must remind herself (so memory-less is she) of the cause of her pain by leaning upon a thorn as she sings beautifully in the night" (Allen Grossman, "Orpheus/Philomela: Subjecting and Mastery in the Founding Stories of Poetic Production," in *The Long Schoolroom* (Ann Arbor: University of Michigan Press, 1997), 32.

68 Stevens, *Collected Poetry and Prose*, 104.

69 Vendler, "The Hunting of Wallace Stevens," 74.

70 Helen Vendler, "The Experiential Beginnings of Keats's Odes," *Studies in Romanticism* 12.3 (1973): 593.

71 Winnicott, "Communicating and Not Communicating Leading to a Study of Certain Opposites," 185.

72 Ibid., 185.

73 Stevens, *Collected Poetry and Prose*, 104.

74 Ibid., 104.

75 Winnicott, "Communicating and Not Communicating Leading to a Study of Certain Opposites," 179.

Chapter 3

1 Randall Jarrell, *The Third Book of Criticism* (New York: Farrar, Straus and Giroux, 1965), 57.

2 Ibid., 66.

3 Ibid., 67.

4 For a longer consideration of Jarrell's relationship to Romantic poetry, especially Wordsworth, see Stephen Burt, *Randall Jarrell and His Age* (New York: Columbia University Press, 2005).

5   Eve Kosofsky Sedgwick, *Touching Feeling* (Durham, NC: Duke University Press, 2003), 27.

6   Mary Jarrell, *Remembering Randall* (New York: Harper Perennial, 1992), 135–136.

7   Ibid., 136.

8   Ibid.

9   Ibid., 25.

10 Ida Kay Jordan, "No Sign of Beatnik behind Poet's Beard," *News and Observer* (Raleigh, NC), June 11, 1961.

11 Note Jack Kerouac's stylized portrait of Jarrell as Random Varnum the "bearded poet" in *Desolation Angels*. Mary Jarrell considers the visit from Corso and Kerouac in *Remembering Randall*, 42–44.

12 For a detailed account of the exchange between Duncan and Ransom, see Ekbert Fass, *Young Robert Duncan: Portrait of the Homosexual Artist in Society* (Santa Rosa, CA: Black Sparrow Press, 1984); Daniel Katz, *The Poetry of Jack Spicer* (Edinburgh: Edinburgh University Press, 2013).

13 Jordan, "No Sign of Beatnik behind Poet's Beard."

14 The tension between Jarrell's espousal of a certain kind of aesthetic nonconformity and his opposition to Beat lifestyles and poetics is, on the one hand, easy to explain, in part, because his friends and contemporaries spent considerable energy criticizing Beat methods. Delmore Schwartz famously questioned the Beats's grounds for feeling victimized by mainstream society and argued that the goals of their revolution—freedom from conformity—had been obtained long before. On the other hand, however, Jarrell may have wished to elide aspects of his work that found a rapport with the Beats, and his beard—and the way it enters into the discourse surrounding his work—signifies the stumbling block such issues presented to him. Delmore Schwartz, *Selected Essays of Delmore Schwartz*, Ed. Donald A. Dike and David H. Zucker (Chicago: University of Chicago Press, 1985).

15 Robert Lowell, "Tribute at Yale," *The Alumni News* (University of North Carolina at Greensboro), Spring 1966, Stuart Wright Collection, J.Y. Joyner Library, East Carolina University, 31.

16 Stanley Kunitz, "Tribute at Yale," *The Alumni News* (University of North Carolina at Greensboro), Spring 1966, Stuart Wright Collection, J.Y. Joyner Library, East Carolina University, 9.

17 Ibid., 9.

18 In a 1965 letter to Robert Penn Warren during his hospitalization, Jarrell notes the proximity of change to madness: "I've always wanted to change, but not to change into what you become when you're mentally ill" (William Pritchard, *Randall Jarrell: A Literary Life* (New York: FSG, 1992), 274).

19 Benjamin, Walter, "On Some Motifs in Baudelaire," in *Selected Writings, Volume 4: 1938-1940*, (Cambridge, MA: Harvard University Press, 2006), 321.

20 Ibid. 321

21   Langdon Hammer, "Who Was Randall Jarrell?" *The Yale Review* 79.3 (Spring 1990):
     389–405; James Longenbach, "Randall Jarrell's Semifeminine Mind," *Southwest
     Review* 81.3 (Summer 1996): 368–386; Stephen Burt, "Men, Women, Children,
     Families," in *Randall Jarrell and His Age* (New York: Columbia University Press,
     2001). Alan Williamson, "Jarrell, the Mother, the Märchen," in *Almost a Girl: Male
     Writers and Female Identification* (Charlottesville, VA: University of Virginia Press,
     2001); Richard Flynn, *Randall Jarrell and the Lost World of Childhood* (Athens,
     GA: University of Georgia Press, 1990). Suzanne Ferguson, "The Woman at the
     Washington Zoo," in *The Poetry of Randall Jarrell* (Baton Rouge, LA: Louisiana State
     University Press, 1971).

22   Randall Jarrell, *The Complete Poems of Randall Jarrell* (New York: Farrar, Straus and
     Giroux, 1981), 279.

23   "Gender can be rendered ambiguous without disturbing or reorienting normative
     sexuality at all … sometimes gender ambiguity can operate precisely to contain
     or deflect non-normative sexual practice and thereby work to keep normative
     sexuality intact." Judith Butler, *Gender Trouble* (New York: Routledge, 1999), xiv.

24   Elizabeth Bishop, *Words in Air: The Complete Correspondence between Elizabeth
     Bishop and Robert Lowell*, Ed. Thomas J. Travisano and Saskia Hamilton (New York:
     Farrar, Straus, and Giroux, 2010), 573.

25   Eve Kosofsky Sedgwick, *A Dialogue on Love* (Boston: Beacon, 1999), 21.

26   Sedgwick, *Touching Feeling*, 33.

27   Jarrell, *The Complete Poems of Randall Jarrell*, 308.

28   Randall Jarrell, *Randall Jarrell's Letters: An Autobiographical and Literary Selection*,
     Ed. Mary Jarrell, Stephen Burt, and Stuart Wright (Charlottesville, VA: University
     of Virginia Press, 2002), 413.

29   Burt, *Randall Jarrell and His Age*, 230.

30   Jarrell, *Remembering Randall*, 133.

31   On the anxiety of beings that emerge from books, see Foucault's "Fantasia of the
     Library."

32   Jarrell, *Randall Jarrell's Letters*, 247. While Jarrell does not specify the title in this
     letter, his later reference, in a letter to Bishop, to the "big Phaidon Donatello"
     suggests that Lowell mailed him the 1941 volume edited by Ludwig Goldscheider.
     (Ibid., 422–423.)

33   Jarrell, *Randall Jarrell's Letters*, 271.

34   Eve Kosofsky Sedgwick, *Epistemology of the Closet* (Berkeley, CA: University of
     California Press, 2008), 62.

35   Ibid., 29.

36   Raymond-Jean Frontain, "Fortune in David's Eyes," *The Gay and Lesbian Review*
     (July–August 2006): 13.

37   Jarrell, *The Complete Poems of Randall Jarrell*, 274.

38   Williamson, "Jarrell, the Mother, the Märchen," 26.

39 "The *David*s were not just erotically pleasing pieces of inexpensive art; they were also signals to visitors in the know that the homeowners were homosexual, functioning as a kind of aesthetic Morse code of sexual identity" (Frontain, "Fortune in David's Eyes," 15).

40 Jarrell, *The Complete Poems of Randall Jarrell*, 273.

41 Ibid., 274.

42 Ibid.,

43 Ibid., 275.

44 Cleanth Brooks and Robert Penn Warren, "How Poems Come About: Intention and Meaning," in *Understanding Poetry*, 3rd ed (New York: Holt, Rinehart, and Winston, 1960), 532.

45 Jarrell, *The Complete Poems of Randall Jarrell*, 215.

46 Ibid., 215.

47 Ibid., 215, 216.

48 Roland Barthes, *Image, Music, Text* (New York: Hill and Wang, 1977), 142.

49 Ibid., 142.

50 Ibid.

51 Brooks and Warren, "How Poems Come About," 532.

52 Cf. Wayne Koestenbaum, *The Queen's Throat: Opera, Homosexuality, and the Myth of Desire* (New York: Da Capo Press, 2001).

53 Burt, *Randall Jarrell and His Age*, 183.

54 Elizabeth Bishop and Robert Lowell, *Words in Air: The Complete Correspondence between Elizabeth Bishop and Robert Lowell*, Ed. Thomas Travisano with Saskia Hamilton (New York: Farrar, Straus, and Giroux, 2008), 573. In other letters, Bishop and Lowell lament the "supreme condescension" of Jarrell's poem, "Women," and his views on women in general. In a humorous aside, Bishop writes, "It just occurred to me that I think Randall and Simone de Beauvoir should exchange a few ideas—or hormones, and then try again." (Ibid., 144.)

55 Eve Sedgwick, *Between Men: English Literature and Homosocial Desire* (New York: Columbia University Press, 1985), 1–2.

56 Sedgwick, *Epistemology of the Closet*, 59.

57 Ibid., 62.

58 Ibid.

59 Kunitz, "Tribute at Yale," 9.

60 Jarrell, *Remembering Randall*, 157–159.

61 Stuart Wright Collection: Randall Jarrell Papers (#1169-005) East Carolina Manuscript Collection, J. Y. Joyner Library, East Carolina University, Greenville, North Carolina, USA.

62 The Henry W. and Albert A. Berg Collection of English and American Literature, The New York Public Library, Astor, Lenox, and Tilden Foundations.

Chapter 4

1 Alan Golding's work on Creeley and serial form is most notable among these. Alan Golding, "George Oppen's Serial Poems," *Contemporary Literature* 29.2 (1988): 221–240.

2 For an appraisal of Creeley's stylistic development, see Ben Lerner, "Of Accumulation: The Collected Poems of Robert Creeley," *boundary 2* 35.3 (2008): 251–262. Lerner argues that, rather than negate the early work's radical syntactic manipulations, the later work achieves the same effects with a syntax startling precisely for its simplicity.

3 Charles Altieri, *The Art of 20th Century American Poetry* (Oxford: Blackwell, 2006), 182.

4 Creeley's name does not appear in the major study of twentieth-century elegy: Jahan Ramazani, *The Poetry of Mourning* (Chicago: University of Chicago Press, 1994).

5 See especially Rachel Blau DuPlessis, Marjorie Perloff, and Benjamin Friedlander in Stephen Fredman and Steve McCaffery's *Form, Power, and Person in Robert Creeley's Poetry* (Iowa City, IA: University Iowa Press, 2010).

6 Ramazani, *The Poetry of Mourning*, 29, xi. R. Clifton Spargo also makes use of the term "anti-elegy." R. Clifton Spargo, "The Contemporary Anti-Elegy," in *The Oxford Handbook of The Elegy*, Ed. Karen Weisman (New York: Oxford University Press, 2010), 213–230.

7 Roland Barthes, *Mourning Diary*, Trans. Nathalie Léger and Richard Howard (London: Notting Hill, 2010), 71, 72.

8 In addition to the elegies I discuss below, see "Four Years Later," "Kid," "Valentine," and "Caves." Robert Creeley, *The Collected Poems of Robert Creeley, 1975–2005* (Berkeley, CA: University California Press, 2006), 132, 224, 272, 620.

9 Alan Golding, "Revisiting Seriality in Creeley's Poems," *Form, Power, and Person in Robert Creeley's Poetry*, 50–65 (51). Without speaking explicitly of mourning, Golding shows that Creeley's serial poems consider related problems of presence and absence at the level of language. (Cf. Alan Golding, "George Oppen's Serial Poems," 238.)

10 Sigmund Freud, "Mourning and Melancholia," in *The Standard Edition of the Complete Psychological Works of Sigmund Freud* (London: Hogarth Press, 1953), 237–258.

11 For a consideration of Howe's own "maternal elegy" and the way in which, like Creeley, multiple poems function "metaleptically, retroactively imparting new frame structures to its various precursors," see Susan Barbour, "'Spiritual Hyphen': Bibliography and Elegy in Susan Howe's *The Midnight*," *Textual Practice* 25 (2011): 143.

12 Marder, *The Mother in the Age of Mechanical Reproduction*, 2.

13 Ibid., 2, 3.

14 Ibid., 7.

15 Robert Creeley, *For My Mother: Genevieve Jules Creeley, 8 April 1887–7 October 1972* (Rushden: Sceptre Press, 1973), Rare Book Literary and Historical Papers, Louis Round Wilson Special Collections Library, University of North Carolina at Chapel Hill.

16 Robert Creeley, *The Collected Poems of Robert Creeley, 1945–1975* (Berkeley, CA: University of California Press, 1982), 594, 596.

17 Ibid., 597.

18 Barbara Johnson, *Mother Tongues* (Cambridge, MA: Harvard University Press, 2003), 66.

19 Creeley, *The Collected Poems of Robert Creeley, 1975–2005*, 200.

20 Robert Creeley and Tom Clark, *Mother's Voice* (Am Here Books/Immediate Editions, 1981), Rare Book Literary and Historical Papers, Louis Round Wilson Special Collections Library, University of North Carolina at Chapel Hill.

21 Creeley, *The Collected Poems of Robert Creeley, 1975–2005*, 201.

22 For an account of this development, see Josh Ellenbogen, "On Photographic Elegy," in *The Oxford Handbook of Elegy*, Ed. Karen Weisman (New York: Oxford University Press, 2010), 681–700.

23 W.G. Sebald and Anne Carson are two prominent examples among many. W.G. Sebald, *The Emigrants*, Trans. Michael Hulse (New York: New Directions, 1996); Anne Carson, *Nox* (New York: New Directions, 2010).

24 Roland Barthes, *Camera Lucida*, Trans. Richard Howard (New York: Hill and Wang, 1981), 8, 64, 85.

25 Ekbert Fass and Maria Trombacco, *Robert Creeley: A Biography* (Hanover, NH: University Press of New England, 2001), 4, 8.

26 My interpretation of Creeley's line is indebted to Allen Grossman's argument that the rules of the blank verse line are not arbitrary, but rather "produce the picture of the speech of a person under those conditions of exteriority … and scale … which characterize social institutions," *The Sighted Singer* (Baltimore, MD: Johns Hopkins University Press, 1992), 282.

27 Eleni Sikelianos, "Notes on a Picture," *Brick* 80.1 (2007): 157.

28 Williams suffered from debilitating vision problems in later life, from "hypersensitiveness to light" and attacks of "blurred" and "double vision" following a stroke. Paul Mariani, *William Carlos Williams: A New World Naked* (New York: McGraw Hill, 1981), 259, 644, 646, 761.

29 Charles Olson, "Proprioception," in *Collected Prose*, Ed. Donald Allen and Benjamin Friedlander (Berkeley, CA: University of California Press, 1997), 181–183, 182.

30   Allen Ginsberg, "On Creeley's Ear Mind," *boundary 2* 6/7.1–2 (1978): 444. *JSTOR*. June 11, 2013, Web. https://www.jstor.org/stable/302636.

31   Barthes, *Camera Lucida*, 96.

32   Ibid., 9.

33   Ibid., 90.

34   Ibid., 89.

35   Marder, *The Mother in the Age of Mechanical Reproduction*, 179.

36   Ibid., 181.

37   Ibid., 182.

38   Ibid., 183.

39   Ibid., 172.

40   Creeley, *The Collected Poems of Robert Creeley, 1975–2005*, 271–272.

41   Ibid., 67–68.

42   W.B. Yeats, *The Collected Works of W.B. Yeats, Vol. 1: The Poems*, Ed. Richard Finneran, 2nd ed. (New York: Scribner, 1997), 216–217.

43   Creeley's "Human Song" addresses similar questions to the infant himself.

44   Barthes, *Camera Lucida*, 91.

45   Ibid., 64.

46   Ibid., 69.

47   Creeley thought highly of "Kaddish," calling it "his never to be forgotten masterpiece." Robert Creeley, "Three Films," in *Was That a Real Poem & Other Essays*, Ed. Donald Allen (Bolinas, CA: Four Seasons Foundation, 1979), 131.

48   Robert Creeley, "Letter to Allen Ginsberg, 28 Jan. 1973," Allen Ginsberg Papers, M0733 Series 1 (Department. of Special Collections, Stanford University).

49   Freud, "Mourning and Melancholia," 255.

50   Barthes, *Camera Lucida*, 72.

51   Emerson, *Essays and Lectures*, 473. My interest in elegy itself as the object of grief derives in part from essays on Emerson's grief by Sharon Cameron and Julie Ellison. Sharon Cameron, "Representing Grief: Emerson's 'Experience'," *Representations* 15 (1986): 15–41; Julie Ellison, "Tears for Emerson: *Essays, Second Series*," in *The Cambridge Companion to Ralph Waldo Emerson*, Ed. Joel Porte and Saundra Morris (New York: Cambridge University Press, 1999),140–161.

52   Stanley Cavell, "Aversive Thinking: Emersonian Representations in Heidegger and Nietzsche," in *Emerson's Transcendental Etudes*, Ed. David Justin Hodge (Stanford, CA: Stanford University Press, 2003), 146.

53   Winnicott, "Anxiety Associated with Insecurity," 98.

54   Barthes, *Camera Lucida*, 91.

55   Charles Altieri, "The Unsure Egoist: Robert Creeley and the Theme of Nothingness," *Contemporary Literature* 13.2 (Spring 1972): 188.

56   Rachel Blau DuPlessis, "The Hole: Death, Sexual Difference, and Gender Contradictions in Creeley's Poetry," in *Form, Power Person*, Ed. Stephen

Fredman and Steve McCaffery (Iowa City: University of Iowa Press, 2010), 89–117.

57 Marder, *The Mother in the Age of Mechanical Reproduction*, 181.

Chapter 5

1   Ted Berrigan, *The Collected Poems of Ted Berrigan*, Ed. Alice Notley (Berkeley, CA: University of California Press, 2005), 43–44.

2   Berrigan, *The Collected Poems of Ted Berrigan*, 56.

3   Ron Padgett, "On *The Sonnets*," in *Nice to See You: Homage to Ted Berrigan*, Ed. Anne Waldman (Minneapolis, MN: Coffee House Press, 1991), 10.

4   Libbie Rifkin, "'Worrying about Making It': Ted Berrigan's Social Poetics," *Contemporary Literature* 38.4 (1997): 649.

5   Barrett Watten, "Entry 08: Homage to Lee Crabtree," *barrettwatten.net*. http://barrettwatten.net/texts/entry-08-homage-to-lee-crabtree/2010/02/.

6   Ted Berrigan, "Reading at Buffalo with Introduction by Robert Creeley." PennSound. https://media.sas.upenn.edu/pennsound/authors/Berrigan/5-6-68/Berrigan-Ted_02_Introduction_Buffalo_5-6-68.mp3.

7   Michael Scholnick, "A Remembrance of Ted Berrigan," in *Nice to See You*, Ed. Anne Waldman (Minneapolis, MN: Coffee House Press, 1991), 161.

8   I prefer the term "introjection" to "incorporation" because the former specifies a psychological rather than a physical interior. (Cf. Laplanche and Pontalis, *The Language of Psychoanalysis*, 230.)

9   Ibid., 230.

10 Leo Bersani finds an early, "nonreparative" Klein with which to oppose claims that art is redemptive; "'The Culture of Redemption': Marcel Proust and Melanie Klein," *Critical Inquiry* 12.2 (1986): 399–421. Mary Jacobus sketches a comprehensive approach to aesthetics based in Kleinian and post-Kleinian psychoanalysis; Mary Jacobus, *The Poetics of Psychoanalysis: In the Wake of Klein* (New York: Oxford University Press, 2005). Robyn Wiegman observes that Eve Sedgwick's engagement with Klein began as early as 1995, long before the 2003 version of "Paranoid Reading and Reparative Reading" published in *Touching Feeling* (Robyn Wiegman, "The Times We're in: Queer Feminist Criticism and the Reparative 'Turn,'" *Feminist Theory* 15.1 (2014): 8, 9.

11 Stephen Mitchell and Margaret J. Black, *Freud and Beyond: A History of Modern Psychoanalytic Thought* (New York: Basic Books, 1995), 87.

12 Ibid., 87.

13 Ibid., 91, 95.

14 Meira Likierman, *Melanie Klein: Her Work in Context* (London: Continuum, 2001), 110.

15   Mitchell and Black, *Freud and Beyond*, 92.

16   Eve Kosofsky Sedgwick, "Melanie Klein and the Difference Affect Makes," *South Atlantic Quarterly* 106.3 (2007): 628.

17   Mitchell and Black, *Freud and Beyond*, 90, 95.

18   Robert D. Hinshelwood, *Dictionary of Kleinian Thought* (London: Free Association Books, 1996), 412.

19   Laplanche, *The Language of Psychoanalysis*, 388, 389.

20   Melanie Klein and Joan Riviere, *Love, Hate, and Reparation* (London: Hogarth, 1937), 65.

21   Melanie Klein, "Infantile Anxiety Situations Reflected in a Work of Art and in the Creative Impulse," in *The Selected Melanie Klein*, Ed. Juliet Mitchell (New York: The Free Press, 1986), 93.

22   Hinshelwood, *Dictionary of Kleinian Thought*, 414.

23   Sedgwick, *Touching Feeling*, 127.

24   Ibid., 134.

25   Ibid., 150, 151.

26   Brian Glavey argues that the reparative reader "assembl[es] fragments in the semblance of a meaningful whole" like "a modernist poet or bricoleur." Brian Glavey, *The Wallflower Avant-Garde: Modernism: Sexuality, Queer Ekphrasis* (New York: Oxford University Press, 2015), 11.

27   Waldman, *Nice to See You*, 9.

28   Berrigan, *The Collected Poems of Ted Berrigan*, xi.

29   Ted Berrigan, *Talking in Tranquility: Interviews with Ted Berrigan*, Ed. Stephen Ratcliffe and Leslie Scalapino, Bolinas, CA: Avenue B/Oakland, CA: O Books, 1991), 19.

30   Berrigan, *The Collected Poems of Ted Berrigan*, 43.

31   Grossman, *The Sighted Singer*, 6.

32   Berrigan, *The Collected Poems of Ted Berrigan*, 70.

33   Ibid., 31, 33–34.

34   Ibid., 56.

35   Berrigan, *The Collected Poems of Ted Berrigan*, 71.

36   Ibid., 71.

37   Ibid., 74.

38   Ibid., 98.

39   Berrigan, *Talking in Tranquility*, 55.

40   Abram, *The Language of Winnicott*, 47.

41   Berrigan, *The Collected Poems of Ted Berrigan*, 69.

42   Christopher Bollas, *Being a Character: Psychoanalysis and Self Experience* (New York: Routledge, 2003), 59.

43   Eve Sedgwick cites these lines in reference to the writing of Gary Fisher. Eve Kosofsky Sedgwick, *Gary in Your Pocket* (Durham, NC: Duke University Press, 1996), 290.

44   Bollas, *Being a Character*, 59.

45   Berrigan, *The Collected Poems of Ted Berrigan*, 661.

46   James Dickey, "Barnstorming for Poetry." *The New York Times*, January 3, 1965.
     http://www.nytimes.com/books/98/08/30/specials/dickey-barnstorming.html.

47   Berrigan, *The Collected Poems of Ted Berrigan*, 237.

48   George Garrett adds that Dickey's account of his reading tour fails to acknowledge
     how damaging, and how expensive, these visits could be. "In fact his extraordinary
     high fees wiped out the budgets of many institutions large and small and, if
     anything, had a counterproductive effect on future poetry readings" George
     Garrett, "Liar, Liar, Pants on Fire: Some Notes on the Life and Art of the Late James
     Dickey," *VQR* Winter 2001. http://www.vqronline.org/essay/%E2%80%9Cliar-liar-
     pants-fire%E2%80%9D-some-notes-life-and-art-late-james-dickey.

49   Berrigan, *The Collected Poems of Ted Berrigan*, 99.

50   Ibid., 516.

51   Ibid., 116. As Andrew Epstein notes, John Wieners had written nearly the same
     lines in "A Poem for Painters," except that his poems, he claimed, contained "no
     / wilde beestes." Andrew Epstein, "Drunk on the Poetry of a New Friend: John
     Wieners and Frank O'Hara." *Locus Solus: The New York School of Poets*. Web.
     https://newyorkschoolpoets.wordpress.com/2015/10/26/drunk-on-the-poetry-of-
     a-new-friend-john-wieners-and-frank-ohara/.

52   Berrigan, *The Collected Poems of Ted Berrigan*, 111.

53   Ibid., 66

54   Waldman, *Nice to See You*, 28.

55   Ibid., 36.

56   Berrigan, *The Collected Poems of Ted Berrigan*, 66.

57   Aaron Kunin, "New Poetries," in *The Handbook of Creative Writing*, Ed. Steven
     Earnshaw (Edinburgh: Edinburgh University Press, 2007), 218.

58   Berrigan, *The Collected Poems of Ted Berrigan*, 111.

59   Izenberg, *Being Numerous*.

60   Brad Gooch, *City Poet: The Life and Times of Frank O'Hara* (New York: Harper
     Perennial, 2014), 399.

61   Ibid., 402.

62   Nick Sturm addresses the prominence of these claims in David Lehman's *The
     Last Avant-Garde* and Marjorie Perloff's *Frank O'Hara: Poet among Painters*. Nick
     Sturm, "'Thinking of you': The Sociality of Reading in Ted Berrigan's Early Books,"
     The Louisville Conference on Literature and Culture since 1900 (Louisville, KY,
     February 23–25, 2017).

63   "Derivative poetics" is a term associated with both Robert Duncan and John Cage,
     and Duncan's use of collage to indicate the poet's reliance on a community bears
     a strong resemblance to Berrigan's practice. As Andy Weaver notes, "Duncan's
     poetry stresses that the individual is proof of the efficacy of the community" (Andy

Weaver, "Divining the Derivers: Anarchy and the Practice of Derivative Poetics in Robert Duncan and John Cage," *Jacket 40* 2010. http://jacketmagazine.com/40/weaver-duncan-cage.shtml).

64 Berrigan, *Talking in Tranquility*, 29.

65 Berrigan, *The Collected Poems of Ted Berrigan*, 67.

66 Frank O'Hara, *The End of the Far West*, Ed. Ted Berrigan (Wivenhoe, England, 1974), [n.p.].

67 Hinshelwood, *Dictionary of Kleinian Thought*, 143.

68 See "Cento: A Note on Philosophy" and "Letter to Sandra Alper Berrigan," in which Berrigan signs off, "My sweet, my dear, we, the world, are in love with you." Waldman, *Nice to See You*, 6.

69 Freud, "Mourning and Melancholia," 244.

70 Ibid., 244.

71 Berrigan, *The Collected Poems of Ted Berrigan*, 380.

72 Berrigan, *Talking in Tranquility*, 29.

73 Likierman, *Melanie Klein*, 119.

74 Melanie Klein, "Mourning and Its Relation to Manic-Depressive States," in *Love, Guilt, and Reparation and Other Works, 1921–1945* (New York: Simon and Schuster, 2002), 353.

75 Berrigan, *The Collected Poems of Ted Berrigan*, 381.

76 As Rona Cran notes, Apollinaire is responsible for giving the name "collage" to the art form pioneered by Pablo Picasso and Georges Braques. Rona Cran, *Collage in Twentieth-Century Art, Literature, and Culture* (Surrey, England: Ashgate, 2014), 1. The line "Guillaume Apollinaire is dead" appears in Sonnet XXXVII, among others.

77 Berrigan, *The Collected Poems of Ted Berrigan*, 614.

78 Ibid., 713.

79 Ibid., 380.

80 Note that Ron Padgett will echo this line in a proleptic elegy for Berrigan, written in 1971, which refers to Berrigan's death as "the end of everything." Ron Padgett, *Ted: A Personal Memoir of Ted Berrigan* (Great Barrington, MA: Figures, 1993), 62.

81 Sedgwick, *Touching Feeling*, 150–151.

82 Alice Notley, "Introduction," in *The Selected Poems of Ted Berrigan* (Berkeley, CA: University of California Press, 2011), vii.

83 Berrigan, *The Collected Poems of Ted Berrigan*, 522.

84 Anne Waldman, "Introduction," in *Nice to See You*, Ed. Anne Waldman (Minneapolis, MN: Coffee House Press, 1991), viii.

85 Charles Bernstein, "Writing against the Body," in *Nice to See You*, Ed. Anne Waldman (Minneapolis, MN: Coffee House Press, 1991), 155.

86 Maurice Blanchot, *The Work of Fire*, Trans. Charlotte Mandel (Stanford, CA: Stanford University Press, 1995), 154.

87 Mitchell and Black, *Freud and Beyond*, 96.

Chapter 6

1 "Like me, Aristotle thinks that the motives behind scholarly study might be the same as the motives behind making art, although, unlike me, he thinks that the former is a superior kind of learning" (Aaron Kunin, "Would Vanessa Place Be a Better Poet If She Had Better Opinions?" *Nonsite.org.* September 26, 2015, Web. http://nonsite.org/editorial/would-vanessa-place-be-a-betterpoet-if-she-had-better-opinions).

2 Aaron Kunin, *Folding Ruler Star* (New York: Fence, 2005), 61, l. 19–21.

3 Aaron Kunin, *Grace Period: Notebooks, 1998–2007* (Tucson, AZ: Letter Machine Editions, 2013), 217.

4 Stephen Burt, "A Review of *The Sore Throat & Other Poems,*" *The Believer.* October 2010, Web. http://www.believermag.com/issues/201010/?read=review_kunin.

5 Kunin, *Folding Ruler Star,* 20, l. 16–18.

6 Aaron Kunin, "Shakespeare's Preservation Fantasy," *PMLA* 124.1 (2009): 92–106.

7 Ibid., 92.

8 Grossman, *The Sighted Singer,* 210; Kunin, "Shakespeare's Preservation Fantasy," 93.

9 Ibid., 93.

10 Ibid., 94.

11 Ibid., 93.

12 Ibid., 94.

13 Ibid.

14 Ibid., 98.

15 Ibid., 102.

16 Ibid., 100.

17 Ibid., 102.

18 Ibid., 103. Kunin's analysis is similar to the premise of Oren Izenberg's recent *Of Being Numerous*, which claims that poetry is not a formal or aesthetic so much as an ontological project, one that has as its purpose ensuring the value of persons. And Izenberg seems to be thinking of Kunin when he argues that the most interesting poetry, for the project of understanding poetry's relationship to the social, occurs in poems that acknowledge that "no style could be adequately capacious to convey the limitless value of the person" (Izenberg, *Being Numerous,* 4). But while Izenberg calls for a poetry that establishes a "new humanism" by "seek[ing] a reconstructive response to the great crises of social agreement and recognition in the twentieth century" (ibid., 4), Kunin would be troubled, I think, by almost any poetic claim for social recognition.

19 Sedgwick and Frank, *Shame and Its Sisters,* 5.

20 Silvan Tomkins, *Affect, Imagery, Consciousness: Vol. 2, The Negative Affects* (New York: Springer, 2003), 133.

21   Grossman, *The Sighted Singer*, 283.

22   "Blank Verse is a regime the rules of which produce the picture of the speech of a person under those conditions of exteriority (seen from the outside) and scale (no larger or smaller than a human being as he or she is seen by other human beings) which characterize social situations" (ibid., 282).

23   Ibid., 282, 283.

24   Sedgwick and Frank, *Shame and Its Sisters*, 23.

25   Kunin, *Folding Ruler Star*, 3, l. 1–3.

26   Ibid., 56, l. 1–7.

27   Ibid., 54, l. 13–15.

28   Halperin and Traub, *Gay Shame*, 3.

29   Kunin has indicated elsewhere that the role or absence of any discernible role for sexuality in all of his work is part of the constraint under which he writes.

30   Kunin, *Folding Ruler Star*, 57, l. 19–21.

31   Ibid., 13, l. 1–14.

32   Aaron Kunin, *The Sore Throat & Other Poems* (New York: Fence, 2010), ix.

33   Sedgwick and Frank, *Shame and Its Sisters*, 20–21.

34   Kunin, *Folding Ruler Star*, 33, l. 2–5.

35   Ibid., 33, l. 11–15.

36   Tomkins, *Affect, Imagery, Consciousness*, 154.

37   Vanessa Place and Robert Fitterman, *Notes on Conceptualisms* (Brooklyn, NY: Ugly Duckling Presse, 2009), 13.

38   Kunin, "Shakespeare's Preservation Fantasy," 93.

39   Kunin, *Folding Ruler Star*, 23.

40   Ibid., 23, l. 7–9.

41   Ibid., 27, l. 3–5.

42   Ibid., 61, l. 10–21.

43   Ibid., 15, l. 4–5. In an interview with Ben Lerner, Kunin announces his desire that the mode of "the possible" rather than the "probable" define the relation of his poems to history (Ben Lerner and Aaron Kunin, "Ben Lerner / Aaron Kunin," in *12 X 12: Conversations in 21st-Century Poetry and Poetics* (Iowa City: University of Iowa Press, 2009), 242).

44   William Shakespeare, *Romeo and Juliet*, (New York: Signet, 1998) III.ii.21–25.

45   Kunin, *Folding Ruler Star*, 56, l. 1–11.

46   Ibid., 61, l. 19–21.

47   Ibid., 54.

48   Kunin, "Shakespeare's Preservation Fantasy," 103.

49   See "The Sore Throat": "I'm inventing a machine / for concealing my desire. / And I'm inventing another / machine for concealing the / machine" (Aaron Kunin, *The Sore Throat & Other Poems* (New York: Fence, 2010), 63).

50 Kunin, *Folding Ruler Star*, 28, l. 9, 2–4, 5, 13.

51 Ibid., 28.

52 Ibid., 54, l. 1–15.

53 Kunin, "Shakespeare's Preservation Fantasy," 99.

54 Elizabeth Wilson, *Affect & Artificial Intelligence* (Seattle: University of Washington Press, 2010), 82.

55 Ibid., 75.

56 Tomkins, *Affect, Imagery, Consciousness*, 216.

57 Lerner and Kunin, "Ben Lerner / Aaron Kunin," 250.

58 Tomkins, *Affect, Imagery, Consciousness*, 136; Wilson, *Affect & Artificial Intelligence*, 81.

59 "Perhaps, then, Kismet is best understood as a robot designed to regulate the production of shame and dampen down its transmission. Perhaps the potency of Kismet has been precisely that it can communicate neither its own shame nor that of its creators" (Wilson, *Affect & Artificial Intelligence*, 82).

60 Sedgwick and Frank, *Shame and Its Sisters*, 138, 139.

61 Robert Creeley, *Selected Poems 1945–2005*, Ed. Benjamin Friedlander (Berkeley, CA: University of California Press, 2008), 60.

62 Stevens, *The Collected Poems of Wallace Stevens*, 18.

63 Kunin, "Shakespeare's Preservation Fantasy," 105n18.

64 Kunin, *Folding Ruler Star*, 62, l. 7–9.

Chapter 7

1 Rankine, *Citizen*, 159.

2 Rankine will explore a form of citizenship that includes even the feeling of not belonging at all, even within the black community: "None of the other black friends feel that way … And so it goes until the vista includes only displacement of feeling back into the body, which gave birth to the feelings that don't sit comfortably inside the communal." (Ibid., 152, 153.)

3 See especially "[When the stranger asks]" (16) and "[When the waitress hands]" (148).

4 Rankine, *Citizen*, 230.

5 Cathy Caruth, *Unclaimed Experience* (Baltimore, MD: Johns Hopkins University Press, 1996), 17.

6 Famously, Freud defines latency with reference to the psychic suffering of a man who had previously emerged physically unscathed from a train crash. Because this man is, at the moment of his escape, only "apparently unharmed," Caruth argues that "the victim of the crash was never fully conscious during the accident itself."

Had he been, the psychic harm he has suffered would not take days or weeks to appear. As a result, "The experience of trauma, the fact of latency, would thus seem to consist, not in the forgetting of a reality that can hence never be fully known, but in an inherent latency within the experience itself" (Caruth, *Unclaimed Experience*, 17).

7   Ibid., 4.

8   Rankine, *Citizen*, 41, 42.

9   Ibid., 42.

10 Ibid.

11 Ibid., 10.

12 Ibid., 43.

13 See Anthony Reed's analysis of Oprah Winfrey's role in "putting African American-identified phrases … in the mouths of white suburbanites" (Anthony Reed, *Freedom Time: The Poetics and Politics of Black Experimental Writing* (Baltimore, MD: Johns Hopkins University Press, 2014), 103).

14 Rankine, *Citizen*, 28.

15 Ibid., 63.

16 Claudia Rankine, "Williams College Museum of Art—Claudia Rankine Reading," November 11, 2014, *youtube.com*. https://www.youtube.com/watch?v=np4ZL8O_sbc.

17 Berlant, *Cruel Optimism*, 71.

18 Rankine, *Citizen*, 30.

19 Ibid., 10.

20 Ibid.

21 Ibid., 11.

22 Ibid.

23 Ibid.

24 Ibid., 13.

25 Lauren Berlant, "Claudia Rankine," *BOMB* 129 (Fall 2014): bombmagazine.org. http://bombmagazine.org/article/10096/claudia-rankine. For a discussion of what the black body contains, rather than the ways in which it is not self-contained, see Fred Moten, *In the Break* (Minneapolis, MN: University of Minnesota Press, 2003), 17, 18.

26 Rankine, *Citizen*, 13.

27 Ibid., 13.

28 For another example of a poem set at the university that regards the black body as an interruption of traditional regimes of temporality, see "[Despite the fact]," Rankine, *Citizen*, 47.

29 Berlant, "Claudia Rankine." For another discussion of this feature of advanced copies of *Citizen*, see Ben Lerner, *The Hatred of Poetry* (New York: Farrar, Straus,

Giroux, 2016), 71, 72. Lerner argues that the virgule is a "virtualizing technique" in *Citizen* (72), a way of gesturing to poetic forms and possibilities the book itself cannot contain.

30 Rankine, *Citizen*, 66.

31 Édouard Glissant, *Poetic Intention*, Trans. Nathalie Stephens with Anne Malena (Callicoon, NY: Nighboat Books, 2010).

32 Moten, *In the break*, 1.

33 For a poem that explicitly theorizes poetry as a defense against external threats, see Timothy Donnelly's "The Dream of a Poetry of Defense," in which poetry figures as a "permanent spark / through American darkness." (Timothy Donnelly, *The Cloud Corporation* (Seattle, WA: Wave Books, 2010), 97.)

34 Rankine, *Citizen*, 14.

35 Berlant refers to Rankine's strategy of developing "counter-uses of the pronoun" (Berlant, "Claudia Rankine").

36 Rankine, *Citizen*, 13.

37 Claire Nouvet argues that Ovid's retelling of Narcissus and Echo reveals something peculiar about the logic of response, namely that the echoing responder is inseparable from the "I" who speaks. As such, the responder undermines the sovereign subjectivity of the "I." See Claire Nouvet, "An Impossible Response: The Disaster of Narcissus," *Yale French Studies* 79 (1991): 103–134.

38 Rankine, *Citizen*, 10.

39 Ibid., 10.

40 *Citizen* already represents an ongoing—in that if follows Rankine's *Don't Let Me Be Lonely*, a book self-consciously marked by melancholic mourning and a struggle to stay alive when one feels dead. The book's melancholy is so saturating that in some poems words cannot sustain themselves and give way to images of words, namely the labels on bottles of prescription antidepressants.

41 Ibid., 10.

42 Ibid.

43 Ibid., 8.

44 Lauren Berlant, "Thinking about Feeling Historical," in *Political Emotions*, Ed. Janet Staiger, Ann Cvetkovich, and Ann Reynolds (New York: Routledge, 2010), 229.

45 Rankine, *Citizen*, 8.

46 Ibid., 8.

47 Ibid., 9.

48 Ibid., 128.

49 Berlant, *Cruel Optimism*, 93.

50 Rankine, *Citizen*, 8.

51 Ibid., 17, emphasis mine.

52 Ibid.

53 Ibid., 32.
54 Claudia Rankine, "The Meaning of Serena Williams," *The New York Times Magazine*. August 25, 2015, Web. https://www.nytimes.com/2015/08/30/magazine/the-meaning-of-serena-williams.html?_r=0.
55 Rankine, *Citizen*, 32.
56 Ibid., 33.
57 Ibid., 29.
58 Ibid., 27.
59 Ibid., 29.
60 Ibid., 25.
61 Ibid., 30.
62 Ibid.
63 Ibid.
64 Ibid., 24.
65 Ibid.
66 Ibid., 36.
67 Berlant, *Cruel Optimism*, 5.
68 Rankine, *Citizen*, 109.
69 Ibid., 122.
70 Ibid., 128.
71 Berlant, *Cruel Optimism*, 81. The body of critical perspectives on traumatic temporality and other varieties of temporal deferral and "afterwardsness" in literature is extensive. The best explication of narrative in light of psychoanalysis and its "temporal analepsis" remains Peter Brooks, "Fictions of the Wolf Man," in *Reading for the Plot: Design and Intention in Narrative* (Cambridge, MA: Harvard University Press, 2003).
72 For an account of the temporality of racist trauma that draws on Caruth's version of trauma theory, see Ronaldo V. Wilson's contribution to *The Racial Imaginary*. Wilson echoes Rankine's use of the pronoun "you": "The event, you correctly suspect, will occur again, and though it will leave you, you continue to hope, untouched by hand, baton, bullet, or fist, what cycles is your narrative's constant repetition and spread" (Ronaldo V. Wilson, "How Do We Invent Language of Racial Identity—That Is Not Necessarily Constructing the 'Scene of Instruction' about Race but Create the Linguistic Material of Racial Speech/Thought?" in *The Racial Imaginary: Writers on Race in the Life of the Mind*. Ed. Claudia Rankine, Beth Loffreda, and Max King Clap (Albany, NY: Fence Books, 2015), 77). One key difference between the accounts is that Wilson and Caruth emphasize the need for traumatic experience to be reintegrated into "narrative language," while Rankine insists that an expanded version of lyric can demonstrate the action of trauma in memory and feeling. Furthermore, in opposing accumulation to

Caruth's "recurrence," Rankine offers an alternative economy of traumatic affect. Rather than the return to awareness what Caruth calls "unassimilated scraps of overwhelming experiences" (Caruth, *Unclaimed Experience*, 153), Rankine's poems suggest that affects accumulate not so much because they are "unassimilated" as because they lack acceptable sites of recognition.

73 For a brief discussion of poetic temporality in Rankine's previous books of poetry, see Anthony Reed. Reed argues that Rankine's *PLOT* "complicates traditional lyric temporality by emphasizing the act of saying … over the experience expressed." As such, Rankine's "postlyric voice … is neither here nor there: the effects of personhood are distributed across the poem" (Reed, *Freedom Time*, 114).

74 James Baldwin, *Collected Essays*, Ed. Toni Morrison (New York: The Library of America, 1998), 83.

75 Ibid., 83.

76 Rankine, *Citizen*, 66.

77 In Lyotard's idiom, not just a damage, but a wrong.

78 Baldwin, *Collected Essays*, 70.

79 Ibid., 70.

80 Ibid.

81 Ibid.

82 Ibid., 71.

83 Ibid., 72.

84 Ibid., 81.

85 Ibid., 93.

86 Ibid., 83.

87 Ibid., 94.

88 Ibid., 95.

89 Ibid., 65.

90 Ann Cvetkovich, *Depression: A Public Feeling* (Durham, NC: Duke University Press, 2012).

91 Caruth, *Unclaimed Experience*, 8.

92 Berlant, *Cruel Optimism*, 3.

Bibliography

Abram, Jan. *The Language of Winnicott*. London: Karnac, 2007.

Ahmed, Sara. *The Promise of Happiness*. Durham, NC: Duke University Press, 2010.

Altieri, Charles. *The Art of 20th Century American Poetry*. Oxford: Blackwell, 2006.

Altieri, Charles. *The Particulars of Rapture*. Ithaca, NY: Cornell University Press, 2003.

Ashbery, John. *Rivers and Mountains*. New York: Ecco, 1977.

Axelrod, Steven Gould, and Helen Deese. "Wallace Stevens: The Critical Reception." In *Critical Essays on Wallace Stevens*. Eds. Steven Gould Axelrod and Helen Deese. Boston, MA: G.K. Hall, 1988.

Bahti, Timothy. "End and Ending: On the Lyric Technique of Some Wallace Stevens Poems." *MLN* 105.5 (1990): 1046–1062.

Baldwin, James. *Collected Essays*. Ed. Toni Morrison. New York: The Library of America, 1998.

Barbour, Susan. "'Spiritual Hyphen': Bibliography and Elegy in Susan Howe's *The Midnight*." *Textual Practice* 25 (2011): 133–155.

Barthes, Roland. "The Death of the Author." In *Image-Music-Text*. New York: Hill and Wang, 1978, 142–148.

Barthes, Roland. *Mourning Diary*. Trans. Nathalie Léger and Richard Howard. London: Notting Hill, 2010.

Bechdel, Alison. *Are You My Mother?: A Comic Drama*. New York: Mariner, 2013.

Benjamin, Walter. "On Some Motifs in Baudelaire." In *Walter Benjamin: Selected Writings, Vol. 4, 1938–1940*. Cambridge: Belknap, 2003, 314–355.

Berlant, Lauren. "Claudia Rankine." *BOMB* 129 (Fall 2014): Web. https://bombmagazine.org/articles/claudia-rankine/.

Berlant, Lauren. *Cruel Optimism*. Durham, NC: Duke University Press, 2011.

Berlant, Lauren. "Thinking about Feeling Historical." In *Political Emotions*, Eds. Janet Staiger, Ann Cvetkovich, and Ann Reynolds. New York: Routledge, 2010, 229–245.

Bernstein, Charles. "Writing against the Body." In *Nice to See You*. Ed. Anne Waldman. Minneapolis, MN: Coffee House Press, 1991, 154–157.

Berrigan, Ted. *The Collected Poems of Ted Berrigan*. Ed. Alice Notley. Berkeley, CA: University of California Press, 2005,

Berrigan, Ted. "Reading at Buffalo with Introduction by Robert Creeley." PennSound. https://media.sas.upenn.edu/pennsound/authors/Berrigan/5-6-68/Berrigan-Ted_02_Introduction_Buffalo_5-6-68.mp3.

Berrigan, Ted. *Talking in Tranquility: Interviews with Ted Berrigan*. Eds. Stephen Ratcliffe and Leslie Scalapino. Bolinas, CA: Avenue B/Oakland, CA: O Books, 1991.

Bersani, Leo. "'The Culture of Redemption': Marcel Proust and Melanie Klein." *Critical Inquiry* 12.2 (1986): 399–421.

Bersani, Leo, and Adam Phillips. *Intimacies.* Chicago: University of Chicago Press, 2010.

Beyer, Chris. "Wallace Stevens and Ludwig Richter." *Wallace Stevens Journal* 18.2 (1994): 197–206.

Bishop, Elizabeth, and Robert Lowell. *Words in Air: The Complete Correspondence between Elizabeth Bishop and Robert Lowell.* Eds. Thomas J. Travisano and Saskia Hamilton. New York: Farrar, Straus, and Giroux, 2010.

Blanchot, Maurice. *The Work of Fire.* Trans. Charlotte Mandel. Stanford, CA: Stanford University Press, 1995.

Blanchot, Maurice. *The Writing of the Disaster.* Trans. Ann Smock. Lincoln, NE: University of Nebraska Press, 1986.

Blasing, Mutlu Konuk. *Lyric Poetry: The Pain and the Pleasure of Words.* Princeton: Princeton University Press, 2007.

Bloom, Harold. *Modern Critical Views.* New York: Chelsea House, 1985.

Bloom, Harold. *Wallace Stevens: The Poems of Our Climate.* Ithaca: Cornell University Press, 1977.

Bollas, Christopher. Being a Character: Psychoanalysis and Self Experience. New York: Routledge, 2003.

Brazeal, Gregory. "Wallace Stevens' Philosophical Evasions." *Wallace Stevens Journal* 31.1 (Spring 2007): 14–26.

Brogan, Jacqueline Vaught. *Stevens and Simile: A Theory of Language.* Princeton: Princeton University Press, 1986.

Brogan, Jacqueline Vaught. *The Violence within the Violence Without.* Athens: University of Georgia Press, 2003.

Brooks, Peter. "Fictions of the Wolf Man." In *Reading for the Plot: Design and Intention in Narrative.* Cambridge, MA: Harvard University Press, 2003.

Bruns, Gerald. "Stevens without Epistemology." In *Wallace Stevens: The Poetics of Modernism.* Ed. Albert Gelpi. Cambridge: Cambridge University Press, 1985.

Burt, Stephen. *Randall Jarrell and His Age.* New York: Columbia University Press, 2005.

Burt, Stephen. "A Review of *The Sore Throat & Other Poems*." *The Believer.* October 2010. Web. http://www.believermag.com/issues/201010/?read=review_kunin.

Butler, Judith. *Gender Trouble.* 2nd ed. New York: Routledge, 1999.

Cameron, Sharon. "Representing Grief: Emerson's 'Experience'." *Representations* 15 (1986): 15–41.

Carson, Anne. *Nox.* New York: New Directions, 2010.

Caruth, Cathy. *Unclaimed Experience.* Baltimore, MD: Johns Hopkins University Press, 1996.

Cavell, Stanley. "Aversive Thinking: Emersonian Representations in Heidegger and Nietzsche." In *Emerson's Transcendental Etudes.* Ed. David Justin Hodge. Stanford, CA: Stanford University Press, 2003, 141–170.

Chodorow, Nancy. *The Reproduction of Mothering: Psychoanalysis and the Sociology of Gender.* Berkeley: CA: University of California Press, 1978.

Cole, Rachel. "Rethinking the Value of Lyric Closure: Giorgio Agamben, Wallace Stevens, and the Ethics of Satisfaction." *PMLA* 126.2 (2011): 383–397.

Cran, Rona. *Collage in Twentieth-Century Art, Literature, and Culture.* Surrey, England: Ashgate, 2014.

Creeley, Robert. *The Collected Poems of Robert Creeley, 1945–1975.* Berkeley, CA: University of California Press, 1982.

Creeley, Robert. *The Collected Poems of Robert Creeley, 1975–2005.* Berkeley, CA: University California Press, 2006.

Creeley, Robert. *For My Mother: Genevieve Jules Creeley, 8 April 1887–7 October 1972.* Rushden: Sceptre Press, 1973. Rare Book Literary and Historical Papers, Louis Round Wilson Special Collections Library, University of North Carolina at Chapel Hill.

Creeley, Robert. "Letter to Allen Ginsberg, 28 Jan. 1973." Allen Ginsberg Papers, M0733 Series 1. Department of Special Collections, Stanford University.

Creeley, Robert. *Selected Poems 1945–2005.* Ed. Benjamin Friedlander. Berkeley, CA: University of California Press, 2008.

Creeley, Robert. "Three Films." In *Was That a Real Poem & Other Essays.* Ed. Donald Allen. Bolinas, CA: Four Seasons Foundation, 1979, 120–131.

Creeley, Robert, and Tom Clark. *Mother's Voice.* Am Here Books/Immediate Editions, 1981. Rare Book Literary and Historical Papers, Louis Round Wilson Special Collections Library, University of North Carolina at Chapel Hill.

Culler, Jonathan. "Apostrophe." *Diacritics* 7.4 (1977): 59–69.

Cvetkovich, Ann. *Depression: A Public Feeling.* Durham, NC: Duke University Press, 2012.

Dickey, James. "Barnstorming for Poetry." *The New York Times.* January 3, 1965. Web. http://www.nytimes.com/books/98/08/30/specials/dickey-barnstorming.html.

Donnelly, Timothy. *The Cloud Corporation.* Seattle, WA: Wave Books, 2010.

DuPlessis, Rachel Blau. "The Hole: Death, Sexual Difference, and Gender Contradictions in Creeley's Poetry." In *Form, Power, and Person in Robert Creeley's Poetry.* Eds. Stephen Fredman and Steve McCaffery. Iowa City, IA: University Iowa Press, 2010, 89–117.

Eeckhout, Bart. *Wallace Stevens and the Limits of Reading and Writing.* Columbia, MO: University of Missouri Press, 2002.

Ellenbogen, Josh. "On Photographic Elegy." In *The Oxford Handbook of Elegy.* Ed. Karen Weisman. New York: Oxford University Press, 2010, 681–700.

Ellison, Julie. "Tears for Emerson: *Essays, Second Series.*" In *The Cambridge Companion to Ralph Waldo Emerson.* Eds. Joel Porte and Saundra Morris. New York: Cambridge University Press, 1999, 140–161.

Emerson, Ralph Waldo. *Essays and Lectures.* Ed. Joel Porte. New York: Library of America, 1983.

Emig, Rainer. "Dominion, Order, Loss: Approaching Wallace Stevens' Poetry through Psychoanalysis and Phenomenology." *Wallace Stevens Journal* 24.1 (Spring 2000): 72–91.

Epstein, Andrew. "Drunk on the Poetry of a New Friend: John Wieners and Frank O'Hara." Locus Solus: The New York School of Poets. Web. https://

newyorkschoolpoets.wordpress.com/2015/10/26/drunk-on-the-poetry-of-a-new-friend-john-wieners-and-frank-ohara/.

Fass, Ekbert, and Maria Trombacco. *Robert Creeley: A Biography*. Hanover, NH: University Press of New England, 2001.

Fass, Ekbert, and Maria Trombacco. *Young Robert Duncan: Portrait of the Homosexual Artist in Society*. Santa Rosa, CA: Black Sparrow Press, 1984.

Filreis, Alan. *Wallace Stevens and the Actual World*. Princeton: Princeton University Press, 1991.

Flatley, Jonathan. *Affective Mapping: Melancholy and the Politics of Modernism*. Cambridge, MA: Harvard University Press, 2008.

Foust, Graham. "Wallace Stevens's Manuscript as if in the Dump." *Jacket 2* 14 (2001). Web. http://jacketmagazine.com/14/foust-on-stevens.html.

Fredman, Stephen, and Steve McCaffery. *Form, Power, and Person in Robert Creeley's Poetry*. Iowa City, IA: University Iowa Press, 2010.

Freud, Sigmund. "Beyond the Pleasure Principle." *The Standard Edition of the Complete Psychological Works of Sigmund Freud*. Eds. Anna Freud, Carrie Lee Rothgeb, and James Strachey. Trans. James Strachey. Vol 18. London: Hogarth Press, 1973, 1–64.

Freud, Sigmund. "The Dissolution of the Oedipus Complex." *The Ego and the Id and Other Works. The Standard Edition of the Complete Psychological Works of Sigmund Freud*. Eds. Anna Freud, Carrie Lee Rothgeb, and James Strachey. Trans. James Strachey. Vol 19. London: Hogarth Press, 1973, 171–180.

Freud, Sigmund. "Inhibitions, Symptoms, and Anxiety." *The Standard Edition of the Complete Psychological Works of Sigmund Freud*. Eds. Anna Freud, Carrie Lee Rothgeb, and James Strachey. Trans. James Strachey. Vol 20. London: Hogarth Press, 1973, 75–176.

Freud, Sigmund. "Instincts and Their Vicissitudes." *The Standard Edition of the Complete Psychological Works of Sigmund Freud*. Eds. Anna Freud, Carrie Lee Rothgeb, and James Strachey. Trans. James Strachey. Vol 14. London: Hogarth Press, 1973, 109–140.

Freud, Sigmund. "The Interpretation of Dreams." *The Standard Edition of the Complete Psychological Works of Sigmund Freud*. Eds. Anna Freud, Carrie Lee Rothgeb, and James Strachey. Trans. James Strachey. Vol 4. London: Hogarth Press, 1973.

Freud, Sigmund. "Lecture XXV: Anxiety." *Introductory Lectures on Psycho-Analysis (Part III). The Standard Edition of the Complete Psychological Works of Sigmund Freud. Eds. Anna Freud,* Carrie Lee Rothgeb, and James Strachey. Trans. James Strachey. Vol 16. London: Hogarth Press, 1973, 392–412.

Freud, Sigmund. "Mourning and Melancholia." *The Standard Edition of the Complete Psychological Works of Sigmund Freud*. Eds. Anna Freud, Carrie Lee Rothgeb, and James Strachey. Trans. James Strachey. Vol 14. London: Hogarth Press, 1973, 237–258.

Freud, Sigmund. "On Narcissism." *The Standard Edition of the Complete Psychological Works of Sigmund Freud*. Eds. Anna Freud, Carrie Lee Rothgeb, and James Strachey. Trans. James Strachey. Vol 14. London: Hogarth Press, 1973, 67–102.

Freud, Sigmund. "On the History of the Psycho-Analytic Movement." *The Standard Edition of the Complete Psychological Works of Sigmund Freud*. Eds. Anna Freud, Carrie Lee Rothgeb, and James Strachey. Trans. James Strachey. Vol 14. London: Hogarth Press, 1973, 1–66.

Freud, Sigmund. "The Question of Lay Analysis." *The Standard Edition of the Complete Psychological Works of Sigmund Freud*. Eds. Anna Freud, Carrie Lee Rothgeb, and James Strachey. Trans. James Strachey. Vol 20. London: Hogarth Press, 1973, 177–258.

Freud, Sigmund. *The Standard Edition of the Complete Psychological Works of Sigmund Freud*. Eds. Anna Freud, Carrie Lee Rothgeb, and James Strachey. Trans. James Strachey. 24 vols. London: Hogarth Press, 1973.

Frontain, Raymond-Jean. "The Fortune in David's Eyes." *Gay and Lesbian Review* 14.2 (2006): 12–15.

Garrett, George. "Liar, Liar, Pants on Fire: Some Notes on the Life and Art of the Late James Dickey." *VQR* Winter 2001. Web. http://www.vqronline.org/essay/%E2%80%9Cliar-liar-pants-fire%E2%80%9D-some-notes-life-and-art-late-james-dickey.

Ginsberg, Allen. "On Creeley's Ear Mind." *boundary 2* 6/7.1–2 (1978): 443–446. *JSTOR*. June 11, 2013, Web. https://www.jstor.org/stable/302636.

Glavey, Brian. *The Wallflower Avant-Garde: Modernism: Sexuality, Queer Ekphrasis*. New York: Oxford University Press, 2015.

Glissant, Édouard. *Poetic Intention*. Trans. Nathalie Stephens with Anne Malena. Callicoon, NY: Nighboat Books, 2010.

Golding, Alan. "George Oppen's Serial Poems." *Contemporary Literature* 29.2 (1988): 221–240. *EBSCOhost*, April 5, 2014, Web. https://www.jstor.org/stable/1208438?seq=1#page_scan_tab_contents.

Golding, Alan. "Revisiting Seriality in Creeley's Poems." In *Form, Power, and Person in Robert Creeley's Life and Work*. Eds. Stephen Fredman and Steve McCaffery. Iowa City: University of Iowa Press, 2010, 50–65.

Gooch, Brad. *City Poet: The Life and Times of Frank O'Hara*. New York: Harper Perennial, 2014.

Green, André. "Anxiety and Narcissism." In *Life Narcissism, Death Narcissism*. Trans. Andrew Weller. London: Free Association Books, 2001, 91–128.

Green, André. "The Bifurcation of Contemporary Psychoanalysis." In *Between Winnicott and Lacan: A Clinical Engagement*. Ed. Lewis A. Kirshner. London: Taylor & Francis, 2011, 29–50.

Green, André. *The Fabric of Affect in the Psychoanalytic Discourse*. Trans. Alan Sheridan. New York: Routledge, 1999.

Grossman, Allen. "London Bridge Is Falling Down." In *Poetry: A Basic Course*. The Teaching Company, Chantilly: VA, 1990 (audiocassette).

Grossman, Allen. "Orpheus/Philomela: Subjecting and Mastery in the Founding Stories of Poetic Production." In *The Long Schoolroom*. Ann Arbor: University of Michigan Press, 1997.

Grossman, Allen. *The Sighted Singer*. Baltimore: Johns Hopkins University Press, 1991.

Halliday, Mark. *Stevens and the Interpersonal*. Princeton: Princeton University Press, 1991.

Halperin, David, and Valerie Traub. Eds. *Gay Shame*. Chicago: University of Chicago Press, 2010.

Hartman, Geoffrey. *Criticism in the Wilderness*. 2nd ed. New Haven: Yale University Press, 2007.

Hinshelwood, Robert D. *Dictionary of Kleinian Thought*. London: Free Association Books, 1996.

Izenberg, Oren. *Being Numerous: Poetry and the Ground of Social Life*. Princeton, NJ: Princeton University Press, 2011.

Izenberg, Oren. "Confiance au monde; Or, The Poetry of Ease." *Nonsite.org*. February 12, 2012, Web. http://nonsite.org/article/confiance-au-monde-or-the-poetry-of-ease.

Jacobus, Mary. *The Poetics of Psychoanalysis: In the Wake of Klein*. New York: Oxford University Press, 2005.

Jakobson, Roman. *Language in Literature*. Eds. Krystyna Pomorska and Stephen Rudy. Cambridge: Harvard University Press, 1987.

Jakobson, Roman. "Linguistics and Poetics." In *Style in Language*. Ed. T. Sebeok. Cambridge, MA: MIT Press, 1960, 350–377.

Jameson, Frederic. "Wallace Stevens." *New Orleans Review* 11.1 (1984): 10–19.

Jarrell, Mary. *Remembering Randall*. New York: Harper Perennial, 2000.

Jarrell, Randall. *Collected Poems*. New York: FSG, 1969.

Jarrell, Randall. *No Other Book: Selected Essays*. Ed. Brad Leithauser. New York: HarperCollins, 1999.

Jarrell, Randall. "Poetry and Art Notebook." Stuart Wright Collection, J.Y. Joyner Library of East Carolina University.

Jarrell, Randall. "A Sad Heart at the Supermarket." In *No Other Book*. Ed. Brad Leithauser. New York: Harper, 2000, 363–.

Jarrell, Randall. "The Woman at the Washington Zoo." In *No Other Book*. Ed. Brad Leithauser. New York: Harper, 2000, 89–97.

Johnson, Barbara. "Apostrophe, Animation, and Abortion." *Diacritics* 16.1 (1986): 28–47.

Johnson, Barbara. *Mother Tongues*. Cambridge, MA: Harvard University Press, 2003.

Jordan, Ida Kay. "No Sign of the Beatnik Behind Poet's Beard." *News and Observer* [Greensboro]. June 11, 1961.

Kahane, Claire. "Gender and Voice in Transitional Phenomena." In *Transitional Objects and Potential Spaces: Literary Uses of D.W. Winnicott*. Ed. Peter Rudnytsky. New York: Columbia University Press, 1993, 278–291.

Katz, Daniel. *The Poetry of Jack Spicer*. Edinburgh: Edinburgh University Press, 1984.

Khan, Masud R. "Introduction." In *Maturational Processes and the Facilitating Environment*. London: Hogarth Press, 1965, xi–l.

Klein, Melanie, and Joan Riviere. *Love, Hate, and Reparation*. London: Hogarth, 1937.

Klein, Melanie, and Joan Riviere. "Mourning and Its Relation to Manic-Depressive States." In *Love, Guilt, and Reparation and Other Works, 1921–1945*. New York: Simon and Schuster, 2002.

Koestenbaum, Wayne. *The Queen's Throat: Opera, Homosexuality, and the Myth of Desire*. New York: Da Capo Press, 2001.

Komura, Toshiaki. "Modern Elegy and the Fiction and Creation of Loss: Wallace Stevens's 'The Owl in the Sarcophagus.'" *ELH* 77.1 (2010): 45–70.

Kostova, Raina. "The Dangerous Voice of the Realist: Wallace Stevens' Extended Critique of Freud's The Future of an Illusion." *The Wallace Stevens Journal* 34.2 (2010): 222–240.

Kunin, Aaron. *Folding Ruler Star*. New York: Fence, 2005.

Kunin, Aaron. *Grace Period: Notebooks, 1998–2007*. Tucson, AZ: Letter Machine Editions, 2013.

Kunin, Aaron. "New Poetries." In *The Handbook of Creative Writing*. Ed. Steven Earnshaw. Edinburgh: Edinburgh University Press, 2007.

Kunin, Aaron. "Shakespeare's Preservation Fantasy." *PMLA* 124.1 (2009): 92–106.

Kunin, Aaron. *The Sore Throat & Other Poems*. New York: Fence, 2010.

Kunin, Aaron. "Would Vanessa Place Be a Better Poet If She Had Better Opinions?" *Nonsite.org*. September 26, 2015. Web. http://nonsite.org/editorial/would-vanessa-place-be-a-betterpoet-if-she-had-better-opinions.

Kunin, Aaron, and Ben Lerner. "Ben Lerner and Aaron Kunin in Conversation." In *12 X 12: Conversations in 21st-Century Poetry and Poetics*. Eds. Christina Mengert and Joshua Marie Wilkinson. Iowa City: University of Iowa Press, 2009, 240–250.

Kunitz, Stanley. "Randall Jarrell." *The Alumni News* 10–11.

Laplanche, Jean. "A Metapsychology Put to the Test of Anxiety." *International Journal of Psycho-Analysis* 62 (1981): 81–89. *PEP Archive*. August 18, 2009, Web. http://0-www.pep-web.org.pugwash.lib.warwick.ac.uk/document.php?id=ijp.062.0081a.

Laplanche, Jean, and J.B. Pontalis. *The Language of Psychoanalysis*. Trans. Donald Nicholson-Smith. London: Hogarth, 1973, 230.

Lauter, Paul. *Canons and Contexts*. Oxford: Oxford University Press, 1991.

Lensing, George. *Wallace Stevens and the Seasons*. Baton Rouge: Louisiana State University Press, 2004.

Lentricchia, Frank. *The Gaiety of Language: An Essay on the Radical Poetics of W.B. Yeats and Wallace Stevens*. Berkeley, CA: University of California Press, 1968.

Lerner, Ben. "Of Accumulation: The Collected Poems of Robert Creeley." *boundary 2* 35.3 (2008): 251–262.

Lerner, Ben. *The Hatred of Poetry*. New York: Farrar, Straus, Giroux, 2016.

Leys, Ruth. "The Turn to Affect: A Critique." *Critical Inquiry* 37.3 (Spring 2011): 434–472. *JSTOR*. December 11, 2011, Web. http://www.journals.uchicago.edu/doi/abs/10.1086/659353..

Likierman, Meira. *Melanie Klein: Her Work in Context*. London: Continuum, 2001.

Litz, A. Walton. *Introspective Voyager*. New York: Oxford University Press, 1972.

Longenbach, James. "Randall Jarrell's Semifemenine Mind." *Southwest Review* 81.3 (1996): 368–387. *EbscoHost.* May 3, 2014. Web. https://www.jstor.org/stable/43471764.

Longenbach, James. *Wallace Stevens: The Plain Sense of Things.* New York: Oxford, 1991.

Lowell, Robert. "Randall Jarrell." *The Alumni News,* 10–11, 30–31. Stuart Wright Collection, J.Y. Joyner Library of East Carolina University.

Lyotard, Jean-François. *The Differend.* Trans. Georges van den Abbeele. Minneapolis, MN: University of Minnesota Press, 1989.

MacKenzie, Gina Masucci, and Daniel T. O'Hara. "Beyond Romance: Wallace Stevens with D.W. Winnicott on the Objects of Insight." *The Wallace Stevens Journal* 34.2 (2010): 241–246.

Marder, Elissa. *The Mother in the Age of Mechanical Reproduction.* New York: Fordham University Press, 2012.

Mariani, Paul. *William Carlos Williams: A New World Naked.* New York: McGraw-Hill, 1981.

Mitchell, Stephen, and Margaret J. Black. *Freud and Beyond: A History of Modern Psychoanalytic Thought.* New York: Basic Books, 1995.

Moten, Fred. *In the Break: The Aesthetics of Black Radical Tradition.* Minneapolis, MN: University of Minnesota Press, 2003.

Nelson, Maggie. *The Argonauts.* Minneapolis, MN: Graywolf Press, 2016.

Ngai, Sianne. *Ugly Feelings.* Cambridge, MA: Harvard University Press, 2007.

Notley, Alice. "Introduction." In *The Selected Poems of Ted Berrigan.* Berkeley, CA: University of California Press, 2011.

Nouvet, Claire. "An Impossible Response: The Disaster of Narcissus." *Yale French Studies* 79 (1991): 103–134.

Nouvet, Claire. "The Inarticulate Affect: Lyotard and Psychoanalytic Testimony." *Discourse* 25.1 (2003): 231–247.

Ogden, Thomas H. "On Potential Space." *International Journal of Psychoanalysis* 66 (1985): 129–141. *PEP Archive.* November 23, 2012.

O'Hara, Frank. *The End of the Far West.* Ed. Ted Berrigan. Wivenhoe, England, 1974, [n.p.].

Olson, Charles. "Proprioception." In *Collected Prose.* Eds. Donald Allen and Benjamin Friedlander. Berkeley, CA: University of California Press, 1997.

Padgett, Ron. "On *The Sonnets.*" In *Nice to See You: Homage to Ted Berrigan.* Ed. Anne Waldman. Minneapolis, MN: Coffee House Press, 1991.

Padgett, Ron. *Ted: A Personal Memoir of Ted Berrigan.* Great Barrington, MA: Figures, 1993.

Perloff, Marjorie. *Radical Artifice: Writing Poetry in the Age of Media.* Chicago: University of Chicago Press, 1991.

Perlow, Seth. "The Other Harmonium: Toward a Minor Stevens." *Wallace Stevens Journal* 33.2 (Fall 2009): 191–210.

Phillips, Adam. *On Flirtation.* Cambridge, MA: Harvard University Press, 1996.

Phillips, Adam. *Winnicott.* Cambridge: Harvard University Press, 1988.

Place, Vanessa, and Robert Fitterman. *Notes on Conceptualisms*. Brooklyn, NY: Ugly
    Duckling Presse, 2009.

Pritchard, William. *Randall Jarrell: A Literary Life*. New York: FSG, 1992.

Ramazani, Jahan. *The Poetry of Mourning*. Chicago: University Chicago Press, 1994.

Rankine, Claudia. *Citizen*. Minneapolis, MN: Graywolf, 2014.

Rankine, Claudia. *Don't Let Me Be Lonely*. Minneapolis, MN: Graywolf, 2004.

Rankine, Claudia. *The End of the Alphabet*. New York: Grove Press, 1998.

Rankine, Claudia. "The Meaning of Serena Williams." *The New York Times Magazine*.
    August 25, 2015. Web. https://www.nytimes.com/2015/08/30/magazine/the-
    meaning-of-serena-williams.html.

Rankine, Claudia. "Race in the Life of the Mind." October 30, 2014. Web. https://www.
    youtube.com/watch?v=np4ZL8O_sbc.

Reed, Anthony. *Freedom Time: The Poetics and Politics of Black Experimental Writing*.
    Baltimore, MD: Johns Hopkins University Press, 2016.

Riddel, Joseph. "'Poets' Politics'—Wallace Stevens' 'Owl's Clover.'" *Modern Philology* 56.2
    (1958): 118–132.

Rifkin, Libbie. "'Worrying about Making It': Ted Berrigan's Social Poetics."
    Contemporary Literature 38.4 (2008): 640–672.

Rodman, F. Robert. *Winnicott: Life and Work*. Cambridge, MA: Perseus, 2003.

Ruskin, John. *Modern Painters*. New York: Wiley & Halstead, 1857–1860. *HathiTrust
    Digital Library*. April 4, 2012, Web. http://catalog.hathitrust.org/Record/001911243.

Scholnick, Michael. "A Remembrance of Ted Berrigan." In *Nice to See You*. Ed. Anne
    Waldman. Minneapolis, MN: Coffee House Press, 1991, 161–163.

Schwartz, Delmore. *Selected Essays of Delmore Schwartz*. Eds. Donald A. Dike and
    David H. Zucker. Chicago: University of Chicago Press, 1985.

Schwartz, M.M. "Introduction: D. W. Winnicott's Cultural Space." *Psychoanalytic Review*
    79 (1992): 169–174. *PEP Archive*. March 30, 2011.

Sebald, W.G. *The Emigrants*. Trans. Michael Hulse. New York: New Directions, 1996.

Sedgwick, Eve Kosofsky. *Between Men*. New York: Columbia University Press, 1985.

Sedgwick, Eve Kosofsky. *Epistemology of the Closet*. Berkeley: University of California
    Press, 2008.

Sedgwick, Eve Kosofsky. *Gary in Your Pocket*. Durham, NC: Duke University Press,
    1996.

Sedgwick, Eve Kosofsky. "Interlude Pedagogic." In *Touching Feeling: Affect, Pedagogy,
    Performativity*. Durham, NC: Duke University Press, 2003,. 27–34.

Sedgwick, Eve Kosofsky. *Touching Feeling: Affect, Pedagogy, Performativity*. Durham,
    NC: Duke University Press, 2003.

Sedgwick, Eve Kosofsky, and Adam Frank. *Shame and Its Sisters: A Silvan Tomkins
    Reader*. Durham, NC: Duke University Press, 1995.

Shakespeare, William. *Romeo and Juliet*. Ed. Brian Gibbons. London: Arden
    Shakespeare, 1980.

Sikelianos, Eleni. "Notes on a Picture." *Brick* 80.1 (2007): 156–158.

Snediker, Michael. *Queer Optimism*. Minneapolis, MN: University of Minnesota Press, 2007.

Spargo, R. Clifton. "The Contemporary Anti-Elegy." In *The Oxford Handbook of the Elegy*. Ed. Karen Weisman. New York: Oxford University Press, 2010, 213–230.

Stevens, Wallace. *The Collected Poems of Wallace Stevens*. New York: Vintage, 1990.

Stevens, Wallace. *Collected Poetry and Prose*. Eds. Frank Kermode and Joan Richardson. New York: Library of America, 1997.

Stevens, Wallace. *The Letters of Wallace Stevens*. Ed. Holly Stevens. New York: Knopf, 1966.

Stevens, Wallace. *The Necessary Angel: Essays on Reality and the Imagination*. New York: Vintage, 1965.

Stevens, Wallace. *Opus Posthumous: Poems, Plays, Prose*. Ed. Milton J. Bates. New York: Vintage, 1990.

Stevens, Wallace. "Particles of Order: The Unpublished Adagia." In *Wallace Stevens: A Celebration*. Eds. Frank A. Doggett and Robert Buttel. Princeton, NJ: Princeton University Press, 1980, 57–77.

Sturm, Nick. "'Thinking of You': The Sociality of Reading in Ted Berrigan's Early Books." The Louisville Conference on Literature and Culture since 1900. Louisville, KY, February 23–25, 2017.

Suleiman, Susan Rubin. "Writing and Motherhood." In *The (M)other Tongue: Essays in Feminist Psychoanalytic Interpretation*. Eds. Shirley Nelson Garner, Claire Kahane, and Madelon Sprengnether. Ithaca, NY: Cornell University Press, 1985.

Sun, Emily. "Facing Keats with Winnicott: On a New Therapeutics of Poetry." *Studies in Romanticism* 46.1 (2007): 57–75.

The Alumni News [University of North Carolina at Greensboro] 54.3 (1966). Stuart Wright Collection, J.Y. Joyner Library of East Carolina University.

Tomkins, Silvan. *Affect, Imagery, Consciousness: Vol. 2, The Negative Affects*. New York: Springer, 2003.

Vendler, Helen. "The Experiential Beginnings of Keats's Odes." *Studies in Romanticism* 12.3 (1973): 591–606.

Vendler, Helen. *On Extended Wings*. Cambridge, MA: Harvard University Press, 1969.

Vendler, Helen. "The Hunting of Wallace Stevens." In *The Music of What Happens*. Cambridge, MA: Harvard University Press, 1988, 75–91.

Vendler, Helen. "The Qualified Assertions of Wallace Stevens." In *The Act of the Mind*. Eds. Roy Harvey Pearce and J. Hillis Miller. Baltimore: Johns Hopkins, 1965, 163–178.

Vendler, Helen. "Wallace Stevens: Men Made Out of Words." In *Voices and Visions: The Poet in America*. New York: New York Center for Visual History, 1988. Video.

Vendler, Helen. *Words Chosen Out of Desire*. Knoxville: University of Tennessee Press, 1984.

Waldman, Anne. "Introduction." In *Nice to See You*. Ed. Anne Waldman. Minneapolis, MN: Coffee House Press, 1991, i–x.

Watson, Mary. "Wallace Stevens and the Maternal Art of Poetry." *Wallace Stevens Journal* 22.1 (1988): 72–82.

Watten, Barrett. "Entry 08: Homage to Lee Crabtree." *barrettwatten.net*. http:// barrettwatten.net/texts/entry-08-homage-to-lee-crabtree/2010/02/.

Weaver, Andy. "Divining the Derivers: Anarchy and the Practice of Derivative Poetics in Robert Duncan and John Cage." *Jacket 40* (2010). Web. http://jacketmagazine. com/40/weaver-duncan-cage.shtml.

Weber, Samuel. *The Legend of Freud.* Expanded ed. Stanford, CA: Stanford University Press, 2000.

Wiegman, Robyn. "The Times We're In: Queer Feminist Criticism and the Reparative 'Turn.'" *Feminist Theory* 15.1 (2014): 4–25.

Williams, William Carlos. "Preface to Kora in Hell (1920)." In *Selected Essays of William Carlos Williams.* New York: New Directions, 1969.

Williamson, Alan. *Almost a Girl: Male Writers and Female Identification.* Charlottesville: University of Virginia Press, 2001.

Wilson, Elizabeth. *Affect & Artificial Intelligence.* Seattle: University of Washington Press, 2010.

Wilson, Ronaldo V. "How Do We Invent Language of Racial Identity—That Is Not Necessarily Constructing the 'Scene of Instruction' about Race but Create the Linguistic Material of Racial Speech/Thought?" In *The Racial Imaginary: Writers on Race in the Life of the Mind.* Eds. Claudia Rankine, Beth Loffreda, and Max King Clap. Albany, NY: Fence Books, 2015, 75–78.

Winnicott, D.W. "Anxiety Associated with Insecurity." In *Through Paediatrics to Psychoanalysis: Collected Papers.* London: Karnac, 1984, 97–100.

Winnicott, D.W. *Babies and Their Mothers.* Reading, MA: Addison-Wesley, 1987.

Winnicott, D.W. "Birth Memories, Birth Trauma, and Anxiety." In *Through Paediatrics to Psychoanalysis: Collected Papers.* London: Karnac, 1984. Print, 174–193.

Winnicott, D.W. "Communicating and Not Communicating Leading to a Study of Certain Opposites." In *The Maturational Processes and the Facilitating Environment.* London: Hogarth Press, 1965, 179–192.

Winnicott, D.W. "Communication between Infant and Mother, and Mother and Infant, Compared and Contrasted." In *Babies and Their Mothers.* Reading, MA: Addison-Wesley, 1987, 89–103.

Winnicott, D.W. "Ego Distortion in Terms of True and False Self." In *The Maturational Processes and the Facilitating Environment.* London: Hogarth, 1965, 140–152.

Winnicott, D.W. "Knowing and Learning." In *Babies and Their Mothers.* Reading, MA: Addison-Wesley, 1987, 15–21.

Winnicott, D.W. "The Location of Cultural Experience." In *Playing and Reality.* London: Tavistock, 1971, 128–139.

Winnicott, D.W. *The Maturational Processes and the Facilitating Environment.* London: Hogarth Press, 1965.

Winnicott, D.W. *Playing and Reality.* London: Tavistock, 1971a.

Winnicott, D.W. "Playing: A Theoretical Statement." In *Playing and Reality.* London: Tavistock, 1971b, 38–52.

Winnicott, D.W. *Psycho-Analytic Explorations*. Eds. Clare Winnicott, Ray Shepherd, and Madeleine Davis. London: Karnac, 2010.

Winnicott, D.W. "String: A Technique of Communication." In *The Maturational Processes and the Facilitating Environment*. London: Hogarth, 1965, 153–157.

Winnicott, D.W. "Theory of the Parent-Infant Relationship." In *Maturational Processes and the Facilitating Environment*. London: Hogarth, 1965, 37–50.

Winnicott, D.W. "Transitional Objects and Transitional Phenomena." In *Playing and Reality*. London: Tavistock, 1971.

Winnicott, D.W. "The Use of an Object and Relating through Identifications." In *Psycho-Analytic Explorations*. Eds. Clare Winnicott, Ray Shepherd, and Madeline Davis. Cambridge, MA: Harvard University Press, 1989, 218–227.

Yeats, W.B. *The Collected Works of W.B. Yeats, Vol. 1: The Poems*. Ed. Richard Finneran. 2nd ed. New York: Scribner, 1997.

Index